The Illustrated Book of
NATURE

*A seasonal guide to the
habitats of the British Isles*

The Illustrated Book of
NATURE

*A seasonal guide to the
habitats of the British Isles*

ARTISTS HOUSE

Executive Manager	Kelly Flynn
Compiling Editor	Margaret Crush
Art Editor	Ruth Levy
Designer	Colin Robson
Design Assistant	Suzie Lanni
Editorial Assistant	Elizabeth Hubbard
Production	Peter Phillips

Mitchell Beazley International Ltd
Michelin House
81 Fulham Road
London SW3 6RB

ISBN 0 86134 088 4

Typeset by Hourds Typographica Limited, Stafford.
Reproduction by La Cromolito s.n.c., Milan.
Produced by Mandarin Offset.
Printed and bound in Malaysia.

Contents

How to Use this Book

This book has been specially designed to make it easier to understand, identify and enjoy the nature of the British Countryside. *The Illustrated Book of Nature* is divided into the six main habitats found in the British Isles and each habitat is sub-divided into the four seasons of the year. Animals and plants are placed within the habitat and season where they are most likely to be found, each with their own illustrated section.

The six main habitats are Meadow and Hedge; Mountain, Moor and Heath; Woodlands; Coast; Marsh and Stream; and the urban habitat familiar as home territory to most of the human population – Town and Garden.

Within each habitat the pages are then seasonally organised as:

Spring: March–May
Summer: June–August
Autumn: September–November
Winter: December–February

Allowances should be made, of course, for fluctuations in climate from year to year and from north to south.

By presenting the species in this way the book both helps in recognizing wildlife in the field and works better as background reference for the "armchair naturalist". If you find yourself in a meadow in the summer, for instance, and spot a wildflower, you will be able to identify it easily by turning to the "Meadow/Summer/Wildflower" pages in this book.

Such a system cannot be rigid, of course, and habitats do tend to merge naturally. For example, a hedgerow with trees could signify a habitat more akin to a small wood than an adjunct to a meadow. Equally, a habitat selected by an animal or plant might vary. The commoner varieties, especially will use several habitats. Some species, too, will be found in more than one season. A flower may bloom from spring to autumn; some birds are resident all the year round and may be seen at any time, but for the most part, remember, habitat is the key to identification.

To identify a particular species, you should first consider its habitat and then what the season is. Turn to the relevant section of the book to find the illustration. If it is not there, try adjacent seasons in the same habitat or other possible habitats.

The species illustrated are selected to represent those you are most likely to see or want to find out about. The rare visitor may not be featured, but the book does include all those species of flowers, butterflies, fungi and birds most often encountered in our beautiful countryside.

There is also a complete index of both common and Latin names by subject which provides a useful cross-checking system for easy identification of species and genera.

FACTSHEET: BUTTERFLIES

The glorious colours of butterflies add richness to the world of nature and offer hours of fascination to the patient watcher. Identification is made easier by the fact that there are only some 50–60 species which are usually seen in Britain and this book includes most of those.

Though most moths fly at night, in Britain there are probably more day-flying moths than butterflies. Accordingly a few of these are also shown. (The antennae of moths tend to be thin or feathery, never clubbed like those of butterflies.)

Each species is illustrated in the habitat where it may often be seen, although other habitats and seasons in which it may occur are also mentioned in the descriptive text. Migrant butterflies such as Red admirals, Clouded yellows, Large whites and the Painted lady can also be seen by the coast *en route* from the Mediterranean to their normal summer habitats.

Most butterflies are illustrated with an upperside and underside view, and where possible both sexes are depicted

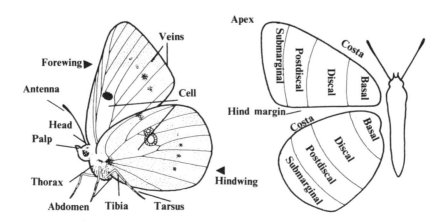

♂ Male
♀ Female

if they differ noticeably. Other information given is the approximate wingspan; the flight period of the butterfly; the number of generations or broods in a year; and the principal foodplant/s of the caterpillar (different from the adult's foodplant). The life cycle of egg – caterpillar – chrysalis – butterfly – egg is well known. Often the eggs are stuck onto the foodplant of the caterpillar.

The fine scales which cover the whole of a butterfly's wings and body give it the colour and pattern which may camouflage it at rest (as does the underside of the Comma) or frighten off small predators (as do the startling eye-spots on the upperside of the Peacock butterfly). The colour, pattern and shape of the wings are of major importance in identification, and entomologists (people who study insects) divide the

wings into various areas to help in this (*see diagram*). Also, certain scales on male butterflies are specially modified to release a scent attractive to females, and these scales may be grouped together to form a sex brand (also indicated).

Butterflies are much less frequent than they used to be. Their natural habitats have been, and are still being, destroyed through the expansion of industry and the introduction of modern farming methods. Nature-lovers everywhere should try to ensure that, while such progress is not necessarily halted, it is tempered to preserve some parts of the environment. You can help in a small way by planting some butterfly-attractors such as Buddleia bushes and Michaelmas daisies in your garden, and by leaving a small patch of nettles and rough grass there.

FACTSHEET: WILD FLOWERS

Wild flowers are lovely just to look at, yet it is possible to enjoy them so much more when casual observation is spiced with a knowledge of their names and habits. And for the armchair naturalist this book is a "must" – depicting as it does in full colour around 500 of the commonest and most easily identified British wild flowers, along with a few rarities for special interest.

The fact that plants, unlike butterflies and birds, are immobile helps greatly in their identification, but it is also a disadvantage since they can be easily destroyed by picking, trampling and misuse.

In this book the flowers are grouped by colour within the habitat and season in which they are likely to be found. If special features like damp and chalky soil are important, these are usually mentioned. To help you identify further, there is often extra information about the actual months in which a plant can usually be found in flower; the average height to which it grows or creeps; and the size of the flowerhead. However, plant heights and sizes of flowers and leaves are extremely variable, and so this average figure should be treated with caution. Colours can vary too.

Botany (the study of plants) has its own special terms. These have been kept to a minimum in this book, but occasionally have had to be used since otherwise the "plain language" explanation would have been over-lengthy for the space available. However, such technical terms are mostly explained pictorially in the diagrams below.

With the development of new farming methods, crop spraying, tearing up of hedgerows, etc., wild flowers are much less common than they used to be. In Britain a recent Act of Parliament has fortunately given them more protection, so it is illegal to uproot not just certain rare species, but *any* wild flowers. However, some seedsmen now offer seeds of plants like Cowslips for the nature-lover to grow.

GLOSSARY

floret one of the small flowers in a composite like a Daisy. Disc florets are tubular; ray florets are strap-shaped.
simple a single leaf, not divided, lobed, or in several parts as a

compound leaf.
spadix elongated, club-like flowerhead.
stipule leaf-like or scale-like outgrowth at the base of a leaf stalk; usually in pairs.

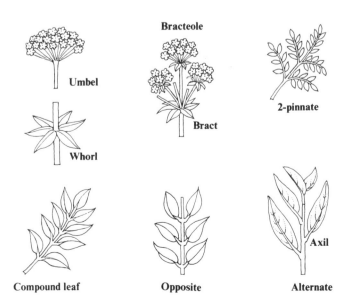

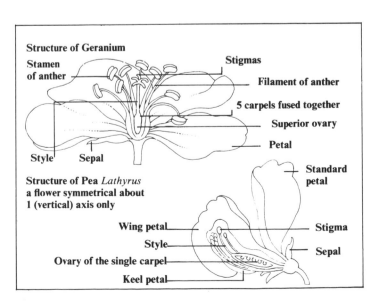

─────── FACTSHEET: FUNGI ───────

The fungi in this book are those commonly known as "mushrooms" and "toadstools", words rather loosely applied to the fruitbodies of fleshy gill-fungi and commonly (if somewhat inaccurately) used for edible and poisonous species respectively. In fact, mushrooms and toadstools are only a small part of the enormous range of organisms known as fungi, and which include puffballs, moulds, mildews, rusts and yeasts. Their essential characteristic (which puts them in a separate kingdom from plants) is the lack of the green pigment chlorophyll.

Fungi are made of filaments called hyphae, which branch out to form an extensive web (the mycelium). This is often hidden underground, so that the part most people notice is the fruitbody. The diagram shows what its various parts are called. This fruitbody is the reproductive part of the fungus and releases masses of tiny spores into the air.

Unlike many plants, mushrooms, toadstools and other fungi do not always have common or English names, probably because of the traditional fear many people seem to share of these strange, fleshy organisms. However, they all have Latin or scientific names. While these may be initially offputting to a beginner, they are the only reliable means of correctly labelling a species.

The species in this book have been grouped by colour in their characteristic habitat and season. The description of each species usually includes the diameter of the cap; the colour range (though colours can vary); the stem height; and the months in which it appears. If the mushroom is edible (raw or after cooking) this is usually indicated. If there is no such indication, *do not* eat. The death's head symbol alongside indicates it is poisonous.

The most delicious edible mushrooms include the Penny bun boletus, the Miller, the Parasol mushroom and the Chanterelle. All edible fungi should be picked young and fresh, and cooked as soon as possible (after removing any tough or slimy parts). *Remember these golden rules whenever picking mushrooms: Never experiment unless an experienced mycologist (fungi expert) has identified them as harmless. Keep to fresh mushrooms which have been thus correctly identified. Ignore folklore giving "tests" on safety.* **If in doubt, don't.** Serious cases of poisoning do appear every year, most of which are caused by a very few species. The Death cap (*Amanita phalloides*) is the most common of the deadly poisonous types in Britain, being responsible for very many deaths by mushroom poisoning. Some other species of Amanita and also species of *Cortinarius, Inocybe, Clitocybe, Tricholoma, Lepiota, Galerina* and the peppery species of *Russula* and *Lactarius* should be avoided. If poisoning is suspected, seek medical help immediately – delay can prevent cure. Where possible supply the doctor with a fragment of the mushroom, however tiny.

GLOSSARY

concave (of cap) with surface curved like the inside of a sphere.
convex (of cap) broadly curved or rounded.
decurrent (of gills, tubes) broadly attached and descending down the stem.
fibrils/fibrillose small fibres or covered with small fibres.
free (of gills, tubes) not attached to stem.
haemolysis haemolysins in some fungi attack blood cells if the fungus is eaten.
pellicle a detachable, skin-like cuticle.
pores the openings of the tubes in the Boletes.
striate lined or grooved.
tubes spore-producing surfaces arranged vertically under the cap in a dense layer, found in Boletes.
veil protective layers of immature fruitbody.

STRUCTURE OF FUNGI

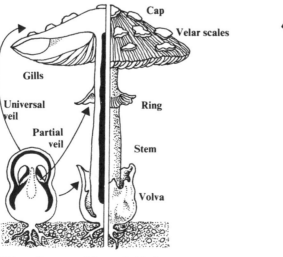

Cap
Velar scales
Gills
Universal veil
Partial veil
Ring
Stem
Volva

Primordium   Mature fruitbody

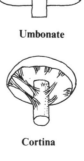

Umbo
Umbonate
Cortina
Bulbous

 Symbol indicates poisonous fungi

FACTSHEET: BIRDS

Birds are perhaps the most varied and noticeable of the wildlife around us. This book illustrates over 200 of the more common British birds, showing them in the habitat where they are likely to be seen and in the season of the year when you may see them there. They are then classified by size, with the smallest first. As an additional check for this, alongside each bird is a small rectangle, showing a silhouette of the bird alongside a sparrow or a pigeon.

However, some birds are widespread, appearing in several habitats, and also many appear in more than one season, most notably those that are resident all year round. Also, wind, weather and migration can land a bird in strange places. Therefore habitats and seasons should be treated with caution.

All the birds illustrated are adult unless otherwise indicated, and males and females are only distinguished if they differ appreciably. However, adults and juveniles can vary in appearance. Also, adults can look different at different seasons of the year, plumage colours often being enhanced at breeding time. A bird with varying seasonal plumages is often illustrated with a picture in each of the relevant seasons, and also cross referenced to the other season/s.

The text supplies much extra information that cannot be shown visually, such as the bird's call, and whether it is a winter or summer migrant, a passage visitor or resident all the year round. When space allows, further facts are given about behaviour, numbers and any special information about distribution. Size is given in centimetres. The expression "Top Sixty" means the bird is among the sixty commonest British species. Technical terms have been used extremely sparingly and the bird outline and key below shows clearly to which part of the bird any ornithological term refers. (Ornithology is the study of birds.)

Below left is a checklist of things to look out for. Basically, when in the field, having established habitat and season, look first at the size, making a rough guess as to whether the bird is sparrow or pigeon-sized to help the process of elimination. Next look at its colouring and pattern. Behaviour and voice provide further pointers, although both of these can be misleading – birds, like all other creatures, often behave unaccountably, and song and calls are difficult to distinguish and even more difficult to interpret from a book.

Birds do not always run true to type in other ways. Plumage not only varies greatly from individual to individual, but generally gets duller as the year progresses towards the pre-winter moult. Numbers seen can also alter radically, as changes in climate or habitat have an effect.

Finally, how you act yourself will greatly affect how much birdlife you and others out with you will see. Avoid disturbing birds and their nests and habitats (remember it is illegal to take eggs or nests), go quietly about (in the breeding season in particular), and a wealth of fascinating birdlife should open before you.

BIRDWATCHER'S CHECKLIST

Habitat

Time of year

Size
Compare with other species (if possible)

Head
Shape, crest, plumage pattern

Bill
Size, shape, colour

Upperparts
Streaked, spotted, barred, plain

Underparts
Streaked, spotted, barred, plain

Wing
Length *Extended, folded (relative to tail)*
Breadth *Extended*
Markings *Upper wing, Underwing*

Tail
Shape, length, markings

Legs
Length, colour

Actions
Flight
Swift/medium/slow Direct/undulating
Ground *Walks/ hops/ runs/ perches/ wades/ swims/ dives*

Calls
Repetitive/varied/ Single note Harsh/melodious

♂ Male

♀ Female

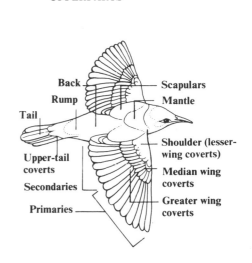

UNDERPARTS

Crown
Forehead
Lores
Nape
Gape
Throat
Mantle and back
Ear coverts
Wing-tip
Chest
Breast
Wing coverts (often pale-tipped forming bars on the wing)
Belly
Flanks
Vent
Under-tail coverts

UPPERPARTS

Back
Rump
Tail
Scapulars
Mantle
Upper-tail coverts
Secondaries
Primaries
Shoulder (lesser-wing coverts)
Median wing coverts
Greater wing coverts

Meadow and Hedge

Hay meadows, pastureland for grazing, turfy downland and the grassy fringes of foot and bridle paths abound in wild flowers. Birds and butterflies flit above them and the field mushroom is well known. Such grassland is one of the most important habitats for wildlife, although it is not as "natural" as people often think, being almost as affected by man as the park and garden of the last section of this book.

Other farmland (the arable fields brown in winter and planted with cereal or green crops in summer) is even more "managed". Arable fields are ploughed, harrowed, sown, fertilised, weeded (usually with sprays devastating to wild flowers), sprayed with insecticide catastrophic to harmless insects like butterflies, and harvested (the huge combines destroying nests of bird and mammal alike). In such an environment, wildlife is greatly endangered and there is usually less there than in an equivalent area of the town, though some "weeds" do flourish on such disturbed ground.

Fortunately, the saving grace of the arable habitat has been the hedgerow whose wealth of shrubby plants gives cover for many creatures and wild flowers. Sadly, modern farming methods are tending to destroy even this precious habitat by rooting up and burning hedges.

SPRING
Butterflies

Orange tip
Anthocharis cardamines
Common in damp fields, woodland edges and country lanes, this butterfly is thought by many to be a true sign of spring. It is the only British species with a distinctive dappled green underside and this occurs in both sexes. The female's hindwing may have a yellow tinge. Orange tip caterpillars feed on Cruciferae (the Cabbage family), especially

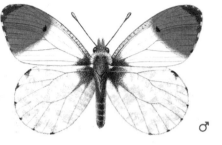

Tower mustard and Lady's smock, and sometimes on the ornamental cabbages in urban parks. There is one brood a year. Wingspan: 38–48 mm. Flight period: Apr–July.

Latticed heath moth
Semiothisa clathrata
This is a mostly day-flying moth which actively seeks the sunshine, though at night it is also attracted to light. It inhabits chalk downland and waste ground (as well as heaths and open woodland). It is widespread. Its caterpillars feed on Lucerne and various species of Clover and Trefoil. Wingspan: 22–26 mm. It has two broods a year and can be seen flying in May and June, and again in July–Sept.

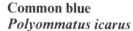

Wall brown
Lasiommata megera
Fluttery in flight, the Wall brown butterfly frequently settles on patches of bare soil to bask in the sun. A widespread species, it is mostly found on rough open farmland and among hedgerows, although it is also seen on heaths and moorland, and even hills. There are two to three broods a year, and the caterpillars feed on grasses. Its wingspan ranges from 36–50 mm, with the female being larger and paler. The adults fly May–June and again late July–mid Sept.

Common blue
Polyommatus icarus
One of the commonest and most widespread of butterflies, found in most open grassy places from sea level up to 1800 m, including heathland, urban parks and gardens and also the coast. Different individuals may have slightly varied markings on the underside. Specimens from the later broods (up to three a year) also tend to be smaller and paler. The caterpillars feed on the underside of leaves of Leguminosae, especially Clover. Wingspan: 28–36 mm. Flight period: Apr–Sept.

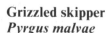

Grizzled skipper
Pyrgus malvae
All skippers are especially active on warm, sunny days, and have a rapid, whirring or skipping flight. The range of the Grizzled skipper is chiefly confined to C and S England, with a few scattered colonies in Wales. It flies rapidly and close to the ground over flowery meadows and bogs up to 2000 m, pausing to rest on bare soil rather than flowers, with its wings held erect over its back. The caterpillar feeds on leaves of Wild strawberry and Cinquefoil, pulling them together to form a tube of silk in which it later pupates. The Grizzled skipper is one of the few British species to overwinter as a pupa. Wingspan: 22–26 mm. Flight periods: Apr–June and July–Aug.

Wild Flowers

White campion
Silene alba
Common on hedge banks and arable ground, its evening-scented, white flowers, 25–30 mm, are pollinated by moths. The lower leaves are hairy. 60 cm. May–Sept.

Common star of Bethlehem
Ornithogallum umbellatum
Widespread in dry, grassy places, its white flowers, 25–40 mm, have a green stripe on the back, and the narrow leaves a centre white stripe. 20 cm. April–June.

Sticky mouse-ear
Cerastium glomeratum
An annual very common in open arable fields, with hairy leaves, stem and sepals, and dense clusters of tiny white flowers. 25 cm. Apr–Sept.

Field mouse-ear (Chickweed)
Cerastium arvense
A perennial of dry chalk and sandy grassland, with loose groups of small white flowers (12–20 mm). There are long rooting shoots. 20 cm. Apr–Aug.

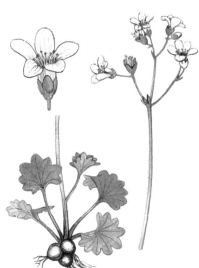

Meadow saxifrage
Saxifraga granulata
Flowering in meadows, with loose clusters of small white flowers, 20–30 mm, on sticky, hairy stalks. The leaves grow in a rosette. In autumn, bulbils form at the base of the leaves. 35 cm. Apr–June.

Field pennycress
Thlaspi arvense
A common arable weed, with tiny white flowers (4–6 mm) and a nasty smell. Pointed toothed leaves clasp the stem and the easily identifiable pods are often seen in winter. 60 cm. May–Sept.

Dropwort
Filipendula vulgaris
On chalk and lime pastures, a small version of Meadowsweet with many more leaflets. Bright pink buds open into creamy florets. 60 cm. May–Aug.

Horse radish
Armoracia rusticana
A tall perennial cultivated for its edible root, also widely naturalised in grassy and waste places. It has huge root-leaves, narrow stem leaves and long spikes of white flowers (8–9 mm). May–June. 1 m.

Field pepperwort
Lepidium campestre
A densely hairy annual with branching stems and tiny white flowers (2–3 mm) on crowded spikes, widespread in dry, bare arable land and roadsides. 40 cm. May–Aug.

Hoary cress
Cardaria draba
A branching perennial on arable farmland and roadsides, with flat-topped clusters of white flowers, 5–6 mm. Narrow, pointed greyish leaves clasp the stem. Up to 90 cm. May–June.

Sweet cicely
Myrrhis odorata
A tall umbellifer growing in hedgerows and roadsides, with a strong smell of aniseed if crushed. Its large dark green leaves are two or three times pinnate. The pods are large. 1 m. May–June.

Cow parsley
Anthriscus sylvestris
The commonest white umbellifer in spring in hedges and woodland. It is tall, with ridged stems and large two or three times pinnate leaves. 80 cm. Apr–June and sporadically thereafter.

Mouse-eared hawkweed
Hieracium pilosella
A low, creeping perennial of meadows and roadsides, with lemon-yellow, red-striped flowers, 20–30 mm, on leafless stalks. The tight rosettes of leaves have white hairs. 20 cm. May–Aug.

Bulbous buttercup
Ranunculus bulbosus
Shorter than the Meadow buttercup (*see p 23*), with all its sepals turned back, and growing in drier meadows. There is a bulbous swelling at the base. 35 cm. May–June.

Crosswort
Cruciata laevipes
Common among hedges and grassland, its pale yellow clusters of flowers, 2 mm, are half hidden by the leaves which are broad, hairy and set in fours. Scrambles to 70 cm. May–June.

Greater celandine
Chelidonium majus
Flowering in hedges and roadsides, this tall perennial has stems which are easily broken and produce orange sap. The flowers are 20 mm across. 60 cm. May–Aug.

Meadow vetchling
(Meadow pea)
Lathyrus pratensis
A scrambling plant common in meadows and roadsides, with clusters of 4–12 flowers, each 15–18 mm. 1 m. May–Aug.

Spotted medick
Medicago arabica
A prostrate creeper in dry meadows and arable land with long-stalked trefoil leaves (each with a black blotch) which almost hide the clusters of yellow flowers, 4–7 mm. (*Compare Black medick, p 187*). 45 cm. Apr–Aug.

Beaked hawksbeard
Crepis vesicaria
Common on dry farmland and roadsides. The yellow flowerheads, up to 15–25 mm across, are in clusters. 60 cm. May–July.

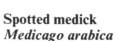

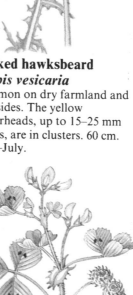

Corn gromwell
Buglossoides arvensis
An arable weed, with tight clusters of creamy-white flowers, 3–4 mm. The stems are usually unbranched except at the top. 35 cm. May–July.

Wild radish
Raphanus raphanistrum
Common on arable and waste land, a tall annual with bristly, lobed lower leaves and yellow or white flowers with lilac veins. (25–30 mm). 40 cm. May–Sept.

Lesser yellow trefoil
Trifolium dubium
Similar to Black medick (*p 187*), but with fewer flowers (up to 15 in a head), no point at the leaf tip and straight pods. On meadows and roadsides. 15 cm. May–Oct.

Cowslip
Primula veris
Rarer these days, especially in Scotland, but can be found in grassland, especially old meadows on chalk. The leaves are wrinkled and hairy and the yellow, bell-shaped flowers (10–15 mm) have orange spots. 20 cm. Apr–May.

Wild pansy (Heartsease)
Viola tricolor
Very variable colouring: this mauve and yellow version (15–25 mm) is found on disturbed sandy soils. Another sub-species is found on coastal dunes and is often all-yellow. There is also an all-violet variety. 30 cm. April–Sept.

Charlock
Sinapis arvensis
A tall annual growing on arable and waste ground, with yellow flowers (12–15 mm), bristly hairs and large, unevenly lobed lower leaves. Belonging to the Cabbage family, its pods are beaded. 80 cm. May–July.

Early spider orchid
Ophrys sphegodes
Owing its name to the shape of its swollen, hairy, velvety brownish lip. The outer petals are yellowish-green or greenish. Grows on chalky soil in dry turf and light woodland. 45 cm. Apr–June.

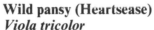

Common fumitory
Fumaria officinalis
A common scrambling weed of arable, wasteland and gardens, especially on sandy soils, having cut leaves and pink, spurred flowers, 7–8 mm long, with darker tips. 10 cm. May–Oct.

Hairy violet
Viola hirta
Unlike the Sweet violet (*p 43*), these flowers are paler and not scented, leaves hairier and more pointed. Chalk and lime grassland and hedges. 20 cm. Apr.

Cuckoo flower (Lady's smock)
Cardamine pratense
Very common in damp grassland. The flowers, 12–20 mm, are lilac or white. 60 cm. Apr–June.

Fritillary
Fritillaria meleagris
A fast declining species of damp meadows with large nodding flowers, 30–50 mm, varying from dull purple-red to creamy white. 50 cm. Apr–May.

Pasque flower
Pulsatilla vulgaris
A declining plant on dry chalk and limestone grassland, with a rosette of long-stalked, hairy, very cut leaves and striking, purple, bell-shaped flowers, 50–80 mm. 20 cm. Apr–May.

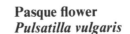

Early purple orchid
Orchis mascula

The first orchid to flower, with a dense spike of flowers (from purple to almost white) above a rosette of (usually) blotchy leaves. Widespread in grassland and woods, usually on limestone. 45 cm. Apr–June.

Bush vetch
Vicia sepium

Very common in rough grass and hedgerows, a tall scrambling perennial with pinnate leaves in 5–9 pairs. The short spikes of two to six flowers, 12–15 mm, are a dull purplish-blue. 60 cm. Apr–Aug.

Common vetch
Vicia sativa

In similar habitats to the Bush vetch (*left*), this annual has three to eight pairs of pinnate leaves. Its purple to pink flowers, 10–30 mm, are usually larger than Bush vetch and often in pairs. 1 mm. Apr–Sept.

Sheepsbit scabious
Jasione montana

On dry acid grassland and heaths, with flowers up to 35 mm. Compare Scabious (*p 39*) which grows on chalk. 35 cm. May–Aug.

Germander speedwell
Veronica chamaedrys

Common in dry, grassy places (meadows and roadsides), having hairy leaves and spikes of blue flowers (10–12 mm) with white centres. The prostrate floppy stems can reach 40 cm. Mar–July.

Hoary plantain
Plantago media

Widespread in chalk and limestone grassland, with a much shorter flower spike than that of Greater plantain (*p 201*). The stalk is considerably longer. Though basically greenish, the flower has purple filaments and creamy anthers. 30 cm. May–Aug.

Venus' looking glass
Legousia hybrida

A fairly common arable weed in the S, with stiff hairs, wavy-edged leaves and small clusters of purplish-blue flowers (8–15 mm) which close up in dull weather. 20 cm. May–Aug.

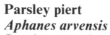

Slender speedwell
Veronica filiformis

Grows in damp grassland and lawns, with kidney-shaped leaves and single flowers (unlike Germander speedwell, (*left*). The flowers are on very long stalks. The creeping stems can be 40 cm long. Apr–June.

Parsley piert
Aphanes arvensis

Growing on sandy arable and wasteland, this insignificant annual has tiny three-lobed leaves not unlike those of the garden herb Parsley, together with minuscule green flowers (2 mm across) in clusters. Creeps up to 20 cm. Apr–Oct.

Salad burnet
Sanguisorba minor

On chalk and limestone grassland, with up to 12 pairs of pinnate leaves and round heads of greenish flowers (6–12 mm). The upper ones have red styles and the lower ones yellow stamens. Scrambles up to 60 cm. May–Aug.

Fungi

St George's mushroom
Calocybe gambosa

A common springtime mushroom, never found in autumn, which forms large fairy rings on chalk grassland. It has a smell of damp meal and a good flavour, which is brought out to the full in soups. Do not confuse it with *Clitocybe dealbata* (*p 40*), which is poisonous and can grow in similar situations. The cap is 5–12 cm, fleshy, uniformly white, greyish or apricot. The gills are white to cream, narrow, thin and very crowded. The stem is 3–8 cm, robust and short, powdery above and whitish. The flesh is thick and white. Apr–June.

Carpet-pin mycena
Gerronema fibula

The cap of this tiny, common fungi is 3–10 cm and is convex, flat and grooved. It is a pale orange-yellow in colour and translucent. The broad gills are white or yellow. The stem is 2–5 cm in height and darker below. Jan–Dec.

Macrolepiota excoriata

A common variety which occasionally forms large troops, especially on cultivated land and grassy meadows. The cap is 4–8 cm, conical to convex in shape, cream to greyish in colour with very fine scales. The gills are white and crowded. The stem is 7–8 cm, all white, silky and smooth, with a double ring encircling the stem. May–Nov.

Birds

Lesser whitethroat
Sylvia curraca

Widespread in England and Wales, sparse in Scotland, the Lesser whitethroat is a smaller, shorter-tailed bird than the closely related Whitethroat (*p 18*). It is also distinctly greyer in tone but with buff wing edges. The legs are bluish-grey, unlike the Whitethroat's reddish ones, and the Lesser whitethroat has no reddish tinge to its wings. It often looks very pale against the background of its tall hedge and scrub habitat, where it forages quietly for insects. The male in spring sometimes has a pink-flushed breast. The bird is fairly secretive, unlike the brasher Whitethroat. The call is a distinctive rattle. 13–14 cm. Summer visitor: mid Apr–Oct.

Whitethroat
Sylvia communis

Widespread among hedges and scrubland, and also heaths, but much less common since 1968. The Whitethroat is a lanky, restless, nervously energetic bird with a long tail and expressive face. The male's display flight involves rocketing climbs and plummeting dives into cover. Over a distance, flight is undulating and, after brief evasion tactics, the bird dives into the cover of hedges and scrub where it scolds the intruder. It is best identified by its white throat, reddish wings, the grey head of the male and its dancing song flight (*see Lesser whitethroat, p 17*). The female lacks the grey head and pinkish breast. The crown feathers are often raised during the bird's pleasant, scratchy song, or when it is inquisitive or angry. 14 cm. Top Sixty. Summer visitor: Apr–Oct.

Turtle dove
Streptopelia turtur

The smallest of the doves, feeding on the ground and nesting low down in bushes and hedges. It is most often seen in flight, which is very swift and direct with a curious intermittent tilting and bent wings. There is a soaring display flight (*see picture, top right*). Its call, a soft, purring "rooorrr-roorrr" is a clear harbinger of spring. Slightly smaller than the Collared dove (*p 206*), it has more striking plumage (especially its rich orange and black which catches the eye during take-off, as does the white band in the tail). The breast is pink. The unique checkered pattern on the upperparts and the multiple black and white marks on each side of its neck identify a Turtle dove. It is found in farmland and open country, including large gardens, as well as in woodland. Top Sixty, yet protected by law against shooting. Distributed mostly in S and E. 27 cm. Summer visitor: Apr–Oct.

Golden plover
Pluvialis apricaria

Dense flocks of Golden plovers fanning out as they land to feed are common on certain inland fields and meadows from autumn to spring, though in summer the birds breed in upland moorland. The summer plumage (*see p 33*) is striking with golden brown upperparts and black and white underparts, but the bird is less distinctive in winter. However, at all times, an all-white underwing, together with yellow spangling above and a dark rump, will easily separate it from the Grey plover (*p 141*) and its pointed wings from the Lapwing (*p 33*). It has a square, bullet head held high, a delicate bill and a deep chest. The juvenile is yellower above, than the adult. The bird often runs rapidly on the ground, with a "pause-dip" method of feeding. It also often stands sentinel on a rock. Its flight is very fast with rapidly beating wings. There is a lovely aerial display with much calling. It has a liquid, plaintive "kleep" whistle. 28 cm. Resident.

Southern

Northern

Northern   Southern

"Southern" forms of Golden plovers, which breed from Ireland to Southern Scandinavia, have black mainly restricted to belly in summer. "Northern" forms (breeding Iceland to central Russia) have black on face and throat as well, surrounded by a distinct white band. Winter plumage is identical.

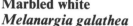

SUMMER
Butterflies

♀

Marbled white
Melanargia galathea

A variable species, whose uppers have a distinctive black and white chequered pattern, with the extent of the black varying in both sexes. It is widespread in grassy areas, especially on chalk downs in S and C areas, and also in parkland. The female is usually larger than the male. Her underside hindwing is tinted ochre-yellow. The male's forewing central cell lacks any narrow black cross bars. The submarginal band encloses eye-spots broken in the middle. The eye-spots are not always visible on the uppers. The female lays

♂

her eggs in flight; they fall on grasses (the food plant) at random. There is one brood a year. Wingspan: 46–56 mm. Flight period: June–Aug.

Large skipper
Ochlodes venatus

A common species of meadows, chalk downs and woodland edges, the Large skipper may also occur in coastal areas. It is a very active butterfly, rarely staying long at any one flower. The male has a conspicuous sex brand on the forewing. There is usually one brood a year and the caterpillars feed on various grasses. Wingspan: 28–34 mm. Flight period: June–Aug.

♂

Small skipper
Thymelicus flavus

The Small skipper has the typical rapid flight of skippers, often pausing to rest on the ground with its hindwings spread out flat and its forewings raised. The uppers are tawny brown with a long, curving sex brand in the male. The underside of the forewing is orange-red. The butterfly is common in flowery fields and on hills up to 1,800 m. The caterpillars eat various grasses, and there is one brood a year. Wingspan: 26–30 mm. Flight period: June–Aug.

♂

Gatekeeper
Pyronia tithonus

A common butterfly, mostly in S and C areas and found in the habitats its popular name of Hedge brown suggests – hedgerows, fields and wooded lanes, especially where brambles are in bloom. The forewing's black eye-spot often has two white centres. The female has larger, brighter orange areas and lacks the male's sex brand. The caterpillars feed on various grasses and there is one brood a year. Wingspan: 34–38 mm. Flight period: July–Aug.

♂   ♀

Chalk-hill blue
Lysandra coridon

The Blues are by far the most numerous of the Lycaenidae family (which also includes Hairstreaks and Coppers) and may be seen in abundance on chalk downs in summer. In this family, the males are often blue or coppery and the females brown. Most of the family quick in flight and tend to settle when the sun goes in. The Chalk-hill blue used to be found in large numbers in the S, but is now less common. The blue colour is variable. The female has bolder markings on the underside. Its caterpillar, which feeds on Horseshoe vetch, is often attended by ants attracted to the sweet secretion from its honey gland. Wingspan: 30–36 mm. There is one brood which flies in July–Aug.

White-letter hairstreak
Strymonidia w-album

This butterfly may be confused with the Black hairstreak but it is paler on the underside and lacks orange spots on the upper hindwing. Often found near elms (a food plant), feeding at bramble flowers in hedgerows, in meadows and parkland. Another food plant is Lime. A widespread species, it is locally common in the S. The sexes may be distinguished by an oval sex brand on the male's forewing, and the female is slightly paler. On the underside a thin white line forms a distinct W-shape on the hindwing. Wingspan: 30–32 mm. Flight period: June–Aug.

MOTHS

Burnet companion
Euclida glyphica

Flying in sunshine on meadows (especially damp ones), downland, wooded clearings and railway banks. The caterpillars feed in July and August on various Clovers and Trefoils and overwinter as pupae. Wingspan: 26–31 mm. May–June.

Chimney sweeper
Odezia atrata

Day-flying, especially in sunshine, on damp, grassy meadows and gardens, also chalk downland and limestone hills. The eggs overwinter and the caterpillars feed (Apr–early June) on Pignut flowers. Wingspan: 23–26 mm. Flight period: June–July.

Ringlet
Aphantopus hyperantus

A very dark butterfly with a variable number of obscure eye-spots on the upperside and conspicuous, yellow-ringed eye-spots on the underside. The female is paler and has larger, more regular markings. Found in damp open woods, near hedgerows, in parkland and also on sea cliffs. There is one brood which feeds on various grasses. Wingspan: 40–48 mm. Flight period: June–Aug.

Six-spot burnet
Zygaena filipendulae

A common day-flying moth found in grassy places, especially on chalk downs and also on dunes. Its wingspan is 28–35 mm, and its caterpillars' food plants are Clovers, Trefoils and others of the Pea family. Flying June–Aug.

Wild Flowers

Ox-eye daisy (Marguerite)
Leucanthemum vulgare
Very common in dry, grassy places (fields and roadsides) and also dry woodland, with a rosette of toothed leaves and a single daisy-like flower, 25–50 mm, on a long stalk. 70 cm. June–Aug.

Field rose
Rosa arvensis
Common in hedges and woods, though rare in the N, a weak-stemmed, scrambling shrub often forming mounds less than a metre high. The flowers are white with a prominent centre of yellow styles. The green or purplish stems are dotted with curved thorns. The leaves are usually hairless, but pinnate. Unlike the fruit of the (usually pink) Dog rose (*p 27*), the hips from the Field rose are poor in vitamins. 1·5 m. June–July.

Bladder campion
Silene vulgaris
Frequently seen on arable land and roadsides, with thick clusters of white flowers, 18–20 mm, above oval blue-green leaves. The flowers produce abundant nectar and are pollinated by moths. 60 cm. June–Aug.

Corn spurrey
Spergula arvensis
Widespread in sandy, acid soil, with succulent narrow leaves, sticky hairs and tiny white flowers (4–8 mm) on long stalks. 25 cm. June–Aug.

Common cleaver (Goosegrass)
Galium aparine
A very common plant of disturbed ground and hedges, with tiny prickles which cling to clothing or fur. White flowers (2 mm) on long stalks emerge from leaf whorls. 1 m. June–Aug.

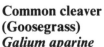

Wild liquorice
Astragalus glycyphyllos
An old medicinal plant of dry hedgerows and woodland, with the creamy-white, sometimes green-tinged, flowers (10–15 mm) of the Pea family to which it belongs. The pinnate leaves are on thick straggling stems. 1 m. May–Aug.

Thyme-leaved sandwort
Arenaria serpyllifolia
Common on dry, sandy, disturbed soils, often near rabbit burrows. Thin greyish stems bear small white flowers, 5–8 mm, and pairs of tiny, pointed, hairy leaves. 20 cm. June–Aug.

Yarrow
Achillea millefolium
Very common on grassy areas, with creeping runners, short, upright, woolly stems, feathery leaves and flat clusters of tiny white flowerets shaded pink. 30 cm. June–Aug.

Greater burnet saxifrage
Pimpinella major
Mostly in dampish grassy meadows and hedgerows, with simply pinnate leaves which smell nasty when rubbed, and rigid brittle stems. 1 m. June–July.

Burnet saxifrage
Pimpinella saxifraga
On dry chalky grassland. Probably most easily distinguished from other white umbellifers by its leaves: the lowest are once pinnate, the next twice pinnate, and the top ones pinnate again. 1 m. July–Aug.

Common gromwell
Lithospermum officinale
Found among hedges and open woods, usually on limestone, a tall, much-branched perennial (compare Corn gromwell, p 14). The narrow leaves have obvious veins and the tiny (3–4 mm) flowers are creamy-white. 80 cm. June–July.

Goatsbeard
Tragopogon pratensis
Common in grassy places, with large flowers partly hidden by overlong green bracts. The leaves are tall and narrow, often twisted. The flowers open only on sunny mornings and the fruits form large "dandelion clocks" from which the plant gets its name. 70 cm. June–July.

Corn marigold
Chrysanthemum segetum
A common plant on light sandy arable land, with coarsely toothed, succulent leaves and single, golden-yellow flowers up to 65 mm across. 50 cm. June–Aug.

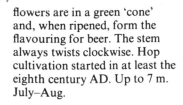

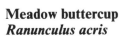

Meadow buttercup
Ranunculus acris
Growing in damper grassland and taller than the Bulbous buttercup (p 14), the sepals of the Meadow buttercup are upright. The leaves are hairy, the upper ones being cut, but the lower ones not. A very common plant. Up to 1 m. June–July.

Hop
Humulus lupulus
Often an escape from hopfields and liking very damp and warm hedgerows and thickets, this woody climber has yellowy-green male flowers and heart-shaped leaves. Female flowers are in a green 'cone' and, when ripened, form the flavouring for beer. The stem always twists clockwise. Hop cultivation started in at least the eighth century AD. Up to 7 m. July–Aug.

Prickly sow thistle
Sonchus asper
Like the Smooth sow thistle (p 194), but with prickly leaves having rounded lobes that encircle the stem; also the fruit is smooth. Common on disturbed ground. 1 m. June–Aug.

23

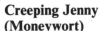

Creeping Jenny (Moneywort)
Lysimachia nummularia
In hedges, damp grass and woodland, and also river banks, a low creeping plant with rounded (coinlike) leaves in opposite pairs. The yellow flowers (15–25 mm) have pointed petals, and often red dots inside. Prostrate to 60 cm. June–Aug.

Wild mignonette
Reseda lutea
Growing on disturbed ground, both fields and roadsides, with a spike of tiny, yellow six-petalled flowers, each 6 mm across. Many small pinnate leaves break from the tall branching stem. 75 cm. June–Aug.

Hoary ragwort
Senecio erucifolius
Found in meadows and roadsides, it can be distinguished from Common ragwort (*p 127*) mostly by its grey downy leaves which have the end lobe pointed. 1 m. July–Aug.

Pineapple mayweed
Chamomilla suaveolens (*Matricaria matricarioides*)
A very common, low aromatic herb of disturbed ground, especially roadsides, paths and farmyards, with many feathery leaves off a branched stem.

Most of the 5–8 mm flowers have disc florets only. Gives off a strong smell of pineapple if crushed. 30 cm. June–July.

Rock rose
Helianthemum nummularium
Common on chalky grassland, a straggling plant, with leaves which are woolly below. The flowers are 20–25 mm and have crinkly petals. 30 cm. June–Sept.

Silverweed
Potentilla anserina
Common in damp meadows and roadsides, a creeping perennial with up to 12 pairs of silvery leaves interspersed with tiny leaflets. The 15–20 mm flowers are not often seen, but are carried on long stems. Creeping up to 1 m. June–Aug.

Wild madder
Rubia peregrina
A tall evergreen scrambling over hedges by means of the prickles on its stems and on the leathery, shiny, dark green leaves set in whorls. The yellow-green flowers, 5 mm, are in many clusters. 1 m. June–Aug.

Tall melilot
Melilotus altissima
Similar to Common melilot and growing on damp arable and wasteland, but to a greater height and with a longer keel to its pea-like flower, Its pods are black and downy. 1.5 m. June–Aug.

Agrimony
Agrimonia eupatoria
Common in grassland, especially roadsides, and below hedges. The hairy hooked spines on the 5–8 mm flowers persist in the fruit which can then cling to clothing and fur. 60 cm. June–Aug.

Treacle mustard
Erysimum cheiranthoides
Another member of the Cabbage family which grows on arable and wasteland. The leaves are long, narrow and slightly toothed, and the flowers are 6 mm across. The four-angled pods can be up to 30 mm long. 90 cm. June–Aug.

Wormwood
Artemisia absinthium
Like Mugwort (*p 200*) and growing on waste ground, but strongly aromatic, with more rounded leaf segments and silky hairs on both sides. 90 cm. July–Aug.

Wild parsnip
Pastinaca sativa
A very common, tall yellow umbellifer, smelling carroty when its leaves are rubbed. It grows on chalk and limestone grassland and by roadsides. The leaves are singly pinnate, with lobed leaflets. 1·2 m. July–Aug.

Pepper saxifrage
Silaum silaus
Another yellow umbellifer of meadows, but with leaves that are two or three times pinnate and have fine-toothed segments. 1 m. June–Aug.

Fly orchid
Ophrys insectifera
Growing on dry chalk and limestone grasses in England, the Fly orchid has yellow-green sepals and brownish-red petals and lip. It is more delicate and sometimes taller than the Bee orchid (*see p 29*), and has narrower leaves. Male flies can be deceived by its similarity to an insect and attempt to mate with it, thus assisting in its pollination. 45 cm. May–July.

White mustard
Sinapis alba
Like Charlock (*p 15*), but with all its leaves pinnately lobed. The flowers are 15–20 mm. Grows on the disturbed chalky soil of fields and wasteland. 60 cm. June–Aug.

Great mullein
Verbascum thapsus
Common on dry, often stony, disturbed land and roadsides, a very tall, robust biennial with a dense woolly covering. The yellow flowers, 15–30 mm, are in a tall dense spike and the leaves are long and rather narrow. 2 m. June–Aug.

Man orchid
Aceras anthropophorum
The reason for this orchid's name is the manikin shape of its flowers, yellowy-green with red margins. It occurs on chalk and limestone grassland in S and C England, but is not very common. 30 cm. June–July.

Carline thistle
Carlina vulgaris
Common on chalk and limestone grassland in the S, a short biennial with a rosette of woolly leaves in the first year which are lost before the flowers (40 mm) appear in the second. The leaves and the outer bracts are spiny, the inner bracts whitish, and the florets purplish. 60 cm. July–Oct.

Musk thistle
Carduus nutans
A tall biennial with woolly stems and spiny leaves. It is common in chalky grassland and roadsides in England. The flowers (30–50 mm) are always nodding and their bracts are spiny. 80 cm. May–Aug.

Greater knapweed
Centaurea scabiosa
Common in dry, chalky meadows and roadsides in England, though scarce elsewhere, this tall perennial has large, reddish-purple flowers, 30–50 mm. The outer florets are spread and the leaves are deeply lobed. 70 cm. July–Sept.

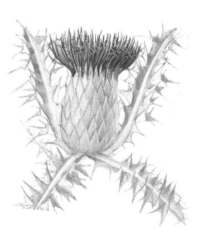

Woolly thistle
Cirsium eriophorum
Scattered on limestone grassland, this majestic thistle has a globular head up to 70 mm across. It is made up of densely woolly bracts and topped by bright reddish-purple flowers. The stems are ridged and the leaves, unique to this type of thistle, are pinnate with narrow lobes and spines. 1·5 m. July–Sept.

Stemless thistle
Carlina acaulis
A low rosette of sharp spiny leaves with bright purplish-red flowerheads, 25–40 mm. A feature of short chalk and limestone turf and the only stemless thistle. 20 cm. July–Sept.

Saw wort
Serratula tinctoria
Liking damp, grassy places, including roadsides and woodland edges, the flowerheads, 15–20 mm across, of this tall perennial look like thistles. However, there are no spines. The leaves are pinnate and finely toothed. Male and female flowers are on separate plants. 65 cm. July–Sept.

Black knapweed
Centaurea nigra
A tough, branching perennial very common in grassy places, with blackish-tipped bracts and reddish-purple flowerheads up to 40 mm in diameter. The narrow leaves are toothed near the bottom and the stems are grooved. 90 cm. June–Sept.

Musk mallow
Malva moschata
Liking dry grassy places, especially in the S, the rose-pink or white flowers (30–60 mm), smelling of musk, stand above deeply cut leaves. (*Compare* Mallow, *p 37*) 60 cm.

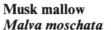

Welted thistle
Carduus acanthoides
Covered with cottony white hairs and common in southern grassland and hedge-foots. The 10–20 mm flowerheads are circled by soft, spiny bracts. The leaves are pinnately lobed and spiny. 1·5 m. June–Aug.

Sainfoin
Onobrychis viciifolia
Deep rose, pea-like flowers (10–12 mm) with deeper pink stripes form long spikes above narrow, pinnate leaves. The ripened pods are warty. On chalk and limestone grassland and roadsides. 60 cm. June–Aug.

Melancholy thistle
Cirsium helenioides
Growing in damp, grassy places with a woolly stem and very hairy leaves. The flowers, 30–50 mm, top green bracts. The leaves are narrow and toothed, but virtually without spines. 1 m. July–Aug.

Downy rose
Rosa tomentosa
A species of the Dog rose, but a deeper reddish-pink and with smaller flowers. The leaves are hairy on the underside and the prickles are just curved. The hips are poor in Vitamin C. 1·5 m. June–July.

Dog rose
Rosa canina
Another rose very common in hedges and woodland, its arching stems covered with curved thorns. The flowers are pale pink or white, 45–50 mm. Unlike Field rose (*p 22*), the styles are flat. The red fruit (hips) are full of vitamins. 2·5 m. June–July.

Long-stalked cranesbill
Geranium columbinum
Liking dry chalky meadows, with larger flowers on longer, branching stalks than the Cut-leaved variety (*p 37*). The petals are unnotched and leaves more feathery. 30 cm. June–July.

Crow garlic
Allium vineale
Bluish-green leaves, like those of Chives, are topped by a tight, round head of green bracts and a few pink or green flowers. On dry grassland and roadsides. 60 cm. June–July.

Hedgerow cranesbill
Geranium pyrenaicum
In hedges and by roadsides, with many sticky hairs and leaves more rounded than the Long-stalked variety (*left*) and cut into lobes. The purplish flowers, 15–20 mm, grow in pairs. 40 cm. June–Aug.

Squinancywort
Asperula cynanchica
A delicate creeping perennial, with clusters of tiny (3–4 mm), bell-shaped, pink flowers, white inside the tube. The leaves are very narrow, and grouped four to a whorl. On dry grassland. Trailing to 40 cm. June–Aug.

Wild clary
Salvia verbenaca
On meadows and roadsides in the S and E, with tall spikes of violet-blue flowers (15 mm), each with two white spots on the lower lip. Leaves are large, oval and sometimes toothed. 60 cm. May-Aug.

Meadow clary (Meadow sage)
Salvia pratensis
On limestone grassland, an aromatic perennial, especially distinguishable from Wild clary (*left*) by its leaf shape. The brilliant blue flowers set on a spike can be up to 25 mm long. 1 m. June–July.

Red bartsia
Odontites verna
A hairy, very branched parasite on the roots of other plants in disturbed ground, with spikes of pinkish-purple flowers (8–10 mm) whose lower lips are toothed, as are the narrow leaves. 50 cm. June–Aug.

Common valerian, All-Heal
Valeriana officinalis
A medicinal plant, whose scent attracts cats, with rounded heads of pale pink flowers, 4–6 mm. The leaves are pinnate and lobed. Found in meadows, usually where it is damp. 1·5 m. June–Aug.

Monkey orchid
Orchis simia
On chalk grassland occasionally in S and E England, with the flowers forming a fascinating monkey shape (the "tail" made by a tooth between the "legs"). There is a rosette of base leaves, as well as a few up the stem. 20 cm. May–June.

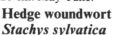

Hedge woundwort
Stachys sylvatica
Very common in hedges and open woodland, with an unpleasant smell. Wine-coloured flowers, 12–15 mm, have white markings on the lower lip. Leaves are heart-shaped. 1 m. July–Aug.

Fragrant orchid
Gymnadenia conopsea
Mostly on chalk and limestone grassland, but also in damp situations. The spikes of sweet-smelling, pale purplish-pink flowers have a very long spur. The leaves are slender. 40 cm. June-Aug.

Pyramidal orchid
Anacamptis pyramidalis
Easily recognised by its densely packed, pyramid-shaped spike of flowers. The spur is not as long as the Fragrant orchid, nor the scent as strong. Chalk and limestone grassland. 35 cm. June–Aug.

Long-headed poppy
Papaver dubium
More frequent in the N and NW, and distinguished from the Common poppy (*right*) by its long, smooth seed capsule and no dark centre in the flower. 40 cm. June–July.

Common poppy
Papaver rhoeas
A common arable and roadside plant, though eliminated by weedkillers from most cornfields. The leaves are pinnately divided, and the stems covered in bristly hairs. Large scarlet flowers, 70–100 mm, often have a black blotch in the middle, and the seedpods are round. 60 cm. June–Aug.

Bistort
Polygonum bistorta
Usually found in dampish hay meadows and roadsides, with a dense spike of pink flowerets. The stems carry nearly triangular leaves with winged scales. 50 cm. June–Aug.

Round-headed rampion
Phyteuma orbiculare
On dryish, chalky pastures, with roundish heads of violet-blue flowers (1·5 cm in diameter). Unlike Scabious (*p 39*) in its long, narrow petals curved like claws. The leaves are narrow and oval. 35 cm. July–Aug.

Cornflower
Centaurea cyanus
Quite a rare arable weed these days, with stiff, cottony, well-branched stems, and bright blue flowerheads (15–30 mm). The lower leaves are deeply lobed, but the upper ones are untoothed. Both leaves and stem have thick grey hairs. 90 cm. June–Aug.

Bee orchid
Ophrys apifera
Typical from its large, brownish-red lower lip, resembling a bumblebee. On semi-dry, chalky turf and sometimes sand dunes. The plant takes 5–8 years to mature and then may flower only once, so should never be picked or uprooted. 30 cm. June–July.

Tufted vetch
Vicia cracca
Clambers in tall grassland and hedges, including roadsides, with up to 12 pairs of pinnate leaflets and tendrils. The blue-violet flowers, 10–12 mm, are in spikes of up to 40. Scrambles to 2 m. June–Aug.

Green-winged orchid
Orchis morio
The name comes from dark parallel lines inside the flower hood. Smaller than the Early purple (*p 16*) with unspotted leaves. Never grows in woods. Now an endangered species. 25 cm. May–June.

Harebell
Campanula rotundifolia
Delicate, blue, nodding bell flowers (15 mm), common on dry grassland, especially sandy soil. Base leaves are rounded, but those on the flower shoots are narrow. 40 cm. July–Sept.

Fungi

Field mushroom
Agaricus campestris
The best known wild mushroom, yet often confused with Horse mushroom (*p 43*). The skin does not bruise yellow, but the thick white flesh discolours pink. The Cultivated mushroom (*p 202*) has a larger ring on the stem. The Field mushroom never occurs in woods. The cap is 3–8 cm, and the gills are pale pink, then blackish brown. Edible. July–Oct.

Leucoagaricus naucinus
Resembles an *Agaricus* but the gills remain whitish. The cap is 4–8 cm, fleshy, white or pale brown at centre, smooth, dry and cracking. The gills are crowded. The stem is 3–7 cm, white with a ring. Edible after cooking. July–Oct.

Dung mottle gill
Paneolus semiovatus
Many of the fungi in this section grow on dung. Released spores which have fallen on vegetation are eaten by cattle, horses, sheep, rabbits or deer, pass through the gut and are finally excreted. This poisonous species was formerly known as *Anellaria separata*. The cap is 2–6 cm, whitish to pale brown and sticky when wet. The gills are grey to black, mottled and crowded. The stem is 7–15 cm, rigid, white or yellowish. The ring is thin and white. July–Nov.

Parasol mushroom
Macrolepiota procera
One of the best edible species, with a nutty flavour, though it is best to reject fibrous stems. Young specimens resemble a drumstick, but in exceptional cases the cap can expand to 40 cm diameter. Grows in grass, generally near trees, sometimes forming fairy rings. The cap has a thick, shaggy margin, the surface covered with large, plate-like brown scales on a greyish-brown background. The stem surface has a snake-skin pattern. July–Oct.

Grey mottle gill
Panaeolus sphinctrinus
A poisonous variety on all dung and rich soil, recognized by its grey-brown to almost black stem and the fringe of white scales on the cap edge. The cap is 2–3 cm, dark grey and the gills are black, white-edged and broad. The stem is 7–12 cm, erect and powdery. July–Oct.

Coprinus radiatus
Although widespread, this tiny ink cap is almost restricted to horse dung (in which it is rooted) and therefore its occurrence depends on the distribution of the horse. The cap, 4–8 mm, has white, curved scales. The gills are few, soon black, and spaced. The stem is 5–25 cm, white and hairy, with a rooting base. May–Nov.

Coprinus niveus
One of the larger ink caps, forming small colonies on cow and horse dung. The cap is 2–4 cm, egg-shaped at first and finally with the margin upturned. It is white with a dense mealy covering. The gills are soon black and crowded. The stem, 4–8 cm, tapers above and is white, with woolly scales. May–Nov.

Agrocybe semiorbicularis

Common on well-established lawns and near roadsides from early summer onwards. The cap is 1–2 cm, hemispherical, yellowish to pale tan in colour and smooth. The gills are pale to deep cinnamon brown and crowded. The stem is 6–8 cm, slender, yellowish-brown, smooth and shiny. June–Oct.

Yellow cow-pat toadstool
Bolbitius vitellinus

Mostly found amongst grass on horse or cow dung, a delicate species with a sticky flat cap and hollow stem. The cap, 2–4 cm, is chrome yellow at the centre, then paler, very thin, and splitting. The gills are brown, crowded and thin. The stem, 6–10 cm, is slender, whitish or yellowish and powdery. Aug–Nov.

Panaeolus campanulatus

Distinguished by its red-brown cap, this poisonous species can cause nausea. It is found only on horse dung. The cap, 2–3 cm, dries a yellow-brown. It is shiny, and often cracked. The gills are black, white-edged and crowded. The stem is 7–10 cm and whitish. Aug–Oct.

Conocybe pubescens

Probably the most common of the several *Conocybe* species found on dung, this is usually smaller than the related *C. rickenii* (p 202). The cap is 1–3 cm, tawny brown, drying paler, and lined when moist. The gills are rusty brown and crowded. The stem, 4–7 cm, is slender, wavy, white above, brown below, and lined. Aug–Oct.

Stropharia coronilla

Commonly grows in groups in fields or at the edge of woods or paths. It is of dubious edibility and easily mistaken for an *Agaricus*, but the gills are attached broadly to the stem, not free. The cap, 2–6 cm, is ochre yellow and paler at the margin. The gills are finally dark brown and crowded. The stem, 5–8 cm, is white to yellowish, slightly scaly below the ring, which is white, narrow, grooved and attached to the upper part of the stem. July–Oct.

Scarlet hood
Hygrocybe coccinea

Colouring similar to *H. punicea* (p 41), but smaller. The cap and upper part of the stem remain blood red. In short grass, sometimes woods. The smooth, dry cap (2–5 cm) is bright scarlet to blood red, fading to orange-buff. The gills are yellow to red. The stem, 4–7 cm, is cap colour and smooth. Edible only after cooking. Aug–Oct.

Pink meadow cap
Hygrocybe calyptraeformis

A fragile mushroom with an easily splitting pointed cap. The lilac or rose-pink tints gradually fade. The cap, 4–10 cm, is very pointed. The gills are white. The stem, 6–12 cm, tapers at both ends and splits. Aug–Oct.

Calocybe carnea

Amongst short grass. The very crowded white gills are distinctive. The smooth, flesh-pink cap, 2–4 cm, is convex, then flattened and finally concave. The stem, 2–3 cm, is slender, flesh pink and tough. The flesh is thin and white. July–Oct.

Birds

Corn bunting
Miliaria calandria

One of the least distinguished-looking British birds, this largest and coarsest-looking of the buntings is to be seen perching conspicuously on wires and fence-posts or feeding quietly on the ground. The male dangles its legs as it flutters off a perch in the breeding season. The song sounds like jangling keys and there is a sharp "quit" call note. The bird occurs in open, usually arable, country and scrub. Its heavy build, odd bill shape and fine streaking are distinctive. The dark speckling streaks on its breast and throat show well against its plain brown plumage. The lack of white in the tail is a distinguishing feature. 18 cm. Resident.

Quail
Coturnix coturnix

Britain's smallest gamebirds, quails stubbornly resist most attempts to flush them and are thus very difficult to see. They do betray their presence by their emphatic, deceptively ventriloquistic "quit-ker-hit" call, heard the end of May to July. When one is seen, it can look rather like a tiny, young Partridge, with its white-flecked, brown upper plumage. But its swift, direct flight and rapid wing-beat differ from the Partridge. The wings are long and thin. Widespread but local in Britain outside Scotland. 16–18 cm. Summer visitor: May–Oct. Some birds winter.

Lapwing (Peewit)
Vanellus vanellus

A common bird of fields, moors and coastal marshes with an atttractive aerial display. Large flocks are usually seen in midsummer on pastures. The lapwing is lowland Britain's commonest inland breeding wader and the only species with a wispy, spiky crest, broad wings and black and white plumage (the green only shows in good light). On the ground the bird runs or walks, tipping up to feed, when its orange undertail shows. Flying birds are striking black and white and orange from below. From above the white upper tail shows well against the dark upperparts. Males have broader wings than females. The "lapwing" name comes from the lapping sound of the wings in flight, and the alternative name of "peewit" from the characteristic, plaintive "peeerst" or "pee-wit" call. Top Sixty. 30 cm. Resident. Also winter visitor.

Golden plover *in summer plumage.* (*see p 19*).

Corncrake
Crex crex

Skulking, elusive birds that will vanish into the smallest area of cover, but are located by their harsh, grating, seemingly endless "rack-rack, rack-rack" call (like a stick drawn across a comb) which can go on all night. They prefer hayfields, but mechanical haycutters have now decimated their nests and young, so numbers have seriously declined. When haymakers flush a bird out, its flight is weak and fluttering and it looks like a buff-coloured Moorhen. The legs trail untidily and the strong marked back shows on take-off, as does the chestnut underwing. 27–30 cm. Summer visitor: mid Apr–Oct.

AUTUMN
Butterflies

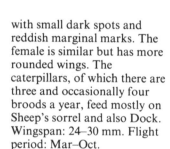

Heath fritillary
Mellicta athalia

A fritillary usually heavily marked with black in the male, but the female is often lighter. The species generally occurs in the drier areas of meadowland, but may also be found in woodland clearings. Restricted to a few counties in S England. The foodplants are Cow-wheat and Plantain and there are one to two broods a year. It hibernates in the caterpillar stage. Wingspan: 34–46 mm. Flight period: May–Sept.

Small copper
Lycaena phlaeas

Widespread except in N Scotland, this bright little butterfly is seen in open, flowery meadows, parkland and even near the sea. The upper forewing of the male is golden red with black spots and a dark border. The upper hindwing is predominantly dark grey with an orange margin. The underside hindwing is brown with small dark spots and reddish marginal marks. The female is similar but has more rounded wings. The caterpillars, of which there are three and occasionally four broods a year, feed mostly on Sheep's sorrel and also Dock. Wingspan: 24–30 mm. Flight period: Mar–Oct.

Wild Flowers

Field pansy
Viola arvensis

Often very similar to Wild pansy (*p 15*), though the flowers, 10–15 mm, are smaller and usually creamy-white, with an orange-yellow mark on the lowest petal. The petals are shorter than the sepals. Common in cornfields. 30 cm. Apr–Oct.

White bryony
Bryonia cretica

A tall, scrambling perennial of hedgerows and sandy soil, with clinging tendrils arising from the bristly stems close to the ivy-shaped leaves. Clusters of greenish-white flowers, 10–15 mm across, produce shiny red berries. The male and female flowers are on separate plants. The veined petals are longer than the sepals. Clambering to 3 m. May–Sept.

White clover
Trifolium repens

One of the Pea family and extremely common on grassland and roadsides, also sown for fodder. The creeping stems root as they grow. White flowers accompany the trefoil leaves which are broader near the tip, with a white V mark. 30 cm. June–Sept.

Black nightshade
Solanum nigrum
Poisonous berries (first green, then black) follow the white flowers, 5–6 mm, on this widespread annual of disturbed ground. The leaves are pointed and the stems are dark. 45 cm. July–Sept.

Greater dodder
Cuscuta europaea
Parasitic on nettles and hops in disturbed ground and roadsides, this leafless climber has clusters of pinkish-white, blunt-petalled flowers on red stems. Fairly rare. 1 m. Aug–Sept.

Hedge bedstraw
Galium mollugo
A stout, scrambling perennial in hedges and meadows. The broad leaves are set in whorls with prickles at their edges. White flowers, 2–3 mm, are followed by dark green, and later black, fruits. 1·2 m. June–Sept.

Hemlock
Conium maculatum
A very tall, extremely poisonous perennial with purple-spotted stems, large leaves (up to four times pinnate) and large dense umbels of tiny flowers, 1–2 mm. Common in damp wasteland and by water. 2 m. June–July.

Hogweed
Heracleum sphondylium
A massive, tall umbellifer, with bristly, hollow stems and once pinnate, hairy leaves up to 60 cm long. Flowers can be 10 mm across, sometimes pink-tinged, and the whole umbel may reach 15 cm in diameter. Very common. 1·5 m. June–Sept.

Eyebright
Euphrasia species
A group of annuals semi-parasitic on the roots of other plants. They are all very similar and grow in meadows, on short chalk grassland. Flowers, 3–15 mm, are white, tinged or blotched with purple, and the lower lip is toothed into three. The leaves are sometimes purplish or bronzed, and the stems often have many branches. 25 cm. July–Sept.

Perforate St John's wort
Hypericum perforatum
Liking chalky meadows and hedgerows, a tall perennial with yellow flowers, 20 mm, edged with black dots. Leaves if held to the light show translucent glands. 70 cm. June–Sept.

Tansy
Tanacetum vulgare
An aromatic plant which used to be cultivated as a herb. The yellow flowerheads, 6–12 mm, have no rays. Common in hedges, disturbed ground and roadsides. 80 cm. July–Sept.

Yellow rattle
Rhinanthus minor
Semi-parasitic on the roots of other plants, but varying in appearance. The yellow flowers, 10–20 mm, are mixed in leafy spikes. On undisturbed grasslands and sometimes cornfields. To 50 cm. May–Sept.

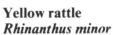

Sharp-leaved fluellen
Kickxia elatine
A prostrate annual having long-spurred flowers, 7–9 mm, with mauve upper and yellow lower lips. The leaves are borne on long stalks and are arrow-shaped. Common on SE arable land. The stems trail to 50 cm. July–Oct.

Large-flowered hemp-nettle
Galeopsis speciosa
The flowers (up to 30 mm) vary in colour, but always have some yellow in them. The plant is widespread on disturbed soils (often peaty), and is similar to Common hemp-nettle (*p 173*), but larger. The leaves are toothed. 1 m. July–Sept.

Round-leaved fluellen
Kickxia spuria
Like *Kickxia elatine* (*above*), but hairy and more robust. The leaves are rounder, the purple-and-yellow long spurred flowers are 10 mm and the stalks are hairy. Trailing. July–Oct.

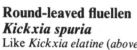

Dwarf spurge
Euphorbia exigua
Growing on arable land, with narrow, grey-green leaves and curious flowers which, like all Spurges, have no sepals or petals. One female and several male flowers are surrounded by a cup-shaped structure with horned glands and triangular bracts. 30 cm. June–Oct.

Dyer's greenweed
Genista tinctoria
A member of the Pea family liking a dampish, loamy soil in grassland. It is a woody plant, without spines, and having slim, yellow flowers, 15 mm, in spikes. The leaves are hairy at the edges. 60 cm. July–Sept.

Ploughman's spikenard
Inula conyza
A robust biennial widespread on chalk and limestone grassland, with red stems, clusters of rayless, yellow flowerheads (8–10 mm) and a rosette of leaves often mistaken for those of Foxglove (*p 87*). 1·3 m. July–Sept.

Yellow bartsia
Parentucellia viscosa
Similar to Red bartsia (*p 28*) but with yellow, lipped flowers and an unbranched stem. Growing in damp meadows, it is stickily hairy, and erect to 50 cm. June–Oct.

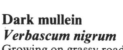

Dark mullein
Verbascum nigrum
Growing on grassy roadside verges, its yellow flowers (20 mm across) have purple hairs on their stamens. The leaves are darker green than Great mullein (*p 25*) and the stem is ridged. 1·2 m. June–Oct.

Alsike clover
Trifolium hybridum
An erect perennial with elliptic leaflets and stipules which are oval, long and with fine points. The flowers are pinkish and long-stalked. Widely cultivated. 40 cm. June–Sept.

Red clover
Trifolium pratense
Very common on grassland and also a forage crop, with large oval flowerheads, 15–18 mm, and leaves having three leaflets which usually have a pale, V mark. Erect or straggling. 30 cm. May–Sept.

Strawberry clover
Trifolium fragiferum
Small round heads of pink flowers on long stalks and trefoil leaves which have serrated leaflets. The fruit look like brownish-pink strawberries. Creeps in grassland. 20 cm. July–Sept.

Zig-zag clover
Trifolium medium
Like the Red clover (*left*), but with narrower leaflets and oblong stipules (Red clover's are contracted to a fine point). A straggling perennial with long-stalked flowerheads. Also in woods. 30 cm. June–Sept.

Dwarf mallow
Malva neglecta
Often prostrate, with paler, smaller flowers than Common mallow (*below*). The leaves are 70 mm across. Grows in weedy places on disturbed ground (wasteland and arable). 40 cm. June–Sept.

Cut-leaved cranesbill
Geranium dissectum
Pinkish-purple flowers, 8–10 mm, with deeply cut, finger-like leaves, are typical of this short, straggly annual which grows well on grassland and roadside verges. 40 cm. May–Aug.

Common mallow
Malva sylvestris
A hairy perennial herb of wasteland and roadside. Its magenta flowers, 25–40 mm across, have darker stripes. The leaves are ivy-shaped, with usually five lobes, and 10 cm across. Most have a dark spot where they join the stalk. To 90 cm. June–Sept.

Basil thyme
Acinos arvensis
A branched, hairy, straggling annual growing on disturbed ground and meadows. The flowers, 8–10 mm, each with a white mark on the lower lip, grow in whorls. The leaves, 15 mm, are oval. 20 cm. May–Sept.

Pale toadflax
Linaria repens
The flowers are 7–14 mm, pale lilac, dark-veined, and with short spurs. Creeping underground stems produce several upright shoots, with narrow, greyish leaves. Grows on disturbed, chalky ground, to 80 cm. June–Sept.

37

Field madder
Sherardia arvensis
Heads of tiny, pale pinkish-purple flowers, 3 mm, crown this short hairy annual with narrow oval leaves in whorls. It is a common plant of disturbed ground, especially arable, and the prostrate shoots may reach 40 cm. May–Oct.

Spearmint
Mentha spicata
A strong-smelling perennial and the mint most often cultivated in gardens, with pale lilac flowers in spikes. Escapees from gardens are usually found by roads and on wasteland. To 90 cm. Aug–Sept.

Common broomrape
Orobanche minor
A curious plant parasitic on Clover and various Hawksbits, Catsear etc, and consequently has no green among its purplish-yellow colour. The stigmas in the tubular flowers (10–18 mm) are purple. The leaves are actually brownish scales, close against the stem. Favours meadows and road verges. 35 cm. June–Sept.

Rest harrow
Ononis repens
This member of the Pea family, with pink flowers (10–15 mm), trefoil leaves and occasional soft spines, creeps over dry grassland. 45 cm. June–Sept.

Wild basil
Clinopodium vulgare
Growing on chalky soils, in scrubby grassland and by hedges, with whorls of bright pinkish-purple flowers, 15–20 mm, each having a white-haired, purplish sepal-tube. The leaves are oval and finely toothed. Hairy. 60 cm. July–Sept.

Marjoram
Origanum vulgare
A tall, aromatic perennial, with heads of clustered pale purplish-pink (7 mm) flowers, with protruding stamens. The leaves are oval. Common in dry, limestone grassland. 60 cm. July–Sept.

Vervain
Verbena officinalis
A stiffly erect, woody perennial common by roadsides in the S, with delicate spikes of dull lilac flowers (3–4 mm across). The plant is often coarsely hairy and the lower leaves are deeply cut, while the upper ones are untoothed. 45 cm. July–Sept.

Field forget-me-not
Myosotis arvensis
Curved spikes of tiny blue flowers (5 mm across), shaped individually like the garden variety. There is a rosette of hairy leaves. The plant is upright. Found on arable land and also in open woodland. 20 cm. April–Sept.

Chicory
Cichorium intybus
A tall, stiff perennial with bright blue flowers, 25–40 mm, in clusters. The root has been used as a flavouring since the 1600's. Common on chalky grassland and roadsides. 1·2 m. July–Oct.

Common milkwort
Polygala vulgaris
The flower colour of this scrambling perennial is variable (blue, purplish-pink, white, or white tipped with purple). The flowers are 8 mm. The lower leaves are only about 10 mm, much shorter than the upper. It is a common grassland plant on chalk and limestone. 20 cm. May–Sept.

Bugloss
Anchusa (Lyocopsis) arvensis
A bristly, upright annual with bright blue flowers, 5–6 mm, and wavy-edged leaves. It grows on arable land and sometimes in sandy places near the sea. 60 cm. May–Sept.

Field scabious
Knautia arvensis
The flowers are 40 mm in diameter and there are narrow, hairy, slightly lobed leaves on the stem, as well as a rosette of pinnately lobed base leaves. There are bigger petals round the rims of the flowers. On dry grassland and by hedges. 70 cm. July–Sept.

Devilsbit scabious
Succisa pratensis
Grows on damp meadows, as well as marshes and damp woods, with deep purplish-blue flowers (15–25 mm across and covered with starlike bracts). The narrow oval leaves have a white midrib and often are blotched. More frequently short than tall, but up to 80 cm. June–Oct.

Meadow cranesbill
Geranium pratense
Growing most often on roadsides in limestone areas as well as in meadows, this tall perennial has big violet-blue flowers, 25 mm in diameter. The stems are hairy and the leaves are deeply cut After flowering the stalks bend down and then stand erect again as the fruit ripens. 50 cm. June–Sept.

Clustered bellflower
Campanula glomerata
A shortish perennial common on chalk or limestone grassland, with deep violet-blue, bell-shaped flowers growing in dense clusters. The stem is thick and hairy, and the leaves are narrow. 20 cm. May–Sept.

Lady's mantle
Alchemilla vulgaris
Usually on grassland, sometimes in upland areas, with tiny, greenish-yellow flowers, 2–3 mm across, in clusters on branched heads. Roughly sycamore-shaped leaves. 30 cm. June–Sept.

Red goosefoot
Chenopodium rubrum
A tall annual common on disturbed ground with shining reddish stems, bright green, toothed leaves and dense greenish flowerheads in spikes. 50 cm. July–Sept.

Fungi

The miller
Clitopilus prunulus
A delicious edible mushroom, with a thick, soft flesh and a strong mealy smell. Do not confuse it with the poisonous white *Clitocybe* species (*below*). The Miller can quite often be found. The cap is 3–8 cm, irregular, dry, whitish and shiny. The gills are whitish-pink and crowded. The stem, 2–5 cm, is solid and white. July–Nov.

Camarophyllus virgineus
Similar to *C. niveus* (*p 43*) but typically larger and more robust. Common on pastures and downland, sometimes in grassy places in woods. Edible only after cooking. The cap is 4–7 cm, convex then flattened or depressed, pure white drying yellow. The gills are white, thick, broad and spaced. The stem is 5–10 cm, white, tapering towards the base. Sept–Oct.

Lepista luscina
With a mealy smell and excellent to eat, but do not confuse with *Clitocybe dealbata* (*right*). The cap is 5–9 cm, convex, finally depressed, pale grey to dark brownish-grey, and typically spotted. The gills are white, then grey, narrow and crowded. The stem is 2–5 cm, solid and grey-brown. The flesh is thick and whitish. Oct–Nov.

Clitocybe dealbata
Do not confuse this dangerous white species with either Fairy ring champignon (*p 188*), the Miller (*above*) or *Lepista luscina* (*left*). Its thin flesh contains muscarine, a toxin that produces blurred vision, sweating and twitching within 30 minutes. It is often on grassland at the edge of woods or in clearings. The cap, 2–4 cm, is white to beige, with pinky-brown zones. The gills are thin, a creamy flesh colour and crowded. The stem, 2–4 cm, is the same colour as the cap. Aug–Nov.

Mycena flavoalba
One of the many species of *Mycena* which have small conical or bell-shaped caps on delicate long stems. *Mycena flavoalba* is common in grass generally as well as in troops on lawns. The cap is 1–2 cm, pale yellow with a darker centre and a prominent umbo. The gills are white and spaced. The stem is 2–3 cm and smooth. The flesh is thin and white and smells radishy. Aug–Nov.

Buff meadow cap
Camarophyllus pratensis
An excellent edible grassland species, also found in broad-leaved woods. The cap, 3–9 cm in diameter, is fleshy, convex, smooth or cracking when dry, buff to tawny yellow in colour. The gills are thick, broad, spaced and pale buff like the stem. The stem is 5–8 cm in height. It is a similar colour to the cap but paler, and tapering below. Sept–Oct.

Melanoleuca grammopodia

In meadows and grassy woodlands, recognized by its thick, fibrous stem and crowded white gills, which discolour creamy brown. It is edible only after cooking. The cap, 7–15 cm, is livid brown to brownish-black in colour, smooth and moist. The gills are white and then brownish. The stem 7–10 cm high, is white with brown fibrils. Sept–Nov.

Mycena aetites

A common species, giving off a faint smell of ammonia. The cap, 1–2 cm in diameter, is dark grey, brownish at the centre, and radially grooved. The gills are white to grey, and interveined. The stem is 3–5 cm high and greyish-brown. Aug–Oct.

Nolanea papillata

The chestnut-brown cap is 2–3 cm across. The gills are pinkish-brown and crowded. The stem, 2–3 cm in height, is the same colour as the cap and shiny. Sept–Oct.

Hygrocybe punicea

These brightly coloured, shiny *Hygrocybe* species are known collectively as Wax agarics. This is the largest and certainly one of the most beautiful. It usually grows singly in long grass and is edible after cooking, but has a brittle, watery texture with little taste. The cap, 5–12 cm, is blood red discolouring yellowish from the centre, and sticky when moist. The gills are at first yellow tinted with red, thick and spaced. Normally the flesh is white. The stem, 6–11 cm, is yellow or blood red, white at the base. Sept–Nov.

Conical slimy cap
Hygrocybe conica

This brightly coloured species differs from *H. nigrescens* (*right*) in its more conical cap and yellow stem base. The cap, 1–4 cm in diameter, is acutely conical. Its colour is orange or yellow with reddish tints, and finally black. The gills are free and white to yellow, not red. The stem is 3–5 cm high, the same colour as the cap. July–Nov.

Hygrocybe nigrescens

Larger and more robust than *H. conica* (*left*), this also has a white stem base. It is a predominantly red fungus but finally turns totally black. Mostly found in grass in fields, occasionally in woods, its cap, 3–8 cm across, is red, scarlet or yellowish, and blackens quickly. The gills are white, tinged yellowish-green, blackening. They are very broad and spaced. The stem, 4–8 cm high, is lemon yellow, flushed red, then streaked with black. Sept–Oct.

Birds

Partridge
Perdix perdix

A gamebird widespread on farmland, heath and moorland, usually in pairs or groups. The orange head, grey breast, grey flanks with chestnut bars and maroon 'horseshoe' on the breast distinguish adults from the Red-legged species (*right*). The bill is cream. If disturbed, partridges fly low in a loose formation, with several wing-beats and long, bow-winged glides. The bird is a fast runner. Its call is a grating "krik-ik". Top Sixty. 29–31 cm. Resident.

Red-legged partridge
Alectoris rufa

More often seen on bare, open ground than the Partridge and often on roofs and fences whereas Partridges never perch. The call is a harsh "chuck-chuck-chuckor" and a measured "check-check". Top Sixty. 32–34 cm. Resident.

Wood pigeon (Ring dove)
Columba palumbus

The largest and commonest British pigeon and the only one with a white collar and large white wing panels. The large body, deep chest and small, erect head also distinguish it from other pigeons. The smallness of its head accentuates the stocky look of the body. Compare the tail extending beyond the wings with the Stock dove's (*right*). Wood pigeons are often seen flocking in huge numbers in autumn and winter. They feed in fields and woodlands, and are also commonly seen in cities and towns with Feral pigeons. Take-off involves a great clatter of wings, but flight is swift and direct. The widespread tail is conspicuous on landing. In its courtship flight, the bird rises steeply, claps its wings and sails around in display. The call is the familiar "coor-cooo, coor-cooo". Top Sixty. 41 cm. Resident.

Stock dove
Columba oenas

Smaller and more compact than the Wood pigeon (*left*), with a squarer head and no significant areas of white visible. The wings are narrower, almost triangular, with a straighter rear surface. The tail is shorter and the wing tips are black. Usually seen in pairs, but flocks do occur. The swift, direct flight has the wings held straighter than the Wood pigeon, and an intermittent slight flicking action. In its display flight the Stock dove soars on angled wings. It calls a monotonously regular "rroo-roo-ro". It is mostly found in farmland and woods and usually nests in holes in trees. Top Sixty. 33 cm. Resident.

WINTER

Wild Flowers

Sweet violet
Viola odorata
Flowering early by hedges and in woods, with sweetly-scented flowers, 15 mm, violet or white. The sepals are blunt and the leaves are round (the more common Dog violet's being heart-shaped). There are down-pointing hairs on the leaf stalks. 10 cm. Feb–Apr.

Snowy meadow cap
Camarophyllus niveus
Excellent to eat but small and thin-fleshed. Grows in large troops on short grass. Distinguished from the white *Clitocybe* species (*see Index*) by its thick gills. It is snow white when dry. The cap, 2–3 cm across, is smooth. The gills are white and very spaced. The stem, 3–5 cm in height, tapers below and is soon hollow. It too is white. Sept–Dec.

Hygrocybe ceracea
All parts of this small, delicate species are a uniform wax yellow. It can be separated from other yellow species by the decurrent gills (meaning they are broadly attached and descend down the stem). It grows in large numbers in short grass. The cap, 1–3 cm in diameter, is convex, soon flat, sticky, with a lined or grooved margin. The gills are triangular, with interveining. The stem, 2–5 cm high, tapers below and is hollow. Sept–Dec.

Fungi

Horse mushroom
Agaricus arvensis
A large, robust species which can occur in great quantities over many years in the same locality, often in circles in fields. It differs from the Field mushroom (*p 30*) in having a large ring and staining yellow, but do not mistake it for the toxic Yellow-staining mushroom (*p 202*). The Horse mushroom is edible and noted for its outstanding flavour. The cap is 8–20 cm, white, then discolouring to yellow, dry and silky. The gills are crowded, pinkish-grey to chocolate brown. The stem, 6–15 cm, is silky, white bruising yellow; its base is not swollen. The large, fleshy, pendent ring is double and white. The white, firm flesh smells of aniseed. June–Dec.

Marasmius graminum
A tiny species growing on dead stems and leaves of grasses, with a cap 0·5–0·7 cm across, red-brown and radially grooved. The cream, very spaced gills are attached to a collar. The stem is 2–4 cm, deep brown and paler at the apex. It is also shiny. July–Dec.

Birds

Yellowhammer
Emberiza citrinella

In winter the Yellowhammer is very much a bird of farmland, frequently in flocks feeding on exposed ploughed fields or roadsides, often with other species. By February the breeding cycle has begun and the birds desert the open ground for the more vegetated areas of the farm or move to heaths and commons. Generally the commonest yellow bird of fields, hedges and open gardens and usually seen in pairs. The chestnut rump distinguishes it from other buntings. It is noticeably long-winged and long-tailed in flight. The song ("A little bit of bread and no cheese") can be heard February onwards from a song perch on wires. There is a ringing "tink" flight call. Top Sixty. 16–17 cm. Resident.

Skylark
Alauda arvensis

One of the commonest birds identifiable by its melodious, bubbling song. It differs from other larks in its longer wings and tail and well-proportioned shape. In its musical song flight, the bird takes off from the ground, climbs vertically to a great height, where it "hangs" before spiralling down with a final plunge to the ground. The call is a rolling chirrup, constantly uttered by flying birds. Especially in winter, the birds are seen in either small parties or enormous flocks, usually over arable land, but sometimes over any open country. If alarmed, they stand erect with raised crests. The streaking on the breast is distinctive. Top Sixty. 18 cm. Resident.

Pheasant
Phasianus colchicus

The only common, long-tailed
gamebird. The young may look
like a lanky, spike-tailed
Partridge before the tail has
grown. Flight is usually short
and low (except at shoots), with
flaps and long glides, though, if
disturbed, the bird rises with a
shocking clatter and echoing
double crow. To clear trees,
birds rise vertically. The female
is identified by her size, long
neck and tail, and buff
plumage. In the male, the wing
coverts vary from maroon to
blue-grey, and the rump may be
greenish or orange. He may or
may not have the white collar.
Top Sixty. 53–89 cm. Resident
(except NW Scotland).

Black-headed Gull
Larus ridibundus

A familiar sight in winter taking
food from freshly turned soil
behind the plough, as well as
from rubbish dumps, city
parks or the beach at low
tide. It is the smallest of
the gulls commonly seen
inland, particularly on arable
land, with a noticeably slender
build and pointed wings. Its
combination of red or orange
legs and red bill are seen on no
other gull (but compare terns).
The distinctive black, white and
grey pattern on its wings
(particularly the white triangle
on the upper wing) and the
brown hood on summer birds
(*p132*) make identification easy.
Young birds also have a white
leading edge on the wing, but
their tails, unlike adults', have a
pronounced dark band. Flight
is much lighter and more
effortless than the larger gulls.
The Black-headed gull makes a
harsh, screeching "kwarrk" and
"kick" call. Top Sixty.
35–38 cm. Resident.

Mountain, Moor and Heath

Mountains, upland moors and lowland heaths are among the most inhospitable habitats, yet even they have their complement of wild creatures and plants, though fewer than in lusher areas. Actually, like the meadow and hedgerow habitat, even the wildest lowland heaths and upland heather moors are manmade. Left alone, the former would become birch or oak woodland and the latter be colonized by birch.

Some ecologists would classify heaths with grassland (arguing that their principal difference is that the former is dominated by heathers rather than grass). But since the soil of both heath and moorland is usually acid and both provide good conditions for heather to flourish, this book has followed other specialists and linked them together.

Lowland heaths tend to be on well-drained, often sandy soils, whereas upland heather moors are on wetter peaty soils. Visually, the purplish tinge of heather is typical of the upland moors, whereas the lowland heaths have their purple spangled with the gold of gorse bushes. Mountain flowers are specialised to cope with the harsh conditions, but they are often extremely beautiful. Few butterflies and fungi exist there, but there are such magnificent birds as the Buzzard and the rarely seen Golden eagle.

200–500 m

over 500 m

SPRING
Butterflies

Green hairstreak
Callophrys rubi

The only British butterfly with a bright green underside, a good camouflage when at rest on green leaves. It has a short, rapid flight and occurs in a wide range of habitats, from moorland bog and heathland to woodland and even parkland. It has many suitable foodplants of the Leguminosae family. There is an oval patch of scales on the male's forewing and the female is a paler brown. There is one brood a year. Wingspan: 26–30 mm. Flight period: Mar–June.

Brown argus
Aricia agestis

A "blue" butterfly in which both sexes are brown! The female is slightly larger, with larger orange markings and a white flash on the underwing, with well defined spots. A common species throughout England and Wales, in the N replaced by the Mountain argus (*p 56*). The Brown argus is very active in sunny weather and flies rapidly over heathland and rough grassy areas up to 900 m. It also occurs in sandy coastal regions. There are usually two broods and it overwinters as a caterpillar. The foodplants are Rock rose and Storksbill. Wingspan: 22–28 mm. Flight period: Apr–Aug.

MOTHS

Kentish glory
Endromis versicolora

The male flies in sunshine and the female from dusk onwards in late March–Apr on moorland with birch and in open woodland. The caterpillars feed on birch in late May–July. They overwinter as pupae, sometimes spending a second and third winter in this stage. Wingspan: 50–85 mm.

Orange underwing
Archiearis parthenias

Very active in sunshine, flying friskily on edges of birchwoods on heath and hill. The one brood of caterpillars feeds on birch, overwintering in the form of pupae. Wingspan: 33–35 mm. Flight period: Mar–Apr.

Emperor moth
Saturnia pavonia

The male flies by day and the female by night over heath and moorland, open woods and waste ground. There is one brood of caterpillars, feeding on Heather, Bramble and many other plants. They overwinter as pupae. Wingspan: 50–80 mm. Flight period: April–May.

Wild Flowers

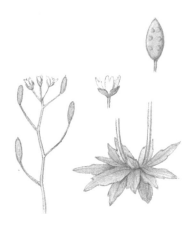

Wood sorrel
Oxalis acetosella
A creeping perennial, growing
from rhizomes, with clover-like
leaves. The white, cup-shaped
flowers, 15–20 mm, have lilac
veins and are carried on long,
thin stems. On mountain rocks,
as well as in woods and by
hedgerows. 10 cm. Apr–June.

Spring sandwort
Minuartia verna
A tufted perennial growing on
chalky rocks and moors. It
makes a loose mat of foliage,
from which white flowers,
8–10 mm, grow up on shoots.
The leaves are narrow, with
three veins. 10 cm. May–Sept.

Common whitlow grass
Erophila verna
A variable, low, hairy annual
found on dry, rocky or bare
ground or walls. The leaves
form a rosette and the white
flowers, 3–6 mm, have very
deeply cut petals. 20 cm.
March–May.

Mossy saxifrage
Saxifraga hypnoides
A tight cushiony mat of
narrow, three to five lobed
leaves, with white flowers. The
stem is hairless. Found on hills
and scree, usually on chalk. The
flower shoots are up to 20 cm
high. May–July.

Horseshoe vetch
Hippocrepis comosa
Named after the shape of its
fruit segments. It has circular
heads of five to eight yellow,
pea-like flowers and pinnate
leaves, with four to five pairs of
leaflets. On chalk hills,
limestone quarries and gravel
embankments. To 40 cm.
May–July.

Petty whin
Genista anglica
A spiny, low shrub of the Pea
family with their typically
shaped flowers, 8–10 mm. The
leaves are narrow, oval and
bluish. On heath and moorland.
45 cm. May–June.

Broom
Cytisus scoparius
No spines and taller than Petty
whin (*above*), with larger
flowers (to 20 mm) and trefoil
leaves. The long, black pods
(30 mm) explode with a loud
crack in dry weather. On heaths
and disturbed ground. 2 m.
May–June.

Rose root
Rhodiola rosea
Growing on mountain rocks
and sea-cliffs, a robust, erect,
greyish-green perennial with
fleshy leaves and a rounded
head of tiny, yellow flowers,
4–6 mm, male and female on
separate plants. 22 cm.
May–Aug.

Gorse
Ulex europaeus
An evergreen shrub on light,
heathy soils with many ridged
spines up to 20 mm long. The
flowers are fragrant, with wings
longer than the keel. 1·5 m. Can
flower all year round, but
mostly Feb–June.

Purple saxifrage
Saxifraga oppositifolia
A perennial with long, prostrate branches, growing on mountain rocks. The stems are covered in tiny, bluish leaves and the flowers are purplish, 10–15 mm. Its erect shoots are only 1–2 cm tall. March–May.

Bilberry
Vaccinium myrtillus
A deciduous shrub of heaths, moors and open woods, with edible purple-black fruits in Aug–Sept. In spring the flowers are flask-shaped, greenish-pink, 4–6 mm long and half-hidden by the leaves. The leaves are oval. 45 cm. Apr–June.

Common cow-wheat
Melampyrum pratense
Common on heath and poor grassland, as well as in woods, with pairs of yellow flowers both facing the same way (sometimes marked with purple). The leaves are long and narrow, without stalks. Can be short or tall, up to 60 cm. May–Oct.

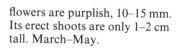

Heath (Dog) violet
Viola canina
On heaths and sand dunes, a creeping perennial, with flowers almost pure blue and having yellow-green spurs. The leaves are not notched at the base as with other *Viola* species. 20 cm. Apr–June.

Sheep's sorrel
Rumex acetosella
A very common plant on bare, dry heathland or rocky, sandy fields, usually on acid soil. It has reddish flower spikes and arrow-shaped leaves. The male and female flowers are separate. 30 cm. May–Aug.

Heath (Common) speedwell
Veronica officinalis
Common on dry heaths and meadow banks, a prostrate perennial, with paler lilac dark-veined, blooms than Germander speedwell (*p 16*), which grow in dense spikes of 15–25 flowers. The stems and leaves are hairy. Creeping to 40 cm. May–Aug.

Thyme-leaved (Heath) milkwort
Polygala serpyllifolia
Growing on heath and moorland, similar to Common milkwort (*p 39*), but with its lower leaves in opposite pairs. Also its blue flowers grow closer together up the stem. 20 cm. May–Aug.

Purple milk vetch
Astragalus danicus
A low, delicate perennial on chalk and limestone hilly grassland, with tight heads of upright, purplish-blue, pea-like flowers, 15 mm. The plant has soft, silky hairs and pinnate leaves, with six to thirteen pairs of leaflets. 25 cm. May–July.

Crowberry
Empetrum nigrum
A prostrate, heather-like, evergreen shrub, with red stems and tiny, six-petalled, pinkish-purple flowers. Many narrow, needle-like leaves clothe the stem. The round (5 mm) fruits are black, and poisonous. Growing on heaths, moorland, and dunes (acid soils). Creeping to 30 cm. May–June.

Fungi

Psilocybe physaloides

One of several small species of *Psilocybe*. *Psilocybe physaloides* is frequently found growing on heaths and moorland, yet may also occur in rich soil near roadsides. The species *P. montana* grows in similar situations, but has a more lined, darker brown cap. The cap of *P. physaloides*, 1–1·5 cm, is convex, dull bay brown to buff-coloured. It is grooved at the edge when moist, but not sticky. The gills are pale brown to blackish-brown. The stem, 2–3 cm high, is slender and paler than the cap. Apr–Oct.

Umbrella navel cap
Omphalina ericetorum

Found on damp peaty ground. The cap, 1–2 cm in diameter, is convex, flat, whitish to olive brown, grooved and with a wavy edge. The gills are triangular, pale yellow and spaced. The stem, 1–2 cm in height, is the same colour as the cap, with a woolly base. Apr–Dec.

Hypholoma ericaeum

A heathland species with a long, tough stem, found only in damp places. The cap is 3–4 cm, sticky when moist, tawny and smooth. The gills are black and crowded. The stem, 6–10 cm high, is slender, yellowish above, tawny below, and smooth. May–Oct.

Birds

The Dartford warbler's cocked tail is about half its body length and is carried high in its weak, bounding flight. The bird has a red eye and rim and is speckled white on its often distended throat. Its tiny size, long tail, stubby wings and dark coloration are unique. Juveniles have short tails and paler breasts. They grow to full size in about ten days. Formerly widespread, the species is now confined to gorse and heath in extreme S England. They are lively, active insect-eaters. A shy, secretive bird, but soft, buzzy "gee-ee-ip" calls betray its presence. It is most often seen in its dancing display flight. Hard winters had reduced the population to a very few pairs, but it is now recovering. 12–13 cm. Resident.

Dartford warbler
Sylvia undata

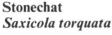

Stonechat
Saxicola torquata

Its tiny size, dumpier profile, short wings and dark, short tail distinguish the Stonechat from the Whinchat (*p 52*), though it is easily missed in its heath and moorland breeding habitat. However, it perches prominently on bushes, wires and fences, constantly flirting its tail and flicking its wings. The flight is somewhat whirring and the call is a constant "tak-tak". Single birds winter out of breeding area in rough ground, often on coastal cliffs, salt marshes and sea walls. The sexes are easily distinguished; the male has a black head and white collar. Juveniles have a more streaked breast than the female. 12–13 cm. Resident.

Whinchat
Saxicola rubetra

A striking small bird of heath and rough grass with suitable perches (including young forestry plantations), often confused with the Stonechat (*p 51*). However, at all times, white in the Whinchat's tail distinguishes it. Its erect posture and constant flicking tail and wings are also distinctive. Its flight is low and jerky from perch to perch and it flicks its wings and tail on landing. The male has black and white in wings and tail. He also has an eye stripe prominent in his strong head and back pattern. The female has a bold eye stripe and a curiously streaked back. The call is a harsh "tik-tik", with a brief simple song. 12–13 cm. Summer visitor: Apr–Oct.

Cirl bunting
Emberiza cirius

Heard throughout March, the rattling trill of the Cirl bunting is more like that of the Lesser whitethroat than the Yellowhammer to which it is usually likened. The call is a thin "zit" or "sip". The female's appearance can be confused with the Yellowhammer, but her rump is streakier and olive (not chestnut). In fact, olive on all birds distinguishes the Cirl bunting. The male's black and greenish-yellow head pattern is unique in buntings. The flight is like the Yellowhammer's but dips more. On scrub, and also hedges and trees, restricted to the S of England. 16–17 cm. Resident.

Wheatear
Oenanthe oenanthe

Among the earliest of the spring arrivals on moors, heaths, dunes and other rough ground. Despite wide variation in plumage between individuals, white and black in the tail make a Wheatear instantly identifiable. Typical in flight is the white rump and black tail band. In spring the male has a grey crown and back contrasting with the black face patch, wings and tail. Wear dulls its bright colours by autumn (*see p 60*). The bird's erect posture, constant bowing and bobbing, with flicking and wagging of its short tail, are characteristic, interspersed with quick scurries to perch on a vantage point. The flight is low, dashing from perch to perch. The bird flies after insects, runs short distances to pick food off the ground, or bolts for cover into holes. It is a hole nester. 14–15 cm. Summer visitor: early Mar–late Oct.

Tree pipit
Anthus trivialis

Very like the Meadow pipit (*p 59*) but with a larger "necklace" on the wing, a more buff breast and larger, more spaced spots. The legs are a brighter flesh colour (dark in Meadow pipit), the wings and tail are longer, and the Tree pipit's stockier build and more erect stance also help to distinguish it. It takes refuge in a tree if flushed, but feeds only on the ground. Distinguished from larks by its wagging tail and the "teez" flight call which is diagnostic. Found in heathland with scattered trees. 15 cm. Summer visitor: Apr–Oct.

Woodlark
Lullaba arborea

One of Britain's finest songbirds, with a mellow, flutelike song, quite distinct from the Skylark's (*p 44*) but delivered on the wing, and a "titlooet" flight call. A singing Woodlark circles at one level before descent, whereas the Skylark continues rising vertically until out of sight. Dumpy build and jerkier movements in flight distinguish the Woodlark from the longer-winged and tailed Skylark. The white eye stripe and streaked breast contrasting with paler belly show well on Woodlarks of all ages. The bold crest is often raised and dropped. On heath and scrub in S England. Decreasing. 15 cm. Resident.

53

Nightjar
Caprimulgus europaeus

During a calm, warm evening, usually after sunset, in late May, the loud "churring" song of the Nightjar can be heard in the S on sandy heathland. It is a mysterious bird of mostly nocturnal habits – and this gives it its name. It may be seen hunting at dusk, bounding and twisting to catch moths. It is rarely seen by day unless flushed from its nest when its cryptic plumage pattern and enormous gape make it unique. A buoyant flight on long, angled wings will identify a flying bird. Only the male bird has white spots at the end of the wings and white in the tail. The bristles (*right hand picture*) save its eyes from insect damage. It nests on suitable heathland and young plantations, but is decreasing. 27 cm. Summer visitor: end Apr–Sept.

Ring ouzel
Turdus torquatus

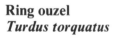

The moorland counterpart of the Blackbird and similar in behaviour and appearance, but the Ring ouzel has longer wings and tail, which show most in flight. It has plumage differences too, though these are confusable with Blackbird mutations. The male's white gorget is visible from a distance. There are faint crescent edges to the feathers. The Ring ouzel is shy, normally shunning habitation. The flight is wild and dashing. The call is a harsh "chack-chack" and there is also a rich, clear, far-carrying song. 24 cm. Summer visitor: Mar–Oct. Some birds winter.

Hobby
Falco subbuteo

At dusk, on southern heathland or wooded farmland, a slim, elegant, handsomely plumaged bird may come scything across the sky. The Hobby is a small falcon, and its head pattern identifies it. The adult female and the smaller male have the same plumage. The juvenile has dark, brownish upperparts. Mercurial in flight, the bird can be overhead and then far distant in a trice. Superb skill on the wing enables it to catch other consummate fliers such as swifts and martins. All insects and some birds are eaten in the air. Insects are caught with the feet and then transferred to the bill. Hobbies soar on angled wings (whereas a Kestrel soars with the front edge of the wing almost straight). The Hobby's tail is shorter than the Kestrel's. Its black head and moustache against a pale chin and collar show well from a great distance. Adults are the only falcons with red thighs. Hobbies call only in the breeding season. A rare breeder (in old crows' nests). 30–36 cm. Summer visitor: Apr/May–Oct.

Golden eagle
Aquila chrysaetos

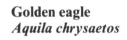

The largest and most powerful of the true eagles and a magnificent and highly accomplished flier, most often seen against the skyline following a ridge, but also soaring overhead. It occupies a huge territory in bare or mountainous country. Flight is deliberate and easy, with much sailing and gliding, the outsplayed primaries being a good clue. When prey is sighted, the great bird folds its wings and plummets. A male Eagle is considerably larger than a Buzzard (*p 67*) and has feathered "trousers". The female is even larger. The white in wings and tails of immature birds gradually disappears. Breeds very occasionally (Mar–June) in Scotland and N England, but otherwise very rare, consistently being illegally persecuted. 80 cm. Resident.

♀

SUMMER
Butterflies

♂

Silver-studded blue
Plebejus argus

Essentially a heathland butterfly (mostly south of the Thames), it will also occur on chalk grassland and dunes. The silver-studded blue male's dark border separates him from the Common blue (*p 12*). His uppers are purplish-blue and the female's are dark brown with orange lunules (though these may be absent). Black marginal spots on the hindwing have tiny, metallic blue-green centres, giving the

centres, giving the "silver-studded" appearance. On the female's hindwing a white band between two rows of black spots is quite prominent. The basic foodplants are Gorse and Broom. Wingspan: 24–34 mm. Flight period: May–Aug.

Dark green fritillary
Mesoacidalia aglaja

One of the more easily identifiable larger fritillaries because of the greenish tinge on the underwing which has silvery spots. The uppers have the typical intricate pattern of fritillaries. The markings are very variable, with the paler females tending to vary more in colour on the upperside than

the males. Some females are particularly pale. A rapid flier, often found in open countryside, such as heaths, dunes and even mountains, but also in woodlands. There is one brood of caterpillars a year, whose foodplant is Violet. Wingspan: 48–58 mm. Flight period: June–July.

♂

Mountain argus
Aricia artaxerxes

The white markings on both wing surfaces are not constant and several subspecies have been described which are more like the Brown argus (*p 48*). Generally the orange lunules are fewer in the Mountain argus and the black spots on the underside are absent or

vestigial. The white spot on the forewing is diagnostic. The females tend to be slightly larger with better developed orange spots. In Scotland and N England it is locally common on moorlands, feeding on Rock rose (*Helianthemum*). One brood a year. Wingspan: 22–32 mm. Flight period: June–Aug.

♂

Mountain ringlet
Erebia epiphron

The less common of the two British mountain butterflies. The Mountain ringlet is a very local species, occurring only in rough moorland in C Scotland and the Lake District, usually above 500 m. Other similar species are found throughout European mountain ranges. The British species is generally dark, the upperside of the forewing being red with the postdiscal band

narrow and often incomplete, usually enclosing four small black spots. The female is similar, but her uppers are sometimes better defined. The caterpillars feed on grasses. Wingspan: 34–42 mm (English specimens being smaller). Flight period: June–July.

MOTHS

Netted mountain moth
Semiothisa carbonaria

Flies in sunshine to the flowers of moorland Bearberry, on which its single brood of caterpillars feed. Also found on mountain hillsides, especially the Scottish Highlands. Wingspan: 20–21 mm. Flight period: Apr–early June.

Beautiful yellow underwing
Anarta myrtilli

Day-flying and preferring hot sunshine, the Beautiful yellow underwing moth inhabits heath and moorland. The caterpillars feed on Heather and Heath. There are probably two overlapping broods, flying between late Apr–Aug. Wingspan: 22–25 mm.

Wild Flowers

Mountain avens
Dryas octopetala
Despite its Latin name, this rare and beautiful mountain plant sometimes has up to ten petals, with black hairs on the sepals. There are many very hairy leaves and a feathery fruit. 6 cm. June–July.

Heath bedstraw
Galium saxatile
Common on peaty heaths, a prostrate, matted plant with prickles at the leaf edges pointing forward. The leaves form whorls of six to eight. White flowers. 20 cm. June–Aug.

Alpine bearberry
Arctostaphylos uva-ursi
The Bearberry bush, found on upland moors and somewhat resembling Bilberry (*p 50*), can live for 100 years. It is a prostrate evergreen, with groups of five to twelve white flowers, and a red berry which tastes dry. The leaves arc blunt. Creeping to 2 m. May–July.

Snowdon lily
Lloydia serotina
A bulbous perennial with flowers (20 mm) which are white with purple veins. There are two to four narrow, grasslike leaves. Only found in Snowdonia. 15 cm. June.

Starry saxifrage
Saxifraga stellaris
Starry white flowers, 10–15 mm, with red anthers grow in clusters above a tight rosette of green leaves. The commonest white mountain saxifrage, liking damp situations. 10 cm. June–Aug.

Common (Round-leaved) sundew
Drosera rotundifolia
Found on moorland, in boggy places, an insectivorous plant exuding a sticky fluid from its red leaf tentacles by which an insect is caught and later digested. The leaves form a low rosette and the few white flowers, 5 mm, are on an upright stalk. 25 cm. June–Aug.

Alpine bistort
Polygonum viviparum
Grows on mountain grassland, with tiny, pale pink flowers on a spike which may have red bulbils lower down. The leaves taper at base and tip. A creeping plant, with some upright shoots. 40 cm. June–Aug.

Alpine enchanter's nightshade
Circaea alpina
Growing in shady places among mountain forests from a tuberous stock, with white or faintly pink flowers and stalked leaves. 20 cm. July–Aug.

Dwarf cornel
Cornus suecica
The striking white "flowers" of this plant of upland moors are really bracts 8 mm, and the actual flowers are tiny, 2 mm. There are up to 25 of them within the bracts. The leaves are in opposite pairs, with parallel veins. 15 cm. July–Aug.

Welsh poppy
Meconopsis cambrica
A native of Wales and SW England, but introduced elsewhere on damp, shady rocks. Not unlike the Greater celandine (*p 14*), but hairier and with yellow, 50–75 mm, four-petalled flowers. 60 cm. June–Aug.

Navelwort
Umbilicus rupestris
Growing in cracks in rocks and stony banks and walls, with round, fleshy leaves and stalks of white or greenish tubular flowers. The name comes from the sunken middle of the leaves – like a navel. 30 cm. June–Aug.

Alpine lady's mantle
Alchemilla alpina
Common on mountain pastures and rock crevices in the N with leaf blades cut almost to the centre. The tiny yellow flowers are 3 mm and the leaves are silky underneath. 15 cm. June–Aug.

Mountain sorrel
Oxyria digyna
Growing on mountains, similar to Common sorrel (*see p 163*), but with fleshy, kidney-shaped leaves. The outer parts of the flowers are spread or bent back. 25 cm. July–Aug.

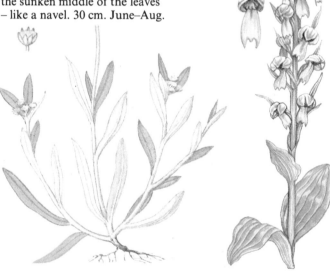

Mossy cyphel
Minuartia sedoides
A densely tufted perennial of Scottish mountains, making a cushion up to 25 cm across by 8 cm high. The leaves are succulent, and the yellow flowers, 5 mm, have five sepals and no petals. June–Aug.

Marsh cudweed
Gnaphalium uliginosum
Common on heaths, sandy fields and roadsides where the soil is damp. A low branching annual, with grey hairs and narrow leaves which almost hide its yellow flowerheads, 3–4 mm, which have brown bracts. 10 cm. July–Aug.

Frog orchid
Coeloglossum viride
On mountain and chalk grassland, with curiously shaped flowers (yellowish but with a hint of orange-brown) in a spike. The leaves start in a rosette and progress up the stem. 15 cm. June–Aug.

Alpine willowherb
Epilobium anagallidifolium
Fond of the bright green mossy carpets that grow by mountain streams, this prostrate plant has flowering shoots erect to 10 cm. The drooping, pink flowers are 5 mm across and the leaves grow in pairs. July–Aug.

Mountain everlasting
Antennaria dioica
Widespread in dry spots in mountains, a creeping perennial with purplish-pink, rounded flowerheads on male plants and long, feathery bracts on female plants. The greyish leaves in rosettes have dense white hairs underneath. 15 cm. June–July.

Wild azalea
Loiseleuria procumbens
On high mountains in Scotland, a prostrate, cushion-like evergreen shrub, with numerous leathery leaves and pinkish-red flowers. The flowers have five stamens. 30 cm. May–July.

Moss campion
Silene acaulis
Growing on mountain rock ledges and cliffs and forming bright green, mossy cushions covered with masses of rose pink flowers, 12 mm and very narrow leaves. 8 cm. July–Aug.

Orange hawkweed
Hieracium aurantiacum
On mountain rocks, screes and grassland, the flower stalks have dark hairs and brown or orange-red flowerheads. The leaves are hairy. 65 cm. June–Aug.

Cowberry
Vaccinium vitis-idaea
A short evergreen shrub growing on moors and wooded hills with acid soils. It has bell-shaped, pinkish-white flowers, 5–6 mm. The red-berried fruit is edible. The leaves are round and glossy above. 20 cm. June–Aug.

Heath spotted orchid
Dactylorhiza maculata
Growing on damp soils on heaths, fairly similar to the Common spotted orchid (*p 163*) except for its habitat preference and its toothed lip. All the leaves are very pointed. Grows to 50 cm. June–Aug.

Birds

Meadow pipit
Anthus pratensis

The commonest of the pipits, to be seen rising erratically with a characteristic "tsiip-tsiip-tsiip" call from rough ground. The song lacks the Tree pipit's distinctive ending. Small flocks seem to "see-saw" in air as if struggling for height. They are ground-feeders and, if flushed, return to the ground, but they will also perch in trees. Found on moorland, wasteland (where they breed) and (especially in winter) on fields and coast. The white in the outer tail, with a darker centre and faint wing-bars, shows both at rest and in flight. The "necklace" is less clear than in the Tree pipit (*p 53*) and the wings and tail are shorter. The legs are darker than the Tree pipit's with a very long rear claw (short in Tree pipit). Top Sixty. 14–15 cm. Resident.

Linnet
Carduelis cannabina

The commonest small brown British finch, differing from the Twite (*below*) and Redpoll (*p 95*) by its grey head and chestnut back. Linnets are tiny birds with long wings and tail, short legs and a small white area in the tail. They breed on heaths and open scrub. The bird's tiny black eye and delicate bill are distinctive and it has an energetic bounding flight. It makes a constant twittering call and song. In winter Linnets form large roving flocks in search of seeds and may occur in gardens and on roadsides. The wings and tail of the male are blacker and with more white than those of the female. The extent of red varies. Top Sixty. 13–14 cm. Resident.

Twite
Carduelis flavirostris

The moorland linnet, breeding in highlands especially in Scotland, but often coastal in winter. It is much less common than the Linnet (*above*). Its bill is grey in summer (the Linnet's is pale) and yellow in winter (dark in the Linnet). Male and female Twites have less white in their wings than Linnets and no obvious white in the tail. The male has a crimson rump, but compare his lack of red generally with Linnets. The female Twite has a tiny white area on her tail and wings. A Twite twitters constantly in flight and has a distinct nasal "twang" call. It feeds with other finches and buntings on rough ground in winter. 13–14 cm. Resident.

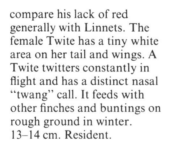

Wheatear
male in July as the bright Spring plumage starts to fade (see p 53).

Dotterel
Charadrius morinellus

A very tame wader with a unique white V on the back of its head, never occuring near water. The chestnut breast separates a breeding adult from any other breeding wader. The female is brighter. The call is a low trill. There is a small breeding population in high mountain tops in the Scottish Highlands and a few in N England and N Wales. 22 cm. Summer visitor and passage birds.

Curlew
Numenius arquata

The commonest and largest of all waders with a very long, down-curved bill, distinguishing it from the godwits (*p 181*). It can only be confused with the Whimbrel (*below*): the dark outer wing and patterned upperparts are almost identical, but note the absence of head pattern on the Curlew. A longer bill (especially in the female – up to 15 cm) and larger size also identify the Curlew. The underwing seems well marked at close range, but looks white (contrasting with the buff chest) at a distance. It is a wary bird, difficult to approach, with a more sedate manner than other

waders. It breeds on moorland, damp pastures, rough land or even in crops. In winter it moves to lowlands and coast, to feed on mud and sand flats and roost on inland fields, marshes and moorland. Flocks are often seen from the beach, flying low over waves out at sea. Flight is fast but the wing-beats are slower and more leisurely than in other waders. The call is diagnostic but very varied, typically a rapid "qui-qui-qui" or a slow "cur-lee". 53–58 cm. Resident.

Whimbrel
Numenius phaeopus

The smaller Whimbrel has build, body and wing shape, and plumage pattern very similar to the Curlew (*above*), Greenshank (*p 168*) and

Bar-tailed godwit (*p 181*), but its shorter legs and bill, conspicuous head pattern and daintier appearance overall distinguish it. Also, its long, down-curved bill sets it apart from all except the Curlew from which it also has a quite different call – a series of seven or eight whistles ("qui-hi-hi-hi-hi-hi-hi-hi")

delivered rapidly. The call will be heard at night and from high-flying passage birds. Its wing-beats are more rapid than the Curlew's and it is less wary, but found in the same habitat – moorlands in N Scotland and Hebrides in summer for breeding, and on sandy coastal shores and estuaries in winter. 41 cm. Summer visitor.

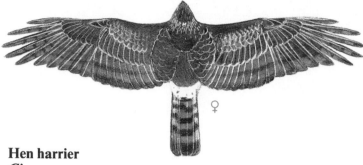

Montagu's harrier

Hen harrier
Circus cyaneus

The commonest British harrier, breeding in moorland and young conifer plantations, and returning in autumn to its winter haunts of lowlying coastal areas and open country. The rump and dark trailing edge of the wing distinguish the male from other harriers. The female and juvenile male may be confused with female Montagu's harriers, except for their heavier build and more defined patterning below (*see pictures left and far left for comparison*). The Hen harrier has five, not four "fingers" on the wing tip. The female Montagu's harrier has three bars in her underwing patterning (the Hen harrier having four). The Hen harrier has a typical harrier flight, quartering the ground with a seemingly lazy flapping and keeping low along a bank or ditch ready to pounce on any small mammal or bird. 44–52 cm. Resident.

Merlin
Falco columbarius

The smallest British falcon, with the male not much larger than a Blackbird. It is declining as a breeding bird, but found in summer in moorland areas, nesting on ground or in trees. It follows every twist and turn of its quarry in a swift, dashing flight. It is sometimes confused with the longer-winged Kestrel (*p 206*), but the male Merlin's blue-grey plumage with a black tail band is distinctive. He is also smaller and has distinctive chestnut streaking on his underparts. Although the female and juvenile look more or less dark brown, their broad-based, sharply pointed wings, bullet-shaped heads and ample, well-barred tails are characteristic. 25–30 cm. A scarce resident.

Ptarmigan
in summer plumage (see p 68).

62

Great skua
Stercorarius skua

Except in the breeding season, when it moves to open moorland colonies on the N coast of Scotland, Orkney, Shetland and Hebrides, the Great skua will only be seen out at sea. The lefthand picture shows one in aggressive display. It is the largest of the skuas, a powerful bird with a slow, ponderous-looking flight, but agile in the pursuit of birds from which it "pirates" food. Like other marine birds of prey, it finds almost all its food by chasing seabirds like Gannets and forcing them to drop or disgorge their latest meal. It looks like an immature Great black-backed gull (*p 149*), a uniform dark brown with white wing flashes at the base of the flight feathers. 58 mm. Summer visitor.

AUTUMN
Butterflies

Small heath
Coenonympha pamphilus
A widespread and common butterfly on all kinds of grassy heaths, downs and dunes. It will fly in both cloudy and fine weather up to 1,800 m. There are, however, many fewer north of the Midlands. The uppers are bright orange with narrow grey wing margins in both sexes. Females are usually paler and larger. The underside forewing has a small black eye-spot, ringed in yellow. The underside hindwing has a darker basal area followed by a whitish band and indistinct eye-spots. There are two broods of caterpillars a year which feed on grasses. Wingspan: 26–34 mm. Flight period: May–Sept.

♂   ♀

♂

Scotch argus
Erebia aethiops
The commoner of the two British mountain butterflies, velvety brown, of variable size, and generally found in open coniferous woodland up to 1,800 m. It is active in sunshine but disappears into the undergrowth as soon as the weather becomes overcast (unless very warm). The male has three white-centred eye-spots on his forewing, and the underside hindwing has four white dots in a pale grey band. The female is a lighter brown and has yellowish bands enclosing bigger eye-spots. The butterfly may be locally common across Scotland, but in England it is confined mainly to the Lake District. The caterpillars (one brood a year) feed on grasses, especially Purple moor-grass. Wingspan: 42–52 mm. Flight period: Aug–Sept.

Wild Flowers

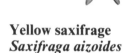

Tormentil
Potentilla erecta
Very common on heaths and moors, as well as bogs, a creeping perennial with four-petalled yellow flowers, 7–11 mm, and leaves forming a rosette. 40 cm. June–Sept.

Trailing St. John's wort
Hypericum humifusum
Another creeping perennial with yellow flowers, but five-petalled ones and narrowly oval leaves with translucent dots on the upper ones. Likes acid soils on heaths and moors, as well as damp, open woodland. 20 cm. June–Sept.

Yellow saxifrage
Saxifraga aizoides
Growing in wet places on mountains, with mats of leafy stems. The flowering shoots are hairy, carrying heads of one to ten flowers, 10–15 mm. The leaves are narrow and slightly fleshy. 20 cm. June–Sept.

Western dwarf gorse
Ulex gallii
Common on heaths and moors in the W, but scarce elsewhere, a low evergreen which forms tighter bushes than the Common gorse (*p 49*). The spines are almost smooth. 60 cm. July–Sept.

Common dodder
Cuscuta epithymum
A curious climbing parasite on Heather and Gorse (*see also* Greater dodder, *p 35*). Uncommon, but usually on SW heaths. The clusters of pink flowers are on red stems and the leaves are actually scales. 1 m. July–Sept.

Bell heather
Erica cinerea
Growing on dry heaths and moors, mostly in the N and W, with deeper, reddish-purple flowers (5–6 mm) than Heather (*below right*) and leaves in whorls of three. The flowerheads are less dense than *E. tetralix* (*right*). Evergreen. 55 cm. July–Sept.

Wild thyme
Thymus praecox (drucei)
On dry chalky grassland and heaths, except in E and C areas. The aromatic flowers are in pinkish-purple heads. 10 cm. June–Sept.

Cross-leaved heath
Erica tetralix
Differing from the other heathers in having its pink, flask-shaped flowers, 6–7 mm, in clusters at the top of the grey, downy stems. Leaves are in whorls of four. On wet heaths and moors. 50 cm. July–Sept.

Heather (Ling)
Calluna vulgaris
Common everywhere on acid soils, heaths and moors, the tightly inrolled leaves overlap. The flowers, 4–5 mm, are a pale pinkish-purple which give their typical mauve tints to autumn hillsides. 60 cm. July–Sept.

Heath cudweed
Omalotheca
(Gnaphalium) sylvatica
Growing in dry places on acid soils, such as heaths and roadsides, and also in light woodland, with loose spikes of brownish-white flowers, 2 mm, and narrow leaves. 45 cm. July–Sept.

Alpine gentian
Gentiana nivalis
Rare, only growing in the Scottish Highlands, but included as one of the most beautiful wild plants. It is a delicate annual, with a petal tube of 15 mm but leaves only 5 mm long. The flowers are deep blue. 15 cm. July–Sept.

Fungi

Cortinarius acutus
A small, non-sticky *Cortinarius* species of heaths and conifer woods. Look out for a faint white cortina between stem and cap edge. The cap, 1–2 cm across, is conical, honey-coloured, drying to ochre. The gills are ochre to cinnamon and fairly crowded. The stem, 5–7 cm high, is wavy, a similar colour to the cap, and soon hollow. Aug–Nov.

Saffron parasol
Cystoderma amianthinum
The Saffron parasol is found in mossy heaths and mixed or coniferous woods. The thin yellow flesh has an unpleasant, mouldy smell. The cap, 2–5 cm in diameter, is convex, with a dry, ochre-yellow, granular surface and a shaggy margin. The gills are widely spaced and white. The stem, 4–8 cm high, is granular up to the fragile, upward pointing ring and is then smooth. Aug–Oct.

Leptonia incana
Grows on heaths and grassland especially on chalk, one of the few green toadstools, but colour varies. The cap is 1–2 cm, yellowish to olive green, and streaked with brown. The gills are pale green then pink. The stem, 2–5 cm, is tough and hard, yellowish green and hollow. The flesh is thin and greenish. It has a strong smell of mice. July–Oct.

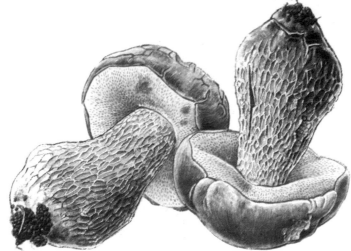

Boletus calopus
One of the most beautifully coloured mushrooms, this species might be confused with *B. luridus* (*p 77*) or *B. erythropus* (*p 78*), both of which have red pores. The thick, veined stem is often swollen and the large, fleshy cap is generally convex, although its size and shape may vary considerably. The creamy-white flesh turns blue when broken and is too bitter to be of any culinary value. Occurs more frequently among trees in mountainous areas on acid soils. The cap, 5–15 cm, is whitish-grey to pale brown, dry, velvety and at times cracked. The tubes are lemon yellow and bruise blue. The stem, 6–10 cm high, is solid, sulphur yellow above, purplish-red below, with network ornamentation. Aug–Oct.

Birds

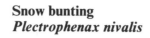

Snow bunting
Plectrophenax nivalis

A rare resident breeding bird of high mountain tops in Scotland, much commoner as a winter visitor to the E coast and also to hilltops. It is a large bunting with very long wings which reach almost to the tip of its tail. It is tame and unobtrusive, taking flight only at the last moment. Flocking birds on the wing make eye-catching patterns of black and white, accompanied by loud, tinkling calls. Females and winter males have some brown. All birds have a dark eye set in a pale face with a dark crown and darkish face patch. Flight is fast with occasional erratic low swoops. The call is a rippling "tirrirrirrip", with "seeoo" or "swapeck" calls from a flock. 16–17 cm. Resident and also a frequent winter visitor: Oct–Mar.

Great grey shrike
Lanius collurio

The Great grey shrike is the largest of the European shrikes and feeds on small mammals, birds and large beetles. It has broad, rounded wings with variable white panels and very splayed wing tips of uneven length. Its favoured winter habitat is gorse-covered heathland with scrub and fringe woodland, and the same bird apparently returns to the same area for several years in succession. It tends to perch very conspicuously on wires or bushes, turning its head from side to side on the look-out for prey such as small mammals, large insects and even birds the size of a Song thrush. The flight over a distance looks curiously feeble and undulating, although the Great grey shrike catches birds on the wing. Prey is held in the foot and impaled on thorns to make a "larder". The bird has a typical "chiuk-chiuk" Shrike call. 24 cm. Scarce winter visitor (especially in E): Oct–Apr.

Red kite
Miluus miluus

One of the species that scavenged the streets of London in the days of open sewers. It was almost lost as a breeding species, but has made a small comeback, but only in the wooded hill districts of Wales. A few winter and passage birds can be seen elsewhere. It has an easy flight action, gliding and soaring well, using its tail as a rudder. The wings are very angled and look long and slender from afar. The well-forked orange tail is obvious from both above and below. The white wing patch also shows well. 60–66 cm. Resident.

Buzzard
Buteo buteo

The largest of the commoner British birds of prey, usually seen circling at some height, but, seen from below, plumage varies considerably from white to (more usually) chocolate brown. The lower leg is bare, unlike the Eagle's feathered legs (p 55). Widespread in western hill districts and moorland, though Buzzards may also be seen in some numbers wheeling over mixed woodland and open agricultural country. They prey on rabbits and small mammals such as mice, earthworms and beetles. The normal flight is direct with powerful, regular wing-beats, often interspersed with glides. Its typically full soaring profile is seen (*far left picture*) as the bird wheels round in the air. Wings are held forwards and the tail is fully spread. The left hand picture shows it sailing with wings fully extended and tail closed. The call is a frequently uttered high "whee-eur". 51–57 cm. Resident, though very local in eastern half of England.

WINTER
Birds

Ptarmigan
Lagopus mutus

Smaller than the Grouse (*below*) but similar in shape and appearance in flight. Extremely tame, but very difficult to pick out in its Scottish mountain-top and rocky hillside habitat. It turns all-white in winter as camouflage against the snow, though its tail stays black and the male also keeps its black eye stripe. Although adults change plumage three times annually, being grey-brown above in summer (*see p 62*) and greyer in autumn, the belly and wings are always white. Moulting birds look patchy. Birds have a habit of standing up on a hillside after an Eagle passes, thereby showing as white dots. The call is a hoarse, croaking, rattling "arrrrrruk". 34–36 cm. Resident.

Red grouse
Lagopus lagopus

The familiar moorland game bird, slightly larger than the Partridge (*p 42*) but with a similar plump, broad-winged profile in flight. The plumage is a dark red brown with brown flight feathers and tail. Despite slight variations, the bird usually looks very dark. Females and immature birds are less red than males, with more buff plumage above and below. Both sexes have bright red patches over the eye and whitish legs in all plumages. Flight is rapid and low over ground. The bird usually calls when flushed: a guttural "kow-kok-ok-ok-ok". There is also a deep "go-bak" call. Top Sixty. 37–42 cm. Resident.

Black grouse
Tetrao tetrix

Found where forest fringes meet heath and moorland in N and W, the male's lyre-shaped tail and black and white plumage distinguish the

Black grouse from other game birds. (Immature males in eclipse plumage are not jet black.) The bird is smaller than the Capercaillie (*p 117*). The plumage of the female (Greyhen) is a rich reddish-brown with two pale wing-bars. She and immatures differ from the similar-sized

Red grouse (*opposite*) in their narrow wing-bar and forked tails. Both sexes have a pure white underwing. Males spread their tails, droop their wings and raise their combs in a spectacular group courtship display. Flight is fast, with rapid wing-beats and long glides. 40–55 cm. Resident.

Raven
Corvus corax

Its huge size (larger than the Buzzard, *p 67*) and easy, soaring flight with regular, powerful wing-beats identify the all-black Raven, which for all its bulk is a great aerial acrobat. In January, the display fighting of a breeding pair is spectacular, with rolls, tumbles, upside-down flight and somersaults. On closed wings, the bird drops from a great height to swing upwards again on its own momentum, using air currents to the best effect. A Raven has a long head, huge

bill, shaggy "beard", relatively narrow, pointed wings and a long, wedged tail. The call is a deep, often repeated "pruk-pruk" and "grok". Usually seen in pairs, although flocks are not uncommon. Occurs in mountain and moorland, and on sea cliffs, in W Britain and Ireland. The substantial nest is built on a ledge. 64 cm. Resident.

69

Woodlands

Woodlands (both deciduous and coniferous), plantations, spinneys and coppices provide a wonderfully sheltered environment for scores of creatures and plants. An oak or beechwood in early summer is a glorious place, with many flowers such as bluebells blooming before the leaves on the trees have opened sufficiently to shade them from the sun. There are many spring and summer woodland butterflies and the summer and autumn woods are a prime place for mushrooms and toadstools. All the year round many birds make their homes there, building their nests and rearing their young away from the more frequent interference of man that occurs on farmland and in park and garden.

Originally most of Britain was covered in trees, but gradually they were felled for fuel, house-building and ships until only a fraction of what was formerly woodland now remains. Little of this existing woodland has been forest since prehistoric times, but has been replanted or "managed" by foresters. Conifer woods are often planted for their timber, and most broad-leaved woodlands are either fox coverts or pheasant reserves. Some of the rarer plants survive only in the more ancient woodlands, since many woodland plants reproduce by rhizomes, suckers, bulbs and tubers and do not easily recolonize planted woods.

SPRING
Butterflies

Green-veined white
Artogeia (Pieris) napi

Unfortunately the Green-veined white, which is not a garden pest, is often mistaken for the harmful Small white, as they both fly over similar terrain. The Green-veined white tends to prefer damp meadows up to 1,500 m, and is commoner in the countryside than the two Cabbage whites (*pp 186 and 199*), especially in woods. The Green-veined species has many variations in colour and spotting, but always a green-veined underside, especially conspicuous at rest. Distinct differences also occur between spring and summer generations, the latter being larger with paler veins. There are two or more broods a year, and the caterpillars feed on the Cruciferae family, especially Wild mignonette and Hedge mustard. Wingspan: 36–50 mm. Flight period: May–Sept.

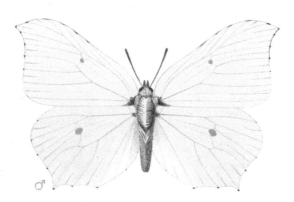

Brimstone
Gonepteryx rhamni

The only all-yellow butterfly in Britain. Any bright yellow butterfly seen in early spring is likely to be the male of this species. The female usually emerges a little later and is sometimes mistaken for a White, but on settling the distinctive leaf-like shape of the wing instantly identifies her. In the male the uppers are uniformly coloured bright yellow, with a small orange spot on each wing. The underside is a duller yellow with prominent veins. The sexes are more difficult to distinguish from the underside, but the uppers of the female are pale green-white with similar markings to the male, It is possible that the Brimstone was once known as the "butter-coloured fly", hence the word "butterfly". The species has a powerful flight and is common in woods, gardens and roadsides. It is one of the few butterflies to hibernate in the adult form, hiding in evergreen plants such as Ivy, where its closed wings provide an effective camouflage. There is one brood of caterpillars whose foodplants are Buckthorn and Alder buckthorn. Wingspan: 52–60 mm. Flight: July–Sept (hibernated specimens appear in April).

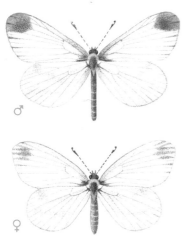

Wood white
Leptidea sinapis
Smaller, more fragile than the other Whites and with a wavering, uncertain flight, the Wood white may be found flying close to the ground in forest clearings and woodland edges. The second generation is whiter with smaller but blacker spots at the apex of the wings. There are two or more broods which feed on Everlasting pea and Birdsfoot trefoil. Wingspan: 36–48 mm. Flight period: May–Aug.

Duke of Burgundy fritillary
Hamearis lucina
Widespread but rarely common, found in woodland clearings, this butterfly's name is a misnomer as it bears only a superficial resemblance to a fritillary, being much smaller and with no silver spots underneath. The female's wings are not so pointed as the male's and her orange markings are wider. The uppers of the male are dark brown with transverse rows of orange spots. The hindwing has two rows of white spots. The two broods a year feed on Cowslip and Primrose. Wingspan: 28–34 mm. Flight: May–June.

Pearl-bordered fritillary
Clossiana euphrosyne
Fritillaries generally have black and warm brown upperparts, and silver spots beneath. The Pearl-bordered fritillary is distinguished from the Small Pearl-bordered species (*right*) by the pattern on its underside hindwing (two bright silver spots in addition to a border of seven "pearls"). A common species in woodlands and meadows up to 1,800 m, and sometimes in parkland, although strangely rare in the E. The sexes are similar. The one brood of caterpillars feeds on Violet. Wingspan: 38–46 mm. Flight period: Apr–Aug.

Small pearl-bordered fritillary
Clossiana selene
The Small pearl-bordered fritillary contains more black on its underside hindwing than *C. euphrosyne* (*left*) and does not have a prominent central silvery spot on this wing, though there is a border of seven "pearls" edged in black and the round black spot in the cell is prominent. The two species often fly together, but *C. selene* prefers damper areas. There is one brood of caterpillars, feeding on Violet. Wingspan: 36–42 mm. Flight period: Apr–Aug.

Wild Flowers

Cuckoo pint (Lords and ladies)
Arum maculatum
An easily identifiable perennial common in woodland with frequently spotted, arrow-shaped leaves and a white-green, pitcher-like surround to the purple "spadix", later the orange-red fruit. 25 cm. Apr–May.

Wood anemone
Anemone nemorosa
Often carpeting the ground in deciduous woodland (unless the soil is very acid), a charming perennial with white, pink-tinged flowers, 20–40 mm, above 3 or 5 lobed leaves. It is propagated by a creeping rhizome. 20 cm. Mar–May.

Lesser stitchwort
Stellaria graminea
Growing in woods, hedges and mountain pastures, on sandy soils, an untidy perennial with starlike white flowers, smaller (12 mm) than those of Greater Stitchwort (*p 74*), and narrow leaves hairy at the base. 50 cm. May–Aug.

Greater stitchwort
Stellaria holostea
Very common among woods and hedges, with larger white flowers, 20–30 mm, than the Lesser species (*p 73*). The flowers have deeply notched petals; the stems are brittle and squarish; the leaves are rough. 45 cm. Apr–June.

Solomon's seal
Paris multiflorum
Very easy to identify when flowering in deciduous woods in spring and early summer, with drooping white flowers like elongated bells, 15 mm, and alternate, unstalked leaves. The berry is black. 80 cm. May–June.

Lily of the valley
Convallaria majalis
In dry woods, usually on chalk or limestone, similar to the cultivated variety, with creamy, sweet-smelling, bell-shaped, nodding flowers and larger, arrow-shaped leaves growing from a rhizome. The fruit is poisonous. 20 cm. May–June.

Woodruff
Galium odoratum
Widespread in woodlands, often in patches, creeping from rhizomes, with clusters of flowers, 6 mm across, and whorls of narrow leaves springing from the erect stems. The leaves have tiny prickles on their edges. 45 cm. May–June.

Wild strawberry
Fragaria vesca
Frequently found in woods and dry, grassy places, a perfect miniature strawberry, with long creeping runners, small white flowers (12–18 mm), trefoil leaves and ultimately tiny red, very sweet strawberries, 20 cm. Apr–July.

Bramble (Blackberry)
Rubus fruticosus
The white or pink flowers, 20–30 mm, are borne on arching, prickly stems, and produce the autumn harvest of blackberries. Very common in woods and hedges and on bare, disturbed ground. 1·5 m. May–Sept.

Garlic mustard
Alliaria petiolata
When crushed, the roots and leaves of this tall perennial smell of garlic. The flowers are white, 6 mm, growing in spikes off the hairy stem. The long fruit is four-angled. Found in open woods and hedgerows. 1 m. Apr–June.

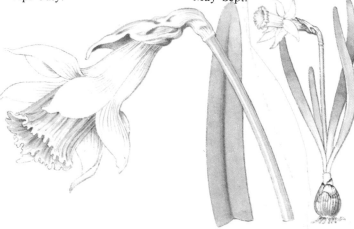

Wild daffodil
Narcissus pseudonarcissus
Found occasionally in woods and meadows and very similar to the basic cultivated variety, except that the "trumpet" is darker yellow and nearly as long as the outer whorl of petals. Greyish narrow leaves. 35 cm. Feb–Apr.

Ramsons
Allium ursinum
Another of the Onion family, smelling of garlic. The white starry flowers (15–20 mm) grow in round clusters on long, ridged stalks, with broad leaves. Clumps grow in damp woodland. 45 cm. Apr–June.

Primrose
Primula vulgaris
Often growing thickly in woods and hedgebanks, very similar to garden cultivated varieties, with yellow flowers, 30 mm, on long, hairy stalks. The large, oval leaves are hairy on the underside. 10 cm. Feb–May.

Wood spurge
Euphorbia amygdaloides
Robust kidney-shaped bracts surround a cup-shaped structure, which in turn encircles one female and several male flowers without sepals or petals. 80 cm. Mar–May.

Red campion
Silene dioica
Like the White campion (*p 13*), with many pinkish-red, slightly smaller flowers (18–25 mm) and wider leaves. The two sometimes produce fertile hybrids. Common in woodlands, hedges and also sea-cliffs. 60 cm. May–June.

Opposite-leaved golden saxifrage
Chrysosplenium oppositifolium
A creeping perennial with rounded, toothed leaves, and tiny yellowy flowers, 3–4 mm, with no petals but noticeable anthers. In damp woods and boggy places. To 15 cm. Apr–July.

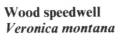

Lesser celandine
Ranunculus ficaria
Grows in damp woodlands and disturbed ground, from root tubers. Some plants may have bulbils at the base of the leaves. The starry, yellow flowers contrast well with the dark green, shiny, heart-shaped leaves. 20 cm. Mar–May.

Spurge laurel
Daphne laureola
An evergreen with glossy, leathery leaves clustered at the tips of the erect shoots and yellowy-green, clustered, bell-shaped flowers. The fruit is black. Liking chalky soils in woodlands. 70 cm. Feb–Apr.

Toothwort
Lathraea squamaria
In damp woods and hedgerows, a parasite on tree roots of Hazel and Elm, with no green at all. It has a one-sided spike of dull purple flowers, and leaves as mere creamy scales against the stem. 20 cm. Apr–May.

Wood speedwell
Veronica montana
Paler lilac flowers (7 mm) than Heath speedwell (*p 50*), with longer stalked leaves and liking damp woods. The stems are hairy all round. A creeping perennial with upright shoots. 40 cm. Apr–July.

Goldilocks buttercup
Ranunculus auricomus
This has much more rounded lower (and three-lobed upper) leaves than the Meadow buttercup (*p 23*), and the flowers have up to five petals of uneven size. A woodland plant. 30 cm. Apr–May.

Yellow archangel
Lamiastrum galeobdolon
Frequently seen in woodlands, with two-lipped flowers, 20 mm, the top lip being hooded. They grow in whorls at the base of the toothed oval leaves. A creeping perennial with upright flowering stems. 40 cm. May–June.

Rhododendron
Rhododendron ponticum
Naturalised in woods, with dense clusters of impressive, bell-shaped flowers (60 mm) and evergreen, hairless leaves. 3 m. May–June.

Ground ivy
Glechoma hederacea
Whorls of tiny, two-lipped, violet flowers (15–20 mm) grow along the stems of this hairy creeping perennial. There are also round, kidney-shaped leaves. In woodland, hedges and grassland. Erect shoots to 30 cm. Mar–May.

Lesser periwinkle
Vinca minor
A prostrate shrub in woods and hedges, with blue-violet flowers (25–30 mm), narrowly oval, evergreen leaves and rooting stems. Creeps to 60 cm. Mar–May.

Columbine
Aquilegia vulgaris
Scattered in woods and scrub, also a garden escape, with unmistakable bluish-purple, long-spurred flowers (25–30 mm) and three greyish-green, three-lobed leaflets on long stalks. There are pink- and white-flowered forms. 70 cm. May–June.

Bluebell
Hyacinthoides non-scripta
Perhaps the archetypal woodland plant, forming breathtaking sheets of blue where conditions suit it (principally well-drained woodland and hedgerows, also upland grassland and sea-cliffs). Spikes of bell-shaped flowers, 20 mm, rise above narrow, slightly bent leaves. 50 cm. Apr–June.

Wood forgetmenot
Myosotis sylvatica
An erect perennial mostly in woods in N England, with hairs on leaves and stems. The flowers carried on loose spikes are larger (6–10 mm) than the Field forgetmenot (*p 38*). 45 cm. May–Sept.

Bugle
Ajuga reptans
Common in damp woods and meadows, bearing blue flowers with a short upper lip and a larger, three-lobed lower lip. The leaves are hairy, the lower ones growing in a rosette. 20 cm. May–July.

Green alkanet
Pentaglottis sempervirens
Found in grassland, woods and hedgerows, a coarse-haired, tall perennial, with long-stalked blue flowers, 10 mm, which have white scales in the mouth of their petal tubes. The leaves, up to 30 cm, are pointed and oval. 1 m. May–June.

Herb Paris
Paris quadrifolia
An unusual flower with four green sepals surrounding narrow, inconspicuous petals. The leaves are whorled in fours and the fruit is a single, black berry. Growing from rhizomes in woods on limestone. 40 cm. May–Aug.

Moschatel
Adoxa moschatellina
A delicate, all-green carpeting plant, of woods and shady hedges (also on mountains), having trefoil leaves and tiny green flowers (5–6 mm). From rhizomes. 10 cm. Apr–May.

Fungi

Lentinus lepideus

Always on coniferous wood, this species will even grow on creosoted railway sleepers. The cap is 5–10 cm, pale yellow, firm and cracked in concentric zones of brown scales. The gills have a toothed edge and are whitish and broad. The stem 2–8 cm high, is hard and white, with brown scales. May–Oct.

Two-toned pholiota
Kuehneromyces mutabilis

The yellow cap, 4–8 cm, absorbs water easily and turns yellow from the centre as it dries. Grows in dense clusters on stumps and may be confused with Honey fungus (*p 202*). The cap is edible, but not the fibrous stems. Gills are clay to rust brown. The curved stem, 5–8 cm, is brown and scaly up to its ring. Apr–Dec.

Horsehair fungus
Marasmius androsaceus

A fragile species with a black horsehair-like mycelium (web) entangling dead pine needles. The cap is 0·5–1 cm, slightly depressed, wrinkled and reddish-brown. The gills are crowded and white. The stem is 3–6 cm high, black and wiry. May–Nov.

Bonnet mycena
Mycena galericulata

A robust *Mycena* species which occurs in clusters on stumps in broad-leaved woodland, with its stems often sticking together. It has a faint, rancid odour. The cap, 2–6 cm, is grey-brown to yellowish, almost white and grooved. The gills are white to pink. The stem, 3–8 cm high, is tough, smooth and shiny grey. May–Nov.

Psathyrella obtusata

Very common on the ground in shady woodland, especially under oak. The cap is 1–2 cm, date brown drying out from the centre to pale tan, wrinkled, with the margin remaining dark and grooved. The gills are pale to dark brown and rather spaced. The stem, 6–8 cm high, is white, silky, shiny, fragile and hollow. Apr–Nov.

Scurfy cortinarius
Cortinarius hemitrichus

Always with birch, often forming large troops on heathy soil and liking damp places. Scurfy cortinarius is identified by the coating of delicate, white, powdery scales over its cap surface. The cap is 2–5 cm, deep brown and covered with these whitish scales which soon fall off. The gills are brown and very crowded. The stem, 5–7 cm, is slender and greyish, with whitish fibrils forming indistinct zones. Apr–Nov.

Boletus luridus

Much more common than *B. satanas* (*p 92*), with which it is often confused, and similarly found on chalky soil under beech, oak or lime. It is poisonous when eaten raw, yet edible when cooked, although it discolours deep blue. Note the red pores and the elongated red network on the stem. The cap, 6–20 cm, is hemispherical to convex, matt, yellowish-olive at the centre, but elsewhere orange to brick red. The tubes are depressed around the stem, olive yellow, bluing. The pores are round, yellow, blood red to orange, bruising deep blue when broken. The stem, 8–20 cm, is solid, often bulbous, with a red network. May–Dec.

Sulphur tuft
Hypholoma fasciculare
Occurs in large clusters on stumps in mixed woods. Poisonous, it has a bitter taste and acts as a gastro-enteric irritant. Its cap, 2–5 cm, is pale yellow, brown in the centre and smooth. The crowded gills are greenish when young, sulphur yellow and finally purplish-black. The stem, 5–15 cm, is the same colour as the cap, rusty at the base, curved, and has fibrils. Jan–Dec.

Entoloma aprile
Less robust than *E. clypeatum* (*right*) with a greyish-brown stem. The smooth greasy cap, 2–9 cm, is conical to convex, greyish-brown, but paler when dry. The gills are pale to greyish-pink, broad and spaced. The stem, 5–9 cm, is solid and greyish, with grey brown fibrils. The flesh is whitish and smells of meal. Apr–May.

Roman-shield entoloma
Entoloma clypeatum
Common in troops under rosaceous shrubs among grass. Poisonous, it causes a stomach upset if eaten raw. The cap is 4–10 cm, conical to convex, greyish-brown, fibrous and silky. The gills are white to pink and broad. The stem, 4–10 cm high, is solid, firm, whitish and grooved. Apr–June.

Trooping crumble cap
Coprinus disseminatus
Always in large numbers and common from spring onwards: hundreds of individuals can appear overnight, densely clustered on rotten wood in broad-leaved woodland. The gills do not dissolve into liquid like other ink caps. The cap, 0·5–1·5 cm, is thin, fragile, pale yellow then grey with a yellow centre, grooved and glistening. The gills are white to grey, narrow and crowded. The stem is 1–4 cm high, curved and white. Apr–Nov.

Psathyrella spadicea
Main characteristics are the gill colour, the inrolled cap margin when young, and the tufted habit on wood, often in clusters on old roots (although it also occurs singly on the ground). The cap is 3–10 cm, date brown drying paler, smooth and finally cracking. The gills are pinkish-brown to umber and finally turn reddish-brown. The stem, 4–10 cm, is smooth, white and silky. It is edible only after cooking. Apr–Nov.

Boletus erythropus
The firm, bright yellow flesh discolours first blue then green when broken open, so rarely considered edible. But it is excellent when properly cooked, though can cause vomiting raw. Do not confuse with the poisonous *B. satanas* (*p 92*), which always has a pale cap and white flesh. This cap is dark brown with olive or reddish tints, 8–20 cm, convex, dry, velvety, then smooth and shiny. The tubes are free, olive brown staining blue. Pores are small, round, yellow to orange-red, turning blue when touched. The stem, 7–15 cm, is robust, dotted orange-yellow above, brown below and ridged. May–Nov.

Fawn pluteus
Pluteus cervinus
The most common and most variable of all *Pluteus* species, often on fallen trunks and old stumps. Giant specimens sometimes grow on sawdust heaps. Edible only after cooking, but of poor quality. The cap, 3–12 cm, is greyish-brown to umber, sticky when moist. The gills are white to pink, free and broad, and very crowded. The stem, 8–12 cm, is white with dark fibrils and often swollen at the base. Jan–Dec.

Birds

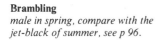

Brambling
male in spring, compare with the jet-black of summer, see p 96.

Long-tailed tit
Aegithalos caudatus

March is nest-building time for this very distinctive small tit, usually seen in small restless feeding parties which cross clearings in ones and twos. Its long graduated tail and pink, black and white plumage show well in flight. Apart from its distinctive patterning and tail-waving flight, constant calls attract attention – most often a trilling "tsurup" and a thin "tzee-tzee-tzee" to keep flock members in contact. The bird has a tiny bill and a white crown. The bold, blackish eye stripe shows clearly in adults. The juvenile has no pink plumage and darker cheeks. Common in woodland, scrub, hedges and well-wooded gardens. Severely hit by hard winters, roosting communally for warmth. Top Sixty. 14 cm. Resident.

Crested tit
Parus cristatus

In spring a very characteristic purring, trilling call betrays the presence of this rarest tit (it also has a thin "tzee-tzee-tzee" contact call). It occurs only in the natural pine woods in central N Scotland and often feeds on trunks like the Treecreeper. Often circles treetops in display flights like Greenfinches. Its whitish underparts, brown upperparts and head pattern (a black and white crest – duller in juveniles – and a black "C" edging the face) are unique. A typical tit, restless and acrobatic. It stores food. 11–12 cm. Resident.

Pied flycatcher
Ficedula hypoleuca

Arriving from its African wintering grounds in late April, the male Pied flycatcher is distinctive with its striking black and white spring plumage including pure white underparts and white wing-bars which show well in flight (*see p 94*). The bird has longish wings, a large dark eye and tiny legs. The male in autumn is like the female: more like the larger Spotted flycatcher (*p 96*). Immature birds are like females, but have buff edges to their wings. All birds wag their tails constantly. They sit quietly on walls or in foliage and then make flitting, gliding flight after insects. The call is a quiet "tik-tak" typical of flycatchers. Found in deciduous woodlands. 13 cm. Summer visitor: mid Apr–Oct.

Goldfinch
Carduelis carduelis

Often seen in flocks in April before breeding starts in May, a very distinctive finch with a red, white and black face, and yellow and black wing pattern all showing in its bouncing flight. (Males and females have dark bill tips in winter.) The juvenile has a brownish head. A bird of woodland fringes, scrub, waste ground and wooded gardens, found wherever there are thistles and weeds, from which its long, sharp bill extracts the seeds. It often feeds head down. Goldfinches often sing from treetops and on roadside wires with a fluent, liquid, twittering "swITT-swITT-swITT" call. The song is an elaboration of this call. Common. Part of the population migrates south in winter. Top Sixty. 12 cm. Resident.

Redstart
Phoenicurus phoenicurus

These slim, delicate birds are always seen in or near trees or perched on walls or wire fences. They make constantly repeated sallies after insects, using a fluttering, hovering flight. The tail is bobbed and constantly "shivered". There is a "houeet" alarm call (not unlike the Willow warbler's) and a soft "whit-ti-tik" contact call. Orange-red tail and rump and pale grey upperparts, together with absence of white in the wing, distinguishes the male from the Black redstart (p 198). The adult female and the young bird can also be picked out by their pale grey-buff above, dark eye set in a pale eye ring, and pale throat. Redstarts prefer deciduous woodlands and also occur in parks, gardens and areas of scattered trees such as heaths. 14 cm. Summer visitor: mid-Apr–Oct.

Nightingale
Luscinia megarhynchos

In mid April the woodlands, scrub and coppices of SE England can be filled with nocturnal song. This famous song, also heard by day, is a slow "pieu-pieu-pieu", then an explosive "chock-chock-chock" and a great crescendo. Singing birds usually have tails cocked and crowns raised. The nightingale is a shy, skulking bird in damp woods, copses and hedges. It is plump and well built with its rich chestnut-brown upperparts and long, rounded tail very evident in flight. The nest is deep in vegetation. Birds accost intruders with a deep scolding call and wing and tail flicking. In display the male fans wings and tail, showing its orange-brown undertail and white belly. The bird has pale throat and underparts. Juveniles have a "scaly" look to breast and upperparts. 16–17 cm. Summer visitor: Apr–Sept.

Great spotted woodpecker
Dendrocopos major

During April the loud drumming of this woodpecker can be heard in the woods. It is distinguished from the Lesser Spotted (*right*) by its red tail vent and white shoulders. The male also has a red nape patch. It has a very undulating flight and an explosive "tchick" call. Common in wooded areas, including gardens. 23 cm. Resident.

Lesser spotted woodpecker
Dendrocopos minor

Much smaller than the Great spotted woodpecker (*left*), and distinguished by its barred back, lack of white on its shoulder and of red in its underparts. The male has a red and the female a white crown. The juvenile is like the adults, but lacking any red and with a dun face. This woodpecker also drums, more weakly but for longer. It has a typical undulating flight and also a moth-like floating display flight. The call is a high "qui-qui-qui-qui". In woods and parks. 14–15 cm. Resident.

Cuckoo
Cuculus canorus

The voice of the cuckoo is widely thought to mark the true beginning of spring and goes on until mid-June. Only the male makes the "cuckoo" sound and also has scolding, growling calls. The female makes a liquid, bubbling sound. Cuckoos do not stay long, since they lay their eggs in other birds' nests (Dunnock, Meadow pipit and Reed warbler) and have therefore no young to

rear. The cuckoo is superficially falcon-like in its pointed wings and long, graduated tail, but the bill shape distinguishes it. The male has a white-spotted, black tail and grey breast and upperparts. Adult and first summer females have buff on the breast. The reddish-brown juvenile resembles a female Kestrel, and a grey phase also occurs. The bird makes a level, lowish flight with shallow wing-beats. Found in woodland, scrub and agricultural land. 33 cm. Common summer visitor.

Sparrowhawk
Accipiter nisus

In March and April Sparrowhawk pairs often make slow, soaring aerial display flights. The most agile of the woodland predators, the combination of a long tail, blunt wings and "flap and glide" motion distinguish it

from the more common Kestrel (*p 206*). Females are grey brown above and white-barred below. The smaller male is identifiable by its blue-grey upperparts and very rich chestnut underparts. All juveniles are like an adult female, but more buff. The Sparrowhawk feeds exclusively on birds caught on the wing or taken from the ground. Widespread in wooded areas

and agricultural land, wherever there is suitable cover (including urban gardens). The population is now recovering from decline due to pesticide poisoning. 28–38 cm. Resident.

Goshawk
Accipiter gentilis

The Goshawk breeds early in spring, and superficially resembles a massive Sparrowhawk, but the female is a Buzzard-sized bird and both adults give an immediate

impression of muscular power with their easy wing-beats. The triangular head, broad, very solid-looking body and wide base to the tail will always distinguish Goshawks. In the male's spring display, the white undertail coverts show at a great distance, especially when soaring (which may be followed by a 200-metre plummet). Adults and juveniles have a bold eye stripe. The Goshawk is a quiet, easily overlooked bird of suitable woodland, which takes mainly rabbits and Wood pigeons, pursuing them with a dashing Sparrowhawk-like flight. Rare but regular breeder and probably increasing. 48–62 cm. Resident.

SUMMER
Butterflies

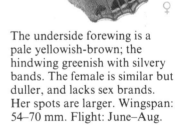

High brown fritillary
Fabriciana (Argynnis) adippe

It is difficult to identify this species by its upperside pattern alone. The most distinctive features are on the underside hindwing, notably the row of reddish, silver-centred postdiscal spots which separate it from the Dark green fritillary (*p 56*). The female is broadly similar to the male, often slightly larger and more heavily marked, with a dark suffusion in the basal area of her uppers. Recently the species has become less common in Britain and is found mainly in wooded areas of the S including gardens. There is one brood of caterpillars a year which feeds on Violet. Wingspan: 50–62 mm. Flight: June–July.

Silver-washed fritillary
Argynnis paphia

Much commoner than the High brown and usually found in woods and wooded gardens, mainly in the S and SW. The adults are partial to Bramble blossom and on sunny days may be seen descending from the trees to feed. The female lays her eggs not on the Violet foodplant but on nearby tree trunks, where the single brood of caterpillars hibernates until spring. This fritillary gets its name from the silvery markings on its underside. Two female forms are illustrated; the dark one, *valesina,* is less common. The male has sex brands on the forewing which occur as thick black stripes along the veins.

The underside forewing is a pale yellowish-brown; the hindwing greenish with silvery bands. The female is similar but duller, and lacks sex brands. Her spots are larger. Wingspan: 54–70 mm. Flight: June–Aug.

Speckled wood
Pararge aegeria

This butterfly has a slow, fluttering flight and is commonly found in shady areas with dappled sunlight, such as woodland edges, pine forest clearings and sometimes gardens, where its creamy white spotted pattern is camouflaged well. The eye-spot is conspicuous on both sides of the forewing. Males and females are similar. There are two broods a year which feed on grasses, especially Couch grass. Wingspan: 38–44 mm. Flight period: Mar–Oct.

White admiral
Ladoga camilla

The White admiral has a slow, measured flight, sometimes gliding, and is locally common in woodland glades, where it feeds freely on Blackberry blossom. Generally it occurs singly, but sometimes numbers may congregate in shady places, especially when feeding. Both sexes lack a clear white spot in the cell of the forewing. The female is larger and slightly paler. There is one brood a year, which feeds on Honeysuckle. Wingspan: 52–60 mm. Flight: June–July.

Purple emperor
Apatura iris

Considered to be a rare species, this large and beautiful butterfly has a powerful flight and is much sought-after by collectors. Elusive rather than rare would perhaps be a more apt description, as it spends most of its time in the tree tops, the males occasionally coming down to feed at damp patches such as sap, dung and carrion. The females seldom descend except to deposit the eggs for their one brood a year on young Willow trees. Well-established oakwoods up to 1,000 m form the main breeding grounds, within which an adequate supply of foodplants (Sallow and Grey willow) must be found. In Britain the species has only been recorded in the S and E. The male's purple iridescence is seen only from certain angles; otherwise the wings appear brownish. The forewing has an obscure round black spot near the middle of the outer margin. Females are not as dark as males and lack the purple sheen, but have larger white markings. Wingspan: 62–74 mm. Flight: July–Aug.

——————— MOTHS ———————

Hornet clearwing
Sesia apiformis

Adult Hornet clearwing moths are frequently found in early morning on the trunks of Poplar and their caterpillars on the lower trunks and upper roots of Black poplar and occasionally other poplar species. Mainly in the S. There is one brood, flying mid June–July. Wingspan: 33–46 mm.

Wild Flowers

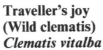

Chickweed wintergreen
Trientalis europaea
Found in pinewoods and also on moors, common in E Scotland, but rare in England, an erect perennial with hairless stems, one or two white flowers, 15–18 mm, with seven petals rising from the leaf whorl. 25 cm. June–July.

Baneberry
Actaea spicata
Very localised (mostly Yorkshire) in woods on limestone, with fluffy white flowers and striking black berries. It is strong-smelling, with pinnate leaves. 40 cm. June July.

Traveller's joy
(Wild clematis)
Clematis vitalba
A woody, climbing perennial, with white, four-petalled flowers, followed by fruits with long, feathery styles (the "Old Man's Beard" of autumn woodland and hedges on chalk). To 30 m. July–Aug.

Wood vetch
Vicia sylvatica
Scrambling through woods, with broader leaflets and larger flowers than Tufted vetch (*p 29*). The flowers are pale violet with darker veins. The plant has tendrils. 1 m. June–Aug.

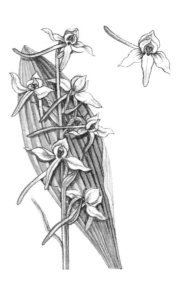

Creeping lady's tresses
Goodyera repens
Fairly rare and exclusively in pinewoods, but an exquisite orchid having fragrant white flowers with pouched lips. The oval leaves are net-veined, in rosettes. 20 cm. July–Aug.

Lizard orchid
Himantoglossum hircinum
One of the easiest orchids to recognise, with nasty-smelling greenish-grey, purple-streaked flowers in spikes. The middle lower lip looks like a long "lizard's tail." The stem is spotted purple. Rare (among woodland edges, hedges, chalky grassland in the S and E). 30 cm. May–July.

Greater butterfly orchid
Platanthera chlorantha
Growing in damp woods, meadows and grassland, with greenish-white flowers, 20 mm, whose lip is narrow and spur long and curved. There are two glossy, broad lower leaves and a few small stem leaves. 30 cm. May–July.

Lesser butterfly orchid
Platanthera bifolia
Smaller than the Greater butterfly orchid (*left*), with parallel pollen sacs (the Greater has them in the shape of an inverted V). The spur is straight, not curved. Woodland, meadows and marsh. 25 cm. May–July.

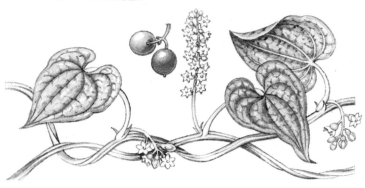

Black bryony
Tamus communis
Tall and twining in woods and hedges, with heart-shaped leaves and tiny, greenish-yellow flowers, 4–5 mm, in spikes.

Male and female flowers are on separate plants, the male ones being stalked. The plant has no tendrils. May–July. To 4 m.

Pignut
Conopodium majus
Growing from swollen edible tubers in dry woods and fields, with tiny white flowers, 1–2 mm, in umbels up to 7 cm across. Delicate, finely divided leaves. 40 cm. May–June.

Herb bennet
Geum urbanum
A common perennial in damp woods and hedges, with small five-petalled, starry flowers, 8–15 mm, and large, lobed leaves. The fruits have hooked awns. 45 cm. June–Aug.

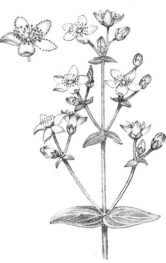

Yellow pimpernel
Lysimachia nemorum
Not unlike Creeping Jenny (*p 24*) but with smaller flat flowers and pointed-tipped leaves. A prostrate plant, growing in damp or shady woodland, hedges and fields. 30 cm. May–Sept.

Honeysuckle
Lonicera periclymenum
A woody climber in woods and hedges with fragrant, two-lipped flowers growing in round heads. Very similar to the cultivated variety. Leaves are oval and a tight cluster of red berries forms. To 6 m. June–Sept.

Birdsnest orchid
Neottia nidus-avis
A parasite on soil fungi and without green pigment, having scale-like leaves. Distinguished from Broomrape (*p 38*) by its two-lobed lipped flowers and by its woodland shade habitat. 35 cm. June–July.

Common figwort
Scrophularia nodosa
In very damp, loamy soil in woods, hedges and occasionally ditches and river banks, with brownish-purple 8–10 mm flowers and oval, toothed leaves. 60 cm. June–Sept.

Small teasel
Dipsacus pilosus
A weak, prickly biennial growing in damp, shady places. The round flowerheads (20 mm, white with purple anthers) are carried above a rosette of leaves. 1·2 m. Aug.

Slender St. John's wort
Hypericum pulchrum
In damp, open woods, the reddish-tinged flower buds, edged with black dots, open to yellow flowers, 15 mm. There are translucent glands on the oval leaves. 45 cm. June–Aug.

Stinking iris
Iris foetidissima
Named after its evergreen
leaves with a nasty smell if
crushed. The flowers, 80 mm,
are usually mauve with dark
veins. The capsules open out to
display the bright orange seeds.
In woods and thickets on
chalky soil. 80 cm. May–July.

Twinflower
Linnaea borealis
A mat-forming flower, with
pairs of nodding, pink,
bell-shaped flowers, 8 mm, and
evergreen leaves on creeping
woody stems. Rare (in Scottish
pinewoods). 7 cm. June–Aug.

Common wintergreen
Pyrola minor
A creeping perennial of woods,
moors and mountain rockledges
with a single spike of pale pink
or white, spherical flowers, 6 mm.
The oval, finely toothed leaves
grow in a rosette. 20 cm.
June–Aug.

Foxglove
Digitalis purpurea
A tall biennial with a spike of
pinkish-purple, tubular flowers
(40–50 mm), large enough for a
bumble bee to crawl inside. The
lower part of the tube is
spotted. The leaves are
wrinkled, with felty hairs, and
form a large rosette. 1·5 m.
June–Sept.

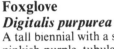

Red helleborine
Cephanlanthera rubra
A rare orchid growing in
beechwoods on chalk in one or
two places in the S. It has
pointed leaves and bright rosy-
purple flowers in a spike. The
stem is stickily hairy. 35 cm.
June–July.

Enchanter's nightshade
Circaea lutetiana
Common in damp woods, with
long spikes of tiny flowers,
4–8 mm, each with two deeply
notched petals. The leaves are
in opposite pairs. 50 cm.
June–Aug.

Bitter vetchling
Lathyrus montanus
Frequent in open woods and
hedges, with reddish-purple
pea-like flowers, 10–15 mm, on
short spikes, which fade to a
bluish-purple. The leaves are
pinnate, in two to four pairs.
30 cm. June–July.

Giant bellflower
Campanula latifolia
Taller and with large (50 mm)
flowers, paler blue than most
other bellflowers (sometimes
even white), growing off a
spike, intermingled with narrow
leaves on stalks. Softly hairy.
Woods and hedges. 1·2 m.
July–Aug.

Broad-leaved helleborine
Epipactis helleborine
Common in S, rarer in N, this orchid has a spike of green to purple flowers with a large round appendage over the stigma. The broad, ribbed leaves are spirally arranged. The downy stem is often purple-tinged. 65 cm. July–Oct.

Narrow-lipped helleborine
Epipactis leptochila
Almost confined to shady beechwoods, with leaves in two opposite ranks up the stem, and greenish-white flowers, the lip being red inside. The stem is softly hairy. 55 cm. June–Aug.

Woody nightshade (Bittersweet)
Solanum dulcamara
A poisonous red berry follows the mauve and yellow potato-like flowers, 10 mm, on this woody scrambling perennial. Woodland, hedges, fens and on disturbed ground. Leaves are oval, often with two lobes or leaflets at the base. To 2 m. June–Sept.

Deadly nightshade
Atropa belladonna
Very poisonous berries (black, glossy and up to 20 mm across) follow the purple, bell-shaped, drooping flowers, 25–30 mm long. A thick-stemmed, branching perennial which grows in open woods and disturbed ground. 1 m. June–Aug.

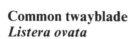

Wood dock
Rumex sanguineus
Differs from Clustered dock (*p 161*) in having flowers on an almost or completely leafless spike and an upright (not zig-zag) stem. The fruit has only a single warty swelling. 1 m. June–Aug.

Green-flowered helleborine
Epipactis phyllanthes
Growing in woods on chalky soil (usually beech), with pale green, drooping flowers. The leaves grow in two opposite ranks. 45 cm. July–Sept.

Common twayblade
Listera ovata
One of the commonest orchids, in wood and grassland, usually in damp situations, with one pair of base leaves growing opposite each other and a spike of yellowy-green flowers, 15 mm, having a two-lobed lower lip. 45 cm. June–July.

Caper spurge
Euphorbia lathyrus
Growing in woods and as a weed in gardens, with greenish flowerheads followed by fruits 20 mm across. The leaves grow oppositely up the stem. 1 m. June–July.

Fungi

Pick-a-back toadstool
Nyctalis parasitica
Grows in clusters on old *Russula* species. The cap is 1–3 cm, white then greyish, and silky. The gills are pale, thick and spaced at first, then brownish. The stem, 1–4 cm high, is slender and greyish. Aug–Oct.

False death cap
Amanita citrina
A species best avoided for risk of confusion with the Death cap (*p 102*). It smells of raw potatoes. The cap, 4–8 cm, is convex, with a thin, unlined margin, lemon yellow to almost white, with loose scales. The gills are free and white. The stem, 6–12 cm, is white, with a large, swollen basal bulb and a grooved ring. Aug–Oct.

Agaricus augustus
One of the largest and most beautiful species of *Agaricus*. The truncated cap is covered with dark brown scales, similar to a *Lepiota* species. It occurs in groups and, although it bruises yellow, it is excellent to eat. The cap, 10–25 cm, is dry, hemispherical to convex, expanding to flat, rusty to yellowish-brown, breaking up into zones of small, brown fibrillose scales. The gills, greyish to chocolate brown, and never pink, are very crowded. The stem, 10–20 cm, is cylindrical, white bruising yellow, its surface loose and scaly below the large, pendent, white ring. The flesh is white, discolouring brownish-yellow, with a smell of bitter almonds. July–Oct.

Lactarius helvus
One of the few poisonous milk caps, rendered harmless by boiling, then dried and used as a spice. In damp conifer woods, it is often distinguished from other wet-loving fungi purely by the large cap size. It has a scant, watery-white milk with a mild taste. The cap, 6–15 cm, is yellowish-grey to coffee brown, with a felty surface and inrolled margin. The gills are pale yellow and crowded. The stem, 4–12 cm, is the same colour as the cap, cylindrical and hollow. It has an unusual smell of liquorice. Aug–Oct.

Common yellow russula
Russula ochroleuca
An exceptionally common fungus, often one of the first to appear in late summer. Recognized by the ochre-yellow cap, pale cream gills and white stem which turns greyish with age. Edible: the taste is variable, ranging from very hot to almost mild. Other yellow species with which it may be confused include: *R. claroflava*, (*p 173*) and R. fellea (*p 103*). The cap is 4–10 cm, convex to depressed with a slightly grooved margin. It is yellow, often with shades of ochre, orange, brown or grey-green. The gills are quite crowded and the stem, 3–8 cm, is firm, cylindric or slightly swollen at the base. Aug–Nov.

Foetid russula
Russula foetens
Recognized by its disgusting, rancid smell and slimy, grooved cap. Mature specimens of *R. foetens* are often infested by insect larvae. The cap is 10–18 cm, convex to flat, splitting, pale ochre to tawny and very slimy. The gills are whitish spotted brown, broad and crowded. The stem, 10–13 cm, is a dirty white. The flesh is white and bruises red. June–Oct.

Russet shank (Penny top)
Collybia dryophila
Frequently occurs amongst dead leaves in oak woods, usually in small groups. The thin flesh is edible after cooking but is mildly poisonous if eaten raw. The cap, 2–5 cm, is flattened, pale yellowish to reddish-brown, with a brown centre and smooth. The gills are white or pale yellow, narrow and crowded. The stem, 4–8 cm, is slender, yellow to light reddish-brown, hollow and smooth. July–Nov.

Chanterelle
Cantharellus cibarius
One of the most popular edible species, with a soft but firm texture and a mild smell of dried apricots. To enjoy it at its best, it should be cooked gently in butter. It grows slowly, always in troops, and is seldom attacked by maggots. Do not confuse it with False chanterelle (*p 101*), which has thin true gills and no smell. The cap, 3–10 cm, is soon depressed to a funnel shape, with a wavy margin, egg yellow to apricot. The gills are thick, formed by forking veins and ridges and widely spaced. The stem, 2–5 cm, is paler than the cap and smooth. July–Nov.

Paxillus atrotomentosus
The short, stout stem with its brown-black felty surface soon identifies this species. The flesh is thick, soft and creamy but its persistent bitter taste makes it inedible. Grows on or near conifer stumps, especially pine and spruce. The large, dry velvety cap, 5–30 cm, yellowish chestnut brown, is often depressed at the centre, with an inrolled margin. It darkens on bruising. The gills are ochre yellow spotting brown, thin, forked, soft and very crowded. They are easily separated from the cap flesh. The densely felty stem is 4–9 cm, robust and solid. July–Oct.

Wood woolly-foot
Collybia peronata
This dry, leathery species is very common, growing in small tufts amongst leaf litter. The flesh is yellowish with a hot, acrid taste. The cap, 3–6 cm, is convex, red-brown drying paler. The gills are yellowish and spaced. The stem, 5–9 cm, tapers above and is yellowish with a woolly base. Aug–Nov.

Small bleeding mycena
Mycena sanguinolenta
Very common amongst leaf litter. The cap, 1–2 cm, is red-brown, bell-shaped and grooved. The gills are spaced, white and the edges are tinged. The very slender stem, 7–10 cm, exudes red juice when broken and has a woolly base. Aug–Nov.

Bitter boletus
Tylopilus felleus
Not poisonous, but intensely bitter and will ruin the flavour of any dish. Easily confused with the Penny bun boletus (*p 104*), but the stem has a brown, not white, network. Usually on sandy soil. The cap, 4–20 cm, has a thick margin and is dry and cracking, pale to dark brown. The pores are round then angular, cream to flesh pink, bruising rusty brown. The stem, 3–15 cm, is thick, cream to yellowish at the apex, rusty brown below, with a net of ridged brownish veins. The flesh is white. June–Nov.

The blusher
Amanita rubescens
A very variable but common species, edible only after cooking since it can cause haemolysis if eaten raw. The flesh reddens when bruised. The cap, 5–15 cm, is spherical to convex, grey to red-brown, with loose, whitish scales. The gills are free, white spotted brown. The stem, 5–15 cm, is white above a lined ring, and red-brown below. The base is scaly and swollen. June–Oct.

Orange birch boletus
Leccinum versipelle (testaceoascabrum)
Growing under birch and recognized by its orange cap and scaly stem. Although edible, the flesh discolours to a dark purplish-grey. The cap, 8–20 cm, is orange to yellowish-red or apricot, and dry. The pores are greyish, minute and round. The tall stem, 10–20 cm, is often club-shaped, and grooved with blackish scales on a white background. June–Oct.

Red-cracked boletus
Xerocomus chrysenteron
Edible but only mediocre and needing to be cooked, this is the most common British bolete. The soft, creamy flesh blues very slowly on exposure. The cap, 4–8 cm, is convex to depressed, dry, velvety, often with red cracks, and pale olive to reddish-brown in colour. The tubes are yellow then greenish. The pores are large, angular and yellow, bruising blue. The stem, 4–8 cm, is slender and solid, and a carmine red. June–Nov.

Bare-toothed russula
Russula vesca
This excellent edible fungus (which must be cooked) is used in many dishes and tastes mildly of hazel nuts. It may be pickled in vinegar, but unfortunately it is prone to insect attack. Prefers sandy soil. The cap, 7–10 cm, is soon depressed. It is finely ridged, flesh pink to purplish-brown with a darker centre, never violet. The gills are white to cream, very forked and crowded. The stem, 3–7 cm, is solid, white and ridged, often with a pink flesh. June–Sept.

Lactarius subdulcis
The copious white milk has a sweetish taste that becomes slightly bitter in the mouth. Edible after cooking, but not recommended. The cap, 3–8 cm, is convex then depressed, smooth, pink to pale cinnamon but darker at the centre. The gills are pinkish and crowded. The stem, 3–5 cm, is red-brown and paler above. Aug–Oct.

Suillus luteus

An edible species prone to insect attack during warm weather. The cap, 5–12 cm, is pale yellowish-brown to chocolate brown, covered by a grey slime and shiny. The tubes are lemon yellow. The pores are angular, pale yellow to golden, finally brownish. The stem, 5–10 cm, is solid, yellow-white with wine-coloured scales; the large, spreading ring is slimy and white. Flesh is thick. July–Oct.

Blackening russula
Russula nigricans

The largest *Russula* species and very common. It is edible after cooking, but the flavour is poor. Often attacked by *Nyctalis* species (*p 89*) when old. The flesh turns from red to black on cutting. All parts blacken with age. The cap, 10–20 cm, is white to brown and finally black. The gills are whitish and widely spaced. The stem, 3–7 cm, is thick. July–Nov.

The devil's boletus
Boletus satanas

One of the largest boletes, though found only occasionally in late summer to early autumn on its own, on chalky soil. It causes severe gastro-intestinal poisoning, even in small amounts, but it is not fatal. The cap, 8–30 cm, has a thick margin. It is whitish, at times greyish or olive brown, shiny and finally cracking. The tubes are short and yellow, bluing when cut. The pores are round, yellow to brick red, growing paler with age, bruising blackish-blue. The stem, 5–10 cm, is very swollen, the upper region yellowish with a fine but distinct red network. It is carmine red elsewhere, bluing to the touch. The flesh is yellowish-white, turning blue when moist, with an unpleasant smell. July–Oct.

Russula pseudointegra

The white stem and ochre gills separate this species from *R. lepida* (*p 105*). Found under oak, beech and hazel. The cap, 5–12 cm, is cinnabar red to scarlet, discolouring pale pink; the margin is grooved. The gills are whitish then ochre, and fairly crowded. The stem, 4–8 cm, is pure white. The flesh is hard and bitter. July–Oct.

Emetic russula
Russula emetica

Has a hot, acrid taste and causes vomiting if eaten raw. Found in damp, mossy places, this species may be confused with *R. lepida* (*p 105*), which has cream (not white) gills. The slimy pellicle of *R. emetica* peels easily, revealing thin red flesh. The cap, 5–9 cm, is light red to cherry red (scarlet in peak condition), fading to pink when wet, convex to depressed. The gills are white and quite spaced. The stem, 3–8 cm, is white and thicker at the base. July–Oct.

Russula cyanoxantha

Probably the most common and best known of all the *Russula* species, appearing from early July onwards. It is also one of the better edible species, though needing to be cooked. Its thick white or greyish flesh has a mild, nutty taste. The cap colour can vary from grey, purple, olive green or brown, but the stem always remains white. The cap, 5–15 cm, is often greenish at the centre, sometimes uniformly green, shiny, radially veined. The gills are white, crowded and forked. The stem, 5–10 cm, is solid, firm and white. July–Nov.

Cortinarius traganus

The yellow-brown flesh and sickly sweet smell are important in separating *C. traganus* from other bluish *Cortinarius* species. It is poisonous. More frequent in Scotland. The young fruitbody is amethyst blue, with the hemispherical cap joined to the stem by a cobweb-like veil. The fully grown cap, 4–12 cm, is convex, fleshy, dry, silky-scaly; first pale blue-violet, then yellowish to rusty ochre. The surface may develop cracks. The gills are pale ochre to rust, discoloured rusty brown by the spores, and fairly crowded. The stem, 6–12 cm, is stout, lilac then pale ochre from the bulbous, club-shaped stem base upwards. July–Oct.

Lilac mycena
Mycena pura

Smells of radish. The pink colour is often washed out and appears whitish. The cap, 2–8 cm, is rose pink to lilac, with a lined margin. The gills are white or pink, broad and spaced. The stem, 4–8 cm, is the same colour as the cap, smooth with a downy base. June–Dec.

Russula queletii

R. queletii is especially associated with spruce in damp places. It has a fruity but unpleasant smell and its acrid taste makes it unsuitable for the table. The white, fragile flesh is pink just under the pellicle. The cap, 3–8 cm, is dark purplish, red to violet, almost black at the centre, flushing dirty olive with age, with a grooved margin. The gills are white, becoming lemon yellow and fairly crowded. The stem, 4–6 cm, is pink to pale violet. July–Oct.

Blackish-purple russula
Russula atropurpurea

The flesh of this fungus is very firm with a vague smell of apples, but is inedible because of its acrid taste. The cap, 5–12 cm, is convex, and irregularly shaped, purplish-red to almost black at the centre, sometimes developing creamy-yellow patches. The gills are cream and fairly crowded. The stem, 5–6 cm, is white. The flesh is white to greyish. June–Oct.

Russula caerulea

The flesh of this species actually has a mild taste, but the whole fungus is considered inedible because of its very bitter pellicle. The cap, 5–7 cm, is almost conical at first, expanding to depressed, and always has a central umbo. The colour is dark violet to purplish-red, blackish at the centre, shiny and slippery when wet. The gills are lemon to ochre and fairly crowded. The stem, 4–8 cm, is white to grey, with a swollen base. June–Oct.

Russula virescens

Regarded as one of the best edible *Russula* species, with a nutty flavour; it can be eaten raw. Often found in grass in small troops, especially near beech. The cap, 6–12 cm, is convex, then depressed. It is grey-green, blue-green, olive to brownish, dry and cracking into small scales. The gills are creamy white and fairly crowded. The stem, 4–8 cm, is solid and white. The flesh is thick, with a fruity smell. June–Oct.

Birds

Wood warbler
Phylloscopus sibilatrix

The largest greenish-plumaged warbler to breed in Britain, a slim, elegant bird with long wings and a short tail. Found in woodland with a good canopy and little ground cover. It is distinguished by its combination of greenish upperparts with pure yellow and white underparts. The large pale eye stripe varies in size. Its sailing, gliding display flight shows the yellow on throat, breast and wing. The bird makes frequent sallies after insects and will hover. Its song is a shivering trill like a spinning coil running down a metal plate. There is also a plaintive bell-like note. Wood warblers build a well-concealed domed nest on the ground, usually with an arch of twigs or small roots across the entrance. 12–13 cm. Summer visitor: Apr–Sept.

Pied flycatcher
male in flight, see p 79.

Chiffchaff
Phylloscopus collybita

A small, delicate warbler with slight physical differences to the Willow warbler (*right*), but otherwise identical. The Chiffchaff has a rounder head, shorter wing tips and, usually, darker legs. Its song, however, is absolutely distinctive: a deliberate "teet-teu" ("chiff-chaff") often repeated, but it also shares a low, anxious, "houeet" call with the Willow warbler. Birds slip quietly through the foliage, picking at food, or take flight to catch insects. Found in woodland and scrub. Top Sixty. 11 cm. Summer visitor: Mar–Oct, but some overwinter.

Willow warbler
Phylloscopus trochilus

A bird of similar habits and appearance to the Chiffchaff (*left*). Both catch flies by flitting, chasing sallies, or hovering. The Willow warbler has greenish upperparts, yellowish underparts and pale legs. There is a pale eye stripe.

It has longer wings than the Chiffchaff. The Willow warbler is a bird of small bushes and young trees and vegetation, but both species will feed high in trees or in low bushes. The Willow warbler is best distinguished by its song (like a tinkling of notes running down the scale) It also has a "hoo-et" call. Top Sixty. 11 cm. Summer visitor: Apr–Oct.

Siskin
Carduelis spinus

A tiny, dumpy bird with a forked tail and long wings, virtually the only small black, green and yellow British bird. Both sexes have black, yellow-banded wings and yellow in the tail. The male has a black cap and bib, but the female's plumage is duller. The call is a high clear "tzu" and "tzy-zing". Sometimes in wooded gardens. Closely associated with conifers for nesting, and with alders and birch in winter when small

flocks of mixed finches including Siskins feed like tits. Siskins twitter quietly but perpetually. 12 cm. Resident.

Lesser redpoll
Carduelis flammea

A small brown finch with a red forehead, distinguished from Linnet (*p 60*) and Twite (*p 60*) by its black chin. Lesser redpolls are tiny birds, highly acrobatic when feeding. The male has a crimson crown, pink flush on its breast, streaky

upperparts and pale wing-bars. The female lacks the pink breast. Both have a black bib. Young birds lack the red cap and black bib. Flight is active and bounding, with a rattling "chi-chi-chi" flight call. In summer, frequents conifer and birch. In winter, often found with Siskins in waterside alders and with finches and tits in weed and scrub. Top Sixty. 13–15 cm. Resident.

Garden warbler
Sylvia borin

A superficially nondescript bird of woodland and scrub, best recognised by its song: a pleasant warble very like the Blackcap's (*p 96*). Its habitat overlaps with the Blackcap's. The Garden warbler breeds in woodland and scrub, but occupies more open areas and is absent from wooded urban areas. It is usually seen flitting from bush to bush. Its rounded

head, a bill relatively short for a warbler and rather blank look are distinctive. Adults have a large dark eye and pale eye ring, juveniles a subtle grey patch and pale eye stripe (the underparts have a yellowish cast). 14 cm. Summer visitor: mid-Apr–Oct.

Spotted flycatcher
Muscicapa striata

Despite the name, adult spotted flycatchers are not spotted, but streaked (though juveniles have spots). Look for a quiet, greyish bird, often slowly wagging its tail or drooping and flicking its wings. Basically it is a long-winged, sparrow-sized bird, with brown underparts and otherwise nondescript plumage. It has a flat bill and large, dark eyes in its pale head, also short, black legs. It intersperses quiet watching from a tree perch with effortless, aerobatic sallies after insects. Its tortuous flight just off the ground is aided by its long wings. The call is a high "tsit" or "tsit-tuk-tuk". Found in woods, scrub, fields and wooded gardens; 14 cm. Summer visitor: late May–Sept.

Brambling
male in summer, see p 108.

Blackcap
Sylvia atricapilla

Distinguished from other warblers by the male's black cap and the female's brown crown. A slim, elegant bird with longish wings and tail. Males have grey nape and breast and olive-brown upperparts. Females have a brownish tinge to the grey breast. An active and lively bird, which usually hugs the cover of woodland trees and bushes. The tail stands out in its swift, jerky flight. The male's song, coming from deep within foliage, is rich and melodious in contrast with the "tack-tack" alarm call and can be confused with the Garden warbler's (*p 95*). Found in open woodland and large wooded gardens in England and Wales. Top Sixty. 14 cm. Summer visitor, though some birds (mostly male) winter and can be seen at bird tables.

Tree sparrow
Passer montanus

A rural replacement for the House sparrow (*p 197*), but distinctly smaller, more compact in appearance and shyer. It has whiter underparts and a generally cleaner look. The sexes are alike, with a chestnut crown, a white collar and black cheek patches which show up clearly when at rest.

The size of the bib varies with the season, but is neater and smaller than in the House sparrow. Tree sparrows pick quietly on the ground for food. They nest in tree holes, quarries and, more rarely, buildings. In late May they sometimes take over (and even build on top of) tits' nests in nestboxes. Flight is direct and sparrow-like, but note the white collar and black cheek patch. The call is a short, sharp "chup" and "tek-tek" on the wing. Fairly common, but often overlooked. Not found in towns. Top Sixty. 14 cm. Resident.

Common crossbill
Loxia curvirostra

In July family parties of Crossbills are present in coniferous woods. The unique crossed bill, used for prising seeds from pine cones, is unmistakable close to. From a distance this unusual finch's long wings, short tail and parrot-like clambering over branches are distinctive. The "gyp-gyp" call attracts attention to flying birds. Plumage varies greatly as the birds mature, from the yellows and greens of juveniles and females through orange to the bright red of adult males. The fledgling's bill is not crossed. Bill size also varies: birds feeding on Scots pine (the Scottish crossbill –*Loxia scotica*) have larger bills than the spruce-feeding Common crossbill. Entirely confined to conifers, breeding mainly in mature plantations. Nests early Dec onwards, but mostly Feb–Apr. Patchy, local distribution. 16–17 cm. Resident.

Common

Scottish

97

AUTUMN
Butterflies

Brown hairstreak
Thecla betulae

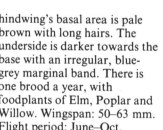

Large tortoiseshell
Nymphalis polychloros
Less common now, found in S England and parts of the Midlands in woodlands and gardens. The sexes are similar. The forewing spots are rounded, and the inner edge of the dark wing border is narrow and well-defined. There is a scalloped wing margin. The hindwing's basal area is pale brown with long hairs. The underside is darker towards the base with an irregular, blue-grey marginal band. There is one brood a year, with foodplants of Elm, Poplar and Willow. Wingspan: 50–63 mm. Flight period: June–Oct.

This butterfly tends to fly in short, sharp bursts, fairly high up, and only when the sun is shining. It is mainly a woodland species, but may also fly near hedgerows and in open spaces. The dark brown colour of the uppers contrasts with the orange-yellow of the underside. The male's upper forewing has a black mark at the end of the cell and an indistinct pale buff area. His underside has thin white lines across both wings.

There are two small orange spots near the hindwing tail, more prominent in the female, as is the orange band on her forewing. Her underside ground colour is more intense than the male's. The eggs of the single brood are laid singly on the foodplants (Sloe and others) in the autumn, and remain without hatching until spring. Wingspan: 34–36 mm; Flight: Aug–Sept.

Purple hairstreak
Quercusia quercus
The iridescent purple varies according to the way the light falls on the wings. An oakwood species, flying mainly in the treetops, in some years it is very common. The caterpillar resembles the leaf buds of the Oak on which it feeds. The male butterfly has uppers of deep purple or violet blue, with dark borders. The underside has a prominent white line on a greyish background. The female is dark brown, with a shiny

violet area on the forewing, less extensive than in the male. There are orange-yellow spots near the corner of the hindwing. Wingspan: 24–28 mm; Flight: July–Sept.

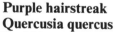

Wild Flowers

Cornish moneywort
Sibthorpia europaea
Rare in damp woodlands in the SW (as its name suggests), a low creeping plant with rounded leaves (2 cm) with five to seven lobes. The pink and yellow flowers are tiny (2 mm). Creeps to 40 cm. July–Oct.

Wood sage
Teucrium scorodonia
Common in woods, rocks, dunes, but always on acid soil, with greenish-yellow flowers, 8–10 mm, on whorled spikes. The flowers have no upper lip. The leaves are wrinkled and heart-shaped. 20 cm. July–Sept.

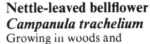

Climbing corydalis
Corydalis claviculata
A scrambling annual of woods and rocks on acid soils, with pinnate leaves ending in tendrils, and clusters of creamy flowers, 5–6 mm, whose petal tube is short-spurred. 50 cm. June–Sept.

Nettle-leaved bellflower
Campanula trachelium
Growing in woods and hedgerows, a tall, hairy perennial, with sharply ridged stems, and violet-blue flowers, 30–40 mm, on leafy spikes. The upper leaves are oval and toothed, the lower ones heart-shaped. 1 m. July–Sept.

Spreading bellflower
Campanula patula
Similar to Nettle-leaved bellflower (*left*), but shorter, with smaller flowers, 15–25 mm, and narrower leaves. The flower-bearing stalks are much branched. 60 cm. July–Sept.

Fungi

Wood mushroom
Agaricus silvicola
May be confused with the deadly *Amanita* species when young, so stem and gills should be examined with care. It smells of aniseed and is edible only when cooked. The cap, 6–12 cm, is creamy white, bruising yellow, dry and smooth. The gills are pale grey then flesh brown, finally chocolate and very crowded. The stem, 6–12 cm, is silky-smooth, with a bulbous base. The ring is persistent but fragile, and hangs down. July–Nov.

Common funnel cap
Clitocybe infundibuliformis (C. gibba)
Very common. The caps are usually eaten with other fungi and must be cooked. Smells of bitter almonds. The flesh is very thin. The cap, 3–8 cm, is flesh-coloured to pale rust brown or cream, convex soon funnel-shaped, dry, with a thin margin. The gills are whitish, narrow and crowded. The stem, 4–8 cm, is solid. Aug–Oct.

Lepiota bucknallii

A small, distinctive species occasionally found amongst grass and dead leaves in woodland; the strong smell of coal gas recalls *Tricholoma sulphureum* (*opposite*), but the two species are not alike. The cap, 2–3 cm, is greyish, with tiny flaky scales. The gills are free, cream and crowded. The stem, 2–6 cm, is lavender blue, with a darker base. Sept–Oct.

Peppery milk cap
Lactarius piperatus

The firm white flesh produces a copious white milk with a very acrid taste which is removed by boiling. Although eaten in Russia and other eastern countries, it is picked only in dry seasons when few other species are around, and it is not recommended for western palates. It is best eaten fried but is of poor quality. Note the exceptionally crowded gills. The cap, 7–20 cm, is creamy white, smooth and rigid. The gills are white to yellow, and forked. The stem, 3–7 cm, is white and smooth. Aug–Nov.

Club-footed clitocybe
Clitocybe clavipes

The watery flesh of this fungus has a mild taste and scent of bitter almonds. Edible after cooking. It is recognized by its club-shaped base which is covered in white down, and pale yellow gills. The cap, 4–8 cm, is greyish-brown with olive tints, darker at the centre, and smooth. The gills are thin and soft. The stem, 5–8 cm, is usually paler than the cap, with a swollen, woolly base. Sept–Nov.

Agaricus langei

A variable species. The cap has more distinct rings of flat, dark brown scales than does *A. silvaticus* (*right*). The white flesh discolours blood red immediately on exposure, far more intensely. The cap, 6–12 cm, is rust brown, darker at centre. The gills are rosy pink then blackish-brown, crowded and free. The stem, 7–12 cm, is white, slightly scaly, not bulbous, but cylindric and bruises red easily. The thick white ring has dark brown scales on the underside. Aug–Nov.

Agaricus silvaticus

Deeply rooted in pine needles. The thin, white flesh reddens when cut but in older specimens it is brownish and does not discolour. May be distinguished from *A. langei* (*left*) by its bulbous base. Edible. The cap, 6–10 cm, is covered with dense, red-brown scales on a white background. The gills are pinkish-grey becoming blackish-brown and crowded. The stem, 7–11 cm, is whitish, rather scaly, soon hollow, with a swollen base and large, thin, persistent ring. Sept–Nov.

Pseudoclitocybe expallens

Looks like a tall, slender *Clitocybe* species, but more closely related to the genus *Melanoleuca*. Edible after cooking. The cap, 2–5 cm, is smoky grey. The gills are pale grey. The stem, 4–8 cm, is cap colour or paler, tough and smooth. Sept–Nov.

Sulphurous tricholoma
Tricholoma sulphureum

An entirely sulphur-yellow mushroom which is locally common, preferring stiff clay soils. It is poisonous with a bitter taste and a strong, unpleasant, sweetish smell of coal gas. The cap, 4–8 cm, is fleshy and irregular, dry and silky-smooth. The gills are thick, spaced and yellow. The stem, 5–10 cm, is slender and curving, yellow discolouring brownish with age. Sept–Nov.

False chanterelle
Hygrophoropsis aurantiaca

Often mistaken for Chanterelle (*p 90*) in colour and shape, but Chanterelle has wrinkled folds, not true gills. False chanterelle occurs in large troops in woods and grassland, and its tough, yellow flesh is best eaten fried, though not recommended. The cap, 3–6 cm, is egg-yellow to orange and has a dry, velvety surface. The gills are thin and forking. The stem, 2–5 cm, is cap colour. Aug–Nov.

Saffron milk cap
Lactarius deliciosus

Thick, fleshy and edible, but its sweet, orange milk has an acrid after-taste. Grows in coniferous woods. The cap, 6–20 cm, is orange-red with darker, concentric zones, bruising green; sticky, with a thin, inrolled margin. The bright orange gills become spotted green with age. The stem, 2–7 cm, is short and thick, with orange spots. The flesh is off-white and discolours slowly. Aug–Oct.

Old man of the woods
Strobilomyces floccopus

Usually solitary and one of the easiest boletes to recognize. Young specimens are all-white and can be eaten, but soon blacken and become too tough for the table. The cap, 4–10 cm, has a shaggy incurved margin. It is dry, covered with large, thick, woolly, blackish-brown scales. The tubes are greyish-white, reddening on exposure. Pores are large, angular, greyish, bruising red. The elongated, scaly, hard stem, 8–14 cm, is cap colour. The flesh is soft and moist, white but discolouring red and finally black. Aug–Oct.

Slimy milk cap
Lactarius blennius

Always under beech, this species may be recognized by its slimy, grey-green cap, which is concentrically zoned with dark, drop-like markings. It produces a very hot white milk, which turns grey on exposure. The cap, 5–10 cm, is olive brown to green-grey. The gills are white staining grey. The stem, 3–5 cm, tapers below and is paler than the cap. The flesh is white. Aug–Nov.

Clouded agaric
Clitocybe nebularis

Regarded as a good edible species by many, although it has been known to cause discomfort and therefore should initially be treated with caution. *C. nebularis* grows well in rich soil and has a strong smell of Swedish turnip. The cap, 6–20 cm, is fleshy, matt or shiny when wet, ash grey to yellow-brown, darker at the centre, with a white, powdery bloom. The gills are cream. The stem, 5–12 cm, is white to grey. Aug–Nov.

Death cap
Amanita phalloides

The most poisonous mushroom, causing 90 per cent of all deaths from fungus poisoning; deadly even cooked and in small amounts. Always wash hands after handling. About the same size as a Horse mushroom (*p 43*), but the cap colour, white, crowded gills and large volva are distinctive. The streaky cap, 6–15 cm, is convex, moist, satiny, yellowish-green to olive, discolouring to cream. The stem, 8–20 cm, cylindric with a bulbous base, is cupped by a fleshy, sac-like volva; white and slightly scaly, with a thin, membranous, persistent ring. The flesh is thick and white, with a smell of honey, soon ammoniacal. July–Nov.

Lepiota friesii
(Cystolepiota aspera)

A large *Lepiota* species, characterized by the numerous erect, pointed scales on the cap. Grows in small groups on sandy soil in woodlands amongst plant debris, also in gardens. The thick white flesh is bitter with a strong, unpleasant smell. The cap, 4–10 cm, has crowded, red brown, small, pointed scales on a pale brown background, which easily break off. The gills are white, crowded and forked. The stem, 7–10 cm, is white above, brown and scaly near the swollen base; the ring is white, rusty underneath. Aug–Nov.

Lactarius pallidus

Usually found under beech, but may also occur with birch; it is often half-hidden in the leaf litter, sometimes in large quantities. Look out for its uniformly pale, smooth cap with inrolled margin. The flesh produces mild white milk. The cap, 6–10 cm, is pale pinkish-brown and sticky. The gills are paler, crowded and narrow. The stem, 5–7 cm, is smooth, the same colour as the cap or paler. July–Sept.

Greasy tough shank
Collybia butyracea

The greasy cap surface lends this species its popular name. The cap pales from the margin inwards when dry, but the pointed top remains coloured, dark and oily. Grows in clusters or rings in mixed woods. The cap, 4–8 cm, is bay brown to olive brown. The gills are white, broad and crowded. The stem, 5–10 cm, is reddish, with a swollen base, lined and tough. Sept–Nov.

The deceiver
Laccaria laccata

Probably the most common toadstool in the northern hemisphere but also one of the most variable, hence the name. Edible after cooking but poor. The cap, 1–5 cm, is convex to depressed, irregular, pinkish to yellowish-brown and scaly. The gills are pinkish, powdery and spaced. The stem, 5–8 cm, is the same colour as the cap. Aug–Nov.

Fairy cake hebeloma (Poison pie)
Hebeloma crustuliniforme
Poisonous – it has a bitter taste and may cause vomiting, cramp and diarrhoea. It is the most common *Hebeloma* species, but varies in size and colour. Note the water drops on the gill edge and the smell of radish. The cap, 5–10 cm, is fleshy, convex, cream to pale olive brown, smooth and sticky. The gills are clay to cinnamon-coloured, and crowded. The stem, 4–8 cm, is whitish, with granules near the apex. Aug–Nov.

Pine spike-cap
Chroogomphus rutilus
(Gomphidius viscidus)
It has a slight scent and is edible after cooking but poor. The cap, 4–15 cm, is sticky, shiny when dry, and smooth. The gills are yellowish to purplish-grey, finally purplish-black, thick, forked and spaced. The stem, 4–12 cm, tapers towards the base; it is reddish at the apex, saffron to chrome yellow at the base; the ring is high with a cobweb-like zone. Aug–Nov.

Cinnamon cortinarius
Dermocybe cinnamomea
This species has bright lemon-yellow gills when young and a dry, silky cap that does not change colour when wet. May occur in large numbers in birch and coniferous woods, often tufted. The thin flesh is lemon to chrome yellow. The cap, 2–6 cm, varies from bright red-brown to yellowish-olive brown. The gills are orange or golden red, and crowded. The stem, 5–8 cm, has brown fibrils. Sept–Nov.

Geranium-scented russula
Russula fellea
A late autumnal species, uniformly coloured and with a distinctive smell of geraniums. Commonly found under beech and oak. All parts are uniformly straw-coloured. The cap, 3–8 cm, is pale to tawny ochre, sticky and shiny. The gills are ochre to cream, and fairly crowded. The stem, 3–7 cm, is solid, and pale yellowish-brown. The flesh is thick, white, and with a very acrid taste. Sept–Nov.

Soft slipper toadstool
Crepidotus mollis
Very common on decaying branches. The soft, horizontal cap contains a gelatinous layer giving an elastic texture when pulled apart. It is 2–7 cm, kidney-shaped, pale ochre brown with scattered brown scales. The gills are cinnamon brown. No stem. May–Dec.

Crepidotus variabilis
This small fungus may be found all year round in troops on dead twigs and straw, although it is more common in the autumn. The cap, 1–2 cm, is kidney-shaped, white and felty. The gills are white, dull yellow to brown. Aug–Oct.

Oak milk cap
Lactarius quietus
Restricted to oaks, its zoned cap and strong oily smell make it easy to recognize. The cap, 4–10 cm, is convex to depressed, a dull reddish-brown, and distinctly zoned with darker spots. The gills are white to reddish, and crowded. The stem, 3–7 cm, is the same colour as the cap or darker, and furrowed; the milk is white and mild. Sept–Nov.

Tricholoma fulvum (flavobrunneum)

Probably the commonest of the brown *Tricholoma* species, it is distinguished by its slimy cap and crowded yellowish gills spotted red. Grows in birch woods. It has an unpleasant smell of rancid meal. The cap, 7–12 cm, is reddish-brown. The stem, 7–12 cm, tapers above. It is slimy at first, reddish-brown and scaly below. The flesh is white, yellow in the stem. Sept–Nov.

Ugly milk cap
Lactarius turpis (necator/plumbeus)

Often in large numbers in damp soil, but always with birch. Edible when cooked. The cap, 6–18 cm, is olive brown to blackish, slimy, with an inrolled margin. The gills are cream to straw yellow, spotted brown on bruising. The stem, 4–6 cm, is cap colour, soon hollow and sticky. The flesh is whitish, with copious white milk and an acrid taste. July–Oct.

The goblet
Pseudoclitocybe cyathiformis

Appears in late summer, continuing through until the first frosts. Grows amongst woody debris in wet areas. Edible when cooked. The moist, watery dark grey-brown cap, 2–6 cm, dries paler. The gills are smoky grey and spaced. The slender stem, 5–10 cm, is the cap colour or paler, and has a downy base. The flesh is thin and watery. Sept–Nov.

Penny bun boletus, Cep
Boletus edulis

Known in France and Italy as the "King of Mushrooms" because of its delicious, white, nut-flavoured flesh. Do not confuse with the bitter *Tylopilus felleus* (*p 90*). The cap, 8–30 cm, hemispherical to convex with a thick margin, is sticky when moist. It is whitish to blackish-brown, often coffee-coloured or chestnut brown. The tubes are free, white then greenish-yellow. The pores are small, round, white to olive yellow, not bluing. The stem, 10–20 cm, is hard, pale brown and always thick. The upper part is covered with a fine network pattern. The base is whitish and swollen. The flesh is white. June–Nov.

Tricholoma ustale

One of a group of *Tricholoma* species in which the gills become spotted red. The dark red-brown slimy cap of *T. ustale* darkens with age. It is 5–8 cm, convex then flat, smooth, with an incurved margin. The gills are white soon spotted red, and crowded. The stem, 5–7 cm, is cream discolouring brownish from the base up. Poisonous. Sept–Oct.

Melanoleuca melaleuca

A very common species although rather variable, becoming much paler as it dries out. Easily confused with species of *Tricholoma*. *M. brevipes* (*p 196*) is similar but has a shorter stem and is less common. *M. melaleuca* also occurs on pastureland. Edible when cooked. The smooth cap, 4–10 cm, is dark brown when moist. The gills are white, broad and crowded. The stem, 5–8 cm, is solid and white, with longitudinal brownish fibrials. The flesh is white to grey and soft. Aug–Nov.

The panther
Amanita pantherina
Differs from *A. rubescens* (*p 91*) in not bruising red and with a cap which is never grey, covered in pure white scales. Poisonous. The cap, 5–12 cm, is black-brown to olive brown then paler. The gills are white. The stem, 6–12 cm, is white and silky, with a swollen base and a fragile, white ring. The flesh is white, purplish-brown with phenol and smells of raw potatoes. July–Oct.

Horn of plenty
Craterellus cornucopioides
Although unattractive and thin-fleshed, these are delicious to eat, usually cut into small pieces before cooking. Can grow in large troops, but the dark colour makes them difficult to see. The cap, 4–8 cm, is trumpet-shaped, dark blackish-brown to brownish-grey, shiny when dry, and scaly. The underside is waxy, pale grey to bluish-grey and powdery. The stem, 4–12 cm, is tubular and brownish-black. Aug–Oct.

Rhodocybe truncata
Usually found growing in clusters or rings in coniferous woods. Edible when cooked. Sometimes mistaken for the toxic *Hebeloma crustuliniformé* (*p 103*). The cap, 4–10 cm, is pink-brown to rust, with a matted surface. The gills are cream to reddish-pink, forked, narrow and crowded. The stem, 3–5 cm, is stocky and white with pink tints below. Sept–Nov.

Russula lepida
A beautiful, pale red species, sometimes discolouring yellowish-white. The hard white flesh has a faint odour of menthol or cedarwood and a bitter taste. The cap, 3–8 cm, has a velvety bloom and is vermilion red at centre, paler near the margin, often pinkish and dry. The crowded gills are cream. The stem, 3–10 cm, is white flushed pink. June–Nov.

Woolly milk cap
Lactarius torminosus
Edible after cooking. Recognized by the zoned woolly cap from which exudes a copious hot white milk. The cap, 4–15 cm, with a shaggy margin and round concentric salmon pink zones is slimy when moist and covered with long, dense, cottony, pink red hairs. The gills are thin, crowded and pinkish-cream. The stem, 3–8 cm, is stocky, soon hollow, creamy, with a pink zone near the apex. Likes damp places. Aug–Nov.

Russula mairei
Resembles *R. emetica* (*p 92*) and will also grow under conifers, but its flesh is hard and firm (not thin and fragile) with a smell of coconuts when young. Typically associated with beech, even growing under isolated trees. It has a very acrid taste. The cap, 4–7 cm, has thick, hard flesh, scarlet to blood red. The gills are whitish and crowded. The stem, 2–5 cm, is hard, solid and white. Sept–Oct.

Brick-red hypholoma
Hypholoma sublateritium
One of the largest *Hypholoma* species; more robust but less common than the Sulphur tuft (*p 78*). Grows in clusters on old stumps and is usually identified by its brick-red cap and stem. The cap, 4–10 cm, is yellowish towards margin, fleshy and smooth. The gills are yellowish to very dark brown. The stem, 5–10 cm, is yellowish-brown, red-brown below, and scaly. Aug–Nov.

Blood-red cortinarius
Dermocybe sanguinea
Even the flesh of this rather vivid species of coniferous woods is red. It is only likely to be confused with *D. cinnabarina* which is wholly scarlet and found in beech woods. The surface has a fine, scaly texture. The cap is 2–5 cm. The gills are crowded. The stem, 6–10 cm, is slender. Sept–Nov.

Fly agaric
Amanita muscaria
The best known toadstool, often illustrated in children's books. Poisonous: only lethal if eaten in enormous amounts, but can induce poisoning similar to drunkenness, and even coma. Used as an intoxicant in northern Europe and Siberia before the introduction of vodka. The cap, 15–25 cm, is scarlet to pale orange, with large white loose scales of the veil. The white free gills are crowded. The stem, 12–25 cm, has a bulbous base and is white with a large, pendant ring near its apex. Aug–Nov.

Russula xerampelina
Considered one of the best edible (after cooking) *Russula* species, but with a smell of crab. The gills, flesh and stem generally discolour yellowish-brown. The cap, 5–12 cm, is dry, but sticky when moist. It is very variable in colour: bright purplish-red, blackish at centre, often with brownish tints. The gills are whitish to pale ochre. The stem, 3–11 cm, is white with wine-red tints. The flesh is also white. Aug–Nov.

Agaricus purpurellus
Edible after cooking. Among pine needles. Differs from most *Agaricus* species in its small size, thin flesh and slender stem. It turns yellow when bruised and smells of bitter almonds. The cap, 2–4 cm, is silky, purplish or reddish with a darker centre. The gills are crowded and grey then pink. The stem, 3–4 cm, is white, the ring being thin and near the middle. July–Sept.

Purple and yellow agaric
Tricholomopsis rutilans
A brightly coloured agaric with a yellow, bitter-tasting flesh. Grows in clusters near old stumps in coniferous woods. The cap, 5–15 cm, is yellow, with the surface covered in dense, purple red scales. The gills are broad, crowded and sulphur yellow. The stem, 6–10 cm, is pale yellow with purple scales. Aug–Nov.

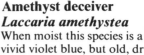

Amethyst deceiver
Laccaria amethystea

When moist this species is a vivid violet blue, but old, dry specimens may be pale lilac or even whitish. Edible after cooking but tasteless. Its cap, 1–6 cm, is finely scaly and often split. The gills are spaced. The stem, 4–10 cm, is curved, the same colour as the cap. The flesh is thin and pale lilac. Aug–Nov.

Cortinarius purpurascens

Belonging to a subgenus which has a slimy cap and dry stem, even in wet weather, *Cortinarius purpurascens* is almost always found tufted on non-chalky soil. The cap, 5–15 cm, is date brown to olive brown, often with darker streaks and a deep violet margin which becomes paler; it is slimy when young. The gills are violet then rusty brown, bruising deep purple. The stem, 5–12 cm, is stout and fibrous, with a bulbous base which often has a distinct rim. It is violet, with remains of a purplish cortina near apex. The flesh is violet. Sept–Nov.

Cortinarius caerulescens

Recognized by its dark bluish sticky cap and deep blue gills which become discoloured rusty brown by the spores. *C. caerulescens* occurs on chalky soil. The centre of the cap, 5–10 cm, discolours yellowish-brown. The gills are crowded. The stems, 5–8 cm, is violet blue with an ochre-yellow, club-shaped base. Aug–Nov.

Entoloma nitidum

Picked for its pretty deep blue colour, but probably best avoided. Found on peat among conifers and birch. The cap, 2–5 cm, is often slightly scaly in the centre. It is dark indigo blue and silky. The gills are white then pink. The stem, 6–9 cm, is lined, with a white, rooting base. Sept–Nov.

Blue-green clitocybe
Clitocybe odora

Edible after cooking and has been used as a condiment for its taste and strong smell of aniseed. Variable in size and colour; typically the cap is uniformly blue-green, but discolours greyish as it dries. The cap is 3–10 cm. The gills are pale bluish green. The stem, 4–10 cm, is curved, cream with a pinkish tint. Flesh is thin and whitish. Aug–Oct.

Verdigris toadstool
Stropharia aeruginosa

Exceptionally attractive when young, but the vivid colours soon fade. Common in grassy woods. The slimy cap, 2–7 cm, is blue-green, with small white scales. The gills are grey-brown. The stem, 4–7 cm, is slimy, paler than the cap, with white, flaky scales; its ring is black with white below. July–Nov.

Birds

Brambling
Fringilla montifringilla

Despite Chaffinch-like wing marks, its white rump sets the Brambling apart from all other finches. Its orange, white, black and grey plumage are further pointers. The male has orange shoulders and white wing-bars (*see also p 79*). In summer his head and back are jet-black (*see p 96*). The yellow armpit is diagnostic. In winter the female has a white rump and wing bars (*see p 115*). Arriving in migrant flocks in October, Bramblings feed on the ground, usually under beech trees (they are much dependent on beech mast), and in fields with other finches. In cold weather, when their natural food source is short, they will feed around farm buildings. The flight call is a rapidly repeated "tchuk-tchuk". 14–15 cm. Common but erratic winter visitor: Oct–Apr. Occasional summer visitor.

Treecreeper
Certhia familiaris

Its cryptic upperparts, silky white underparts and fine, curved bill set the Treecreeper apart from all birds. Tiny and mouse-like in its jerky, spiral movements on tree trunks, it is frequently overlooked, although actually common in woods and large gardens. Treecreepers often join tit flocks in autumn and winter. Their stiff pointed tail feathers sit against the bark of a tree to give them support. They have an undulating, unhurried flight and then their upper wing pattern and curved bill are clear identification pointers. The call is a high, thin "tsee" or "tsit". Top Sixty. 12–13 cm. Resident.

Jay
Garrulus glandarius

A very exotic-looking bird with a mobile crest, but actually a member of the Crow family. Its pink, black, white and blue underparts stand out in flight, and the white rump and blue and white in the wings show well at take-off. It is a raucous and extremely wary bird, an omnivorous feeder on the ground and in trees. Like squirrels, it will bury acorns in autumn. It makes a jerky flight between trees, spending little time exposed. Its harsh, screeching call is part of a wide repertoire. Usually seen in pairs. Found in woodland, parks and large, wooded gardens. Widely distributed. 34 cm. Resident.

Green woodpecker
Picus viridis

Largest of the British woodpeckers, with colours different from any other bird, although its distinctive yellow rump has caused confusion with the rare Golden oriole. The male has a red moustache stripe standing out vividly against his black face. Juveniles have a black-streaked, pale face, without the black area and moustache. Like all woodpeckers, the bird has an extremely long, sticky tongue with which it feeds on ants, alternately probing the ground and pausing to look around. It spends much more time on the ground than other woodpeckers, moving in clumsy hops. The flight is more deeply undulating than other woodpeckers, with a marked closure of wings between beats. The call is a loud, ringing laugh, hence a local name of "Yaffle"

The bird drums very rarely. It moves vertically up a tree trunk, often in a spiral, stopping frequently to hammer at the bark in search of grubs or to lick up insects. The spiky, stiff tail feathers are used as a support. The nest is high up in trees, in an excavated hole (though the bird is often evicted by Starlings). Among trees including heathland and open parkland. 32 cm. Resident.

Jackdaw
Corvus monedula

Smallest of the common "Crows", a perky and inquisitive bird often to be seen strutting on the ground and rooftops. It may be seen alone, but is really highly gregarious. The grey nape, black cap and pale eye are distinctive. It nests on buildings, cliff-faces and trees. The flight is hurried-looking: jackdaws can be seen soaring around cliffs, buildings and rock faces, when the rounded tail is noticeable. They have ringing "keeack" and "kyaw" calls in their wide vocabulary. Generally distributed throughout Britain, but in autumn migratory birds reach the east coast. Top Sixty. 33 cm. Resident.

Little owl
Athene noctua

The Little owl is small, squat and flat-headed, with round yellow eyes, white eyebrows, barred tail, streaked underparts and heavy spotting above. It is often seen in daylight, perched on posts and poles. It occupies small woods and coppices if the Tawny owl (*below*) is not present. It has a very undulating, woodpecker-like flight, and a plaintive "kiew" call. 22 cm. Resident (though very scarce in Scotland).

Tawny owl
Strix aluco

The best-known British owl, always associated with trees and widespread in woodland, but found even in squares in city centres and suburbs with many trees. Its large head, round facial disc and large, dark eye identify it. The upperparts are well marked. Most British Tawnies are rufous, but a grey form also occurs. Black eyes distinguish it from the Short-eared owl (*p 182*). Nocturnal, mostly seen at dawn and dusk, flying on broad, round wings, but, during later autumn and winter, a roosting bird can be discovered by the assembled mobbing of small birds. It has an emphatic "kee-wick" call and a drawn-out hooting. 38 cm. Resident.

Barn owl
Tyto alba

The Barn owl is the only common owl species with pure white wings, usually appearing ghostly in car headlights. The faces and bodies of British birds are mainly white. The upperparts are variable (sometimes very pale). The legs are long. Barn owls are often seen in daylight when gathering food for their young. They nest in old trees and buildings. They have a wavering, quartering flight on rather long, narrow wings over open ground and a loud shrieking call. 34 cm. Resident.

Long-eared owl
Asio otus

The Long-eared owl has long ear tufts (though these are not always visible) and orange-yellow eyes. If the ears cannot be seen, it looks like a slimmer version of the Tawny owl (*left*) but with orange-yellow eyes. Seen in daylight in winter and when feeding young. The finely barred rear half of the wing and the longer tail separates it from the Short-eared owl (*p 182*). It has deep wing-beats in flight. The call is a low "oo-oo-ooh". Breeds widely in woodland (nesting in conifers) and also on moors and heaths. 36 cm. Resident. Also winter visitor.

WINTER
Wild Flowers

Snowdrop
Galanthus nivalis
Growing in thick clumps in damp woods and hedgebanks (also cultivated). Long, narrow leaves grow from a bulb, together with nodding white flowers, which have a green fringe to their lower petals. 20 cm. Jan–Mar.

Winter aconite
Eranthis hyemalis
Not a native flower but naturalised in woodland plantations, with bright yellow flowers very early in the year. The leaves emerge after the flowers. 10 cm. Jan–Mar.

Stinking hellebore
Helleborus foetidus
Often a garden escapee, growing in dry woodland on chalky soils, this is a strong-smelling perennial with bell-shaped flowers, 10–30 mm, purple green in colour. The top leaves are in sheathes and not divided. 80 cm. Mar–Apr.

Barren strawberry
Potentilla sterilis
Rather like a Wild strawberry (*p 74*), except for its fruit. The flowers, 10–15 mm, with notched petals come early in the year. The plant is softly hairy. In woods and hedges, 15 cm. Feb–May.

Mistletoe
Viscum album
A woody evergreen, parasitic on the branches of (mainly) Apple and Poplar trees. It has inconspicuous white flowers Feb to Apr, and the sticky white berries are visible Nov to Jan. The leaves grow in pairs. To 1m. Feb–Apr.

Butcher's broom
Ruscus aculeatus
An evergreen bush growing in woods and by shady hedges, with no real leaves, but leaflike shoots which are leathery and have sharp points. The flowers are tiny, 2–3 mm, and carried on the actual shoots. Large red berries. 80 cm. Jan–Apr.

Green hellebore
Helleborus viridis
Another woodland plant, more often escaped from gardens, with clusters of drooping, widely opened, greenish flowers, 50 mm, and deeply lobed root leaves. 40 cm. Feb–Apr.

Fungi

Pleurotus dryinus
Good to eat when young. The cap, 9–14 cm, is disc- to shell-shaped, greyish and felty, with an incurved margin. The whitish gills, broad and spaced, turn yellow with age. The off-centre stem, 2–5 cm, is hard and scaly, with an ephemeral ring. Sept–Dec.

Herald of the winter
Hygrophorus hypothejus
A late species rarely seen before the frosty weather sets in, and identified by its slimy, yellow-grey cap which has an olive-brown centre and white to orange gills. It prefers acid soil. Edible after cooking. The cap, 3–7 cm, is convex to depressed. The gills are spaced. The stem, 4–10 cm, is yellowish, slimy and tapers below. Oct–Dec.

Magpie ink cap
Coprinus picaceus

A robust, poisonous, ink cap, easily identified by its black and white colouring, which has given rise to its common name "Magpie". Usually solitary in beech woods. The cap, 4–7 cm, is covered when young by a white felty veil, which cracks as the cap expands, leaving large white patches on a dark brown to black background. The gills are white then black, crowded and dissolving into a liquid. The stem, 12–20 cm, is white, fragile, hollow and smooth. Sept–Dec.

Winter funnel cap
Clitocybe brumalis

Only occurs late in the year and usually grows in groups. The cap, 2–5 cm, is dark yellowish-brown with an oily appearance, drying paler. It is thin, always depressed, finally funnel-shaped, with a wavy margin. The gills are pallid, narrow and crowded. The stem, 2–5 cm, is slender, white to grey and smooth. Nov–Dec.

Orange pholiota
Gymnopilus junonius

A handsome, golden yellow, poisonous fungus found clustered on stumps and at tree bases, especially Ash and Apple. The thick, yellow flesh is tough and bitter-tasting. Previously known as *Pholiota spectabilis*. The cap, 6–13 cm, is dry, tawny yellow to golden brown, with an incurved margin. The gills are yellow at first, then rust-coloured. The stem, 6–14 cm, is swollen, and tapers to a short "root", with a high, spreading ring. Aug–Dec.

Baeospora myosura

Sprouts from buried pine cones. A similar species, *Strobilurus tenacellus,* occurs in May. The cap, 1–2 cm, is yellowish to dark brown. The gills are yellowish, very crowded and narrow. The stem, 2–4 cm, is slender, with a rooting base. Oct–Dec.

Shaggy pholiota
Pholiota squarrosa

One of the larger *Pholiota* species which forms dense clusters at the base of old trees. It is weakly parasitic, entering wounds and attacking the living wood, especially of Mountain ash. Young specimens are edible after parboiling, but older fruitbodies are too bitter. They should never be consumed with alcohol. The cap, 3–10 cm, is pale ochre with concentric zones of red-brown, crowded, shaggy scales. The gills are yellow to rust brown and crowded. The stem, 7–15 cm, is the same colour as the cap with upturned scales and bears a small, dark, fibrous ring on the upper part. July–Dec.

Lyophyllum ulmarium

Young specimens are edible after cooking although bitter, but older ones are much too tough. Grows in clusters on Elm trunks, with several fruitbodies on a common base. Sometimes the cap, 7–20 cm, is positioned off-centre. It is flat, fleshy, dirty yellowish, smooth or cracked. The gills are pale ochre yellow and crowded. The stem, 8–12 cm, is thick, whitish, firm and often curved upwards. The flesh is white. June–Dec.

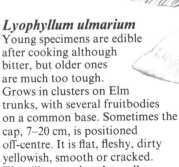

113

Glistening ink cap
Coprinus micaceus
Arises from buried wood or dead roots in dense tufts and common everywhere. The cap, 2–4 cm, is fragile, ochre to tawny brown, and grooved almost to the centre, with a glistening surface. The gills are crowded, pale to dark brown, dissolving into liquid. The stem, 5–8 cm, is white and smooth. Jan–Dec.

Velvet shank
Flammulina velutipes
A widespread fungus, edible after cooking and suitable for soups, valuable because it occurs when few other species are available. Only the caps are edible, but remove the slimy pellicle. It grows tufted on wood, as a wound parasite. The sticky, shiny cap, 3–6 cm, is honey yellow, spotting brown. The gills are yellowish. The dark, velvety stem, 4–10 cm, is tough, black-brown, but pale above. Sept–Mar.

Styptic fungus
Pleurotus stipticus
Common all year, forming crowded tiers on stumps. The tough flesh has a very stringent taste and is claimed to be poisonous, though this has not been confirmed. The cap, 1–3 cm, is roughly kidney-shaped, pale brown, thin, tough and scurfy, with an incurved margin. The gills are yellow to pale brown, thin, narrow and crowded with interveining. The stem is broadest at point of attachment to the stump. Jan–Dec.

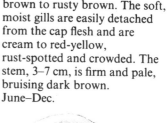

Brown roll-rim
Paxillus involutus
An extremely common species, especially associated with birch on poor soils. It has been stated to be harmless when eaten occasionally, but there is a cumulative poisonous effect if eaten repeatedly over a period of years which has proved fatal. The cap, 5–25 cm, has an inrolled margin and is felty, sticky when wet, and olive brown to rusty brown. The soft, moist gills are easily detached from the cap flesh and are cream to red-yellow, rust-spotted and crowded. The stem, 3–7 cm, is firm and pale, bruising dark brown. June–Dec.

Oyster mushroom
Pleurotus ostreatus
A well-known edible species, grown commercially in Hungary. It forms clusters on broad-leaved trees, especially beech. Best eaten when young. The cap, 7–14 cm, growing off-centre, is ash grey, black, purplish or white, smooth and shiny. The gills are white to cream, and very crowded. The short stem, 1–3 cm, is solid and hard. Jan–Dec.

Wood blewit
Lepista nuda
The lilac blue colour of this excellent edible mushroom makes it one of the best-known. It is slightly toxic eaten raw so parboiling is recommended. In groups, often forming rings on disturbed soil. The flesh is white with a lilac tint. The 7–12 cm, lilac-grey cap discolours grey or brownish. The gills are bright lilac but soon discolour. The stem, 4–8 cm, is bright violet. Sept–Dec.

Birds

Coal tit
Parus ater

The smallest British tit and typically restless and acrobatic. A disproportionately large head, glossy black crown and bib, white cheeks and nape, forked tail and warm buff belly plumage distinguish it. The white wing-bars are evident in its fast, flitting flight. The juvenile is drabber. The call is a thin, clear "tsui", also "susi-susi"; the song a clear repeated "seetoo-seetoo". Common (especially among conifers) and also visits gardens and nut bags in winter. Top Sixty. 11–12 cm. Resident.

Brambling
female in winter plumage
see p.108.

♀

Firecrest
Regulus ignicapillus

Almost the smallest of all the European birds, the Firecrest shares very similar habits with the Goldcrest (*right*), and also has a yellow crown, spread in display to reveal its orange feathers. The Firecrest's bold white eye stripe between two black stripes gives it a quite different look. The nape is copper-coloured. Both species feed mainly high in trees (especially conifers), but may also hunt among low vegetation and bushes. In winter they often join roving parties of tits. They can be extremely tame. The Firecrest is best located by its crescendo of increasingly fast "zit" notes. 9 cm. Resident only a very small population, with about 20 breeding areas (especially in tall Norway spruce) S of line between Severn and Wash. Also occasional winter visitor, and autumn passage migrant (when it is most often seen).

Goldcrest
Regulus regulus

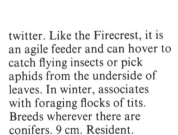

The smallest British bird, weighing just over 5 g. Similar in habits to the Firecrest (*left*), the Goldcrest has a prominent, beady black eye set in a pale face, with a black stripe above and a yellow crown, spread in display to reveal the orange feathers. It does not have the Firecrest's white eye stripe. It is minute-looking in flight, with short, rounded wings and a slightly forked tail. It has a shrill, insistent "zee-zee-zee" call. The song is a thin, high double note ending in a short twitter. Like the Firecrest, it is an agile feeder and can hover to catch flying insects or pick aphids from the underside of leaves. In winter, associates with foraging flocks of tits. Breeds wherever there are conifers. 9 cm. Resident.

Willow tit
Parus montanus

Very similar to the Marsh tit (*left*) but rarely seen together. (The northern Willow tit is paler and very like the Marsh tit.) Flight in both is typical of tits – fast and flitting. The bull-headed, puff-cheeked look of the Willow tit is its best guide. The head is larger and the cap longer and less glossy. The Willow tit is shy and subdued for a tit but has a buzzing call. Never exclusively associated with willows and may be found in a variety of woodland, including wooded gardens. Attracted to bird feeders. 11–12 cm. Resident.

Marsh tit
Parus palustris

Commoner than the Willow tit (*right*), the adult has crown feathers, which can be very glossy, no pale wing panel, a rounder head and generally it is browner and slimmer than the Willow tit. Distinguished from the Coal tit (*p 115*) by lack of white nape patch. Young Marsh and Willow tits are indistinguishable. The Marsh tit has a "sst-choo" call and typical fast, flitting flight. Has never been exclusively associated with marshes, and may be found in a variety of woodland, including wooded gardens. In winter it may go to peanut bags. Top Sixty. 11–12 cm. Resident.

Hawfinch
Coccothraustes coccothraustes

The largest finch, with a huge bill to crack fruit stones, long wings with white wing-bars and a short, square, pale-tipped tail. The bill is bluish in summer and horn-coloured in winter. The bird is extremely shy and wary, but in February flocks may roost communally in dense woodland cover. It moves about by very long hops along the ground. The flight is strong and undulating, often high. The loud explosive "tick" call is the best means of locating it. It sounds rather like a Robin. Also visits large gardens. 18 cm. Resident.

Capercaillie
Tetrao turogallus

Size (the unmistakable male is almost as large as a turkey) prevents confusion with other species. Young males have shorter tails and show an odd mixture of plumage. In summer females and young feed on the ground and in autumn may be found in stubble fields or even heather, some way from their coniferous forest habitat. They may be distinguished from the much smaller Greyhen (*p 69*) by the chestnut patch on the breast, the rounded tail and no wing-bar. The males feed on pine shoots in the trees. The bird is extremely noisy when taking off but silent in flight, which is swift and strong, with a series of flaps followed by a tilting glide. Males are extremely territorial in late winter/early spring and have an elaborate courtship display (*below*), accompanied by an extraordinary cacophony of calls, intermittent leaps into the air, and noisily flapping wings. N of Firth of Forth, recently reintroduced in the Lake District. 60–87 cm. Resident.

Coast

The face of the coastline is fascinating and immensely varied, ranging from tall cliffs and craggy stacks to flat estuaries, bleak salt marshes, mud flats, shingle and sandy beaches, and the constantly shifting dunes. And then there are offshore islands, many of which are renowned for a wealth of gulls and terns whirling and screaming around rocks and promonteries. The coastal habitat boasts a great variety of wildlife, all of it influenced by the overwhelming proximity of the sea and the salty environment which persists several miles inland on exposed coasts.

Although many plants also found in other habitats do manage to tolerate the salt and the ever-blowing wind, this section includes mostly those wild flowers which are *only* found near the sea. Fungi are few – a scattering appears on sand dunes and seaside meadows, though, in the dune slacks (sheltered damp hollows between the dunes) small, delicate mushrooms may flourish in the more stable soil.

Most species of butterfly may occasionally be found in coastal habitats, but migrants – splendid varieties such as the Painted lady and Red admiral butterflies – can be seen crossing the coast regularly each spring. And then there are the magnificent seabirds which haunt the shore with their cries: gulls, terns, waders and wild geese.

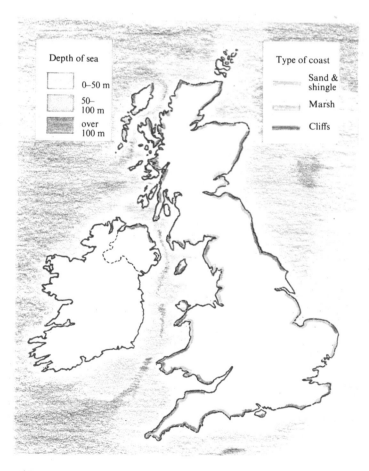

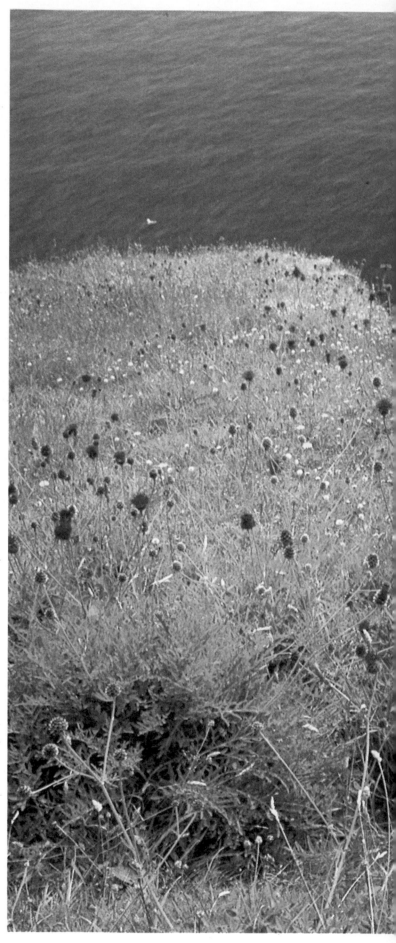

SPRING
Butterflies

♂

Red admiral
Vanessa atalanta

Many migrant butterflies may be seen passing over the coast in spring, including the Red admiral. At rest, the Red admiral is unmistakable, with its red and black wings outspread. The uppers are a dark velvety brown, with a regular scarlet band across the forewing. The underside hindwing is mottled brown and black. A visitor to gardens and parkland, the Red admiral is attracted to a variety of flowers and over-ripe fruit. It is territorial in habit and may be observed patrolling the same area each day. The sexes are similar. The caterpillars feed mostly on Stinging nettle. Wingspan: 56–63 mm. Flight: May–Oct (hibernated specimens appear early spring).

MOTHS

Silver y
Autographa gamma
Flying by day and night from spring to late autumn, migrants are seen at the coast. The caterpillars feed in summer and autumn on almost every kind of low-growing plant and can be a pest on green vegetables. Wingspan: 37–42 mm.

Hummingbird hawk-moth
Macroglossum stellatarum
Usually seen by day in sunshine, on the coast, since it is a migrant. It also visits the flowers of many wild and garden plants. The caterpillars hatch July–Aug and feed on Hedge bedstraw, Lady's bedstraw and Wild madder. Wingspan: 45–51 mm. Flight: Spring to autumn.

Cinnabar
Tyria jacobaeae
A resident, night-flying moth which rests by day in low herbage from which it is easily disturbed. It is mainly coastal in the S half of Scotland and common in meadows and hills elsewhere. The single brood of caterpillars feed July–Aug on Common ragwort and Groundsel and overwinter as pupae. Wingspan: 33–44 mm. Flight: late May–July.

Wild Flowers

Burnet rose
Rosa pimpinellifolia
A bush growing on sand dunes with creamy white flowers, 20–40 mm, which become dark purple hips. The stems have straight prickles and stiff hairs and the leaves are in three–five pairs. 1 m. May–July.

Sea sandwort
Honkenya peploides
A prostrate succulent of sand and shingle, flowers having 6–10 mm, male and female on separate plants. The leaves are fleshy and a pointed oval. 15 cm. May–Aug.

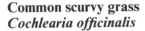

Common scurvy grass
Cochlearia officinalis
On salt marshes and cliffs, with fleshy leaves and small flowers, 8–10 mm, which become pods, 5 mm round. The lower leaves are long-stalked; the upper ones clasp the stem. 35 cm. May–Aug.

Herb Robert
Geranium robertianum
Pale pink flowers, 20 mm, with orange anthers, on much-branched, delicate, reddish stems. This plant can be annual or biennial. By the sea on shingle, or woods and rocks. 30 cm. May–Sept.

Thrift
Armeria maritima
Growing on salt marshes, sea-cliffs and sometimes upland inland areas, and forming dense cushions of narrow leaves, with round heads of pink or white flowers. 30 cm. Apr–Oct.

Spring squill
Scilla verna
A bulb producing a lowish spike of pale violet-blue flowers, 10–15 mm, above narrow, slightly curly, dark green leaves. On grassland by the coast, mostly in the W. 20 cm. Apr–May.

Cornsalad
Valerianella locusta
Tiny lilac flowers, 1–2 mm, in small dense heads, surrounded by narrow bracts, crown this erect, branched annual with unlobed leaves. Grows on sand dunes and dry waste and arable land. 40 cm. Apr–June.

Dove's foot cranesbill
Geranium molle
On sand dunes, disturbed ground, meadows and roadsides, with purplish-pink flowers, 8–12 mm, and rounded, cut leaves. A creeping annual covered with soft white hairs. 30 cm. Apr–Sept.

Hairy tare
Vicia hirsuta
On grassy sea-cliffs, waste and arable land, with narrow leaflets, tendrils and spikes of pale violet flowers, 4–5 mm long. The pod is hairy. Scrambles to 70 cm. May–Aug.

Buckshorn plantain
Plantago coronopus
Common on sandy places, especially near the sea, with normal flowers for a plantain but unusual leaves pinnately cut into narrow segments. 10 cm. May–July.

Birds

Ringed plover
Charadrius hiaticula

A bullet-shaped head, short bill and contrasting plumage pattern set the Ringed plover apart from other common waders. In spring and summer, the adult has a diagnostic black-and-white head and neck pattern and a black-tipped orange bill. (*For winter plumage, see p 145*.) Plain upperparts and the white wing-bar identify flying birds. Often seen running, then pausing to tilt forwards and pick up food. Plumage varies between individuals, and the juvenile shows a scaly pattern and black bill with an absence of black on its head. Flight is swift and erratic with very fast wing-beats. The lilting "turwilk" call is diagnostic. Widely distributed, breeding on coastal sand and shingle and on some inland spots including the artificial beaches round gravel pits. In winter also on muddy shores and estuaries. 19 cm. Resident.

Little tern
Sterna albifrons

Smallest of the terns by far with long angular wings and no tail streamers, also identified by the large head and dumpy body. Spring birds have a line from eye to bill. At close range, the black-tipped yellow bill is diagnostic, as well as the bird's small size, squat profile, head pattern and yellow legs. The hurried-looking flight and prolonged hovering identify Little terns at a distance. Birds hover on rapidly flicking wings, with head held low, before plunging. There is a sharp "kit-kit" and grating "kree-ick" call. Breeds along coasts, nesting on beaches in very exposed situations from April onwards. The most endangered tern, because it has to share its nesting sites with holidaymakers. 24 cm. Summer visitor: Apr–Oct.

Common scoter
Melanitta nigra

Usually seen as a snaking line of black dots over the sea, and in most circumstances a strictly marine species. Birds are usually seen flying low over water or floating, tails held high. They may occur on coastal pools or on reservoirs during passage. The adult male is the only completely black duck. The female has a different bill shape, and brownish plumage similar to that of the female Eider, from which she is distinguished by her different build, bill shape and pale head panel. Juveniles are like the female. The Common scoter feeds by diving for mussels on the seabed. A few birds breed in Scotland and Ireland, arriving by May. 44–54 cm. Seen offshore at all times of the year, but principally a winter visitor.

Eider
Somateria mollissima

A duck of coastal waters whose large size, peculiar head shape and the male's pied plumage with black, white and lime green head distinguish it from all other ducks. The head of the female (similar to the juvenile) shows the odd head and sloping bill shape, with the feathers extending down on to the bill. This distinguishes it from the Mallard (*p 178*). Immature birds have patchy plumage. The Eider is exclusively marine, seen on open shores and islands, and highly gregarious. It is an expert diver and swimmer. The call is a soft "coo-ooh". Breeds round coast of Scotland, N England and N Ireland, settling on eggs by the end of April under a small clump of vegetation. The female shows little fear of man, but her drab plumage gives camouflage against predators. 50–70 cm. Resident.

Avocet
Recurvirostra avosetta

Its pied plumage, long, black upturned bill and grey legs make the Avocet unmistakable at close quarters, yet birds may be "lost" among resting gulls on water. Young Avocets have dark brown where the adult has black, and a slight brownish tinge to the upperparts where the adult has white. Rapid wing-beats in flight give the bird a peculiar flickering appearance and an elongated flight profile. The black patches and tips to the wings are unique. The only black below is on the wing tips.

When feeding (never on land), the birds sweep the water with their bills. Breeds mainly in E Anglia. 43 cm. Summer visitor: Mar–Oct, though there is a small winter population, mainly on SW coast.

Sandwich tern
Sterna sandvicensis

Largest of the common breeding terns, and one of the first of the summer migrants, arriving in March. At all times, the long, black, yellow-tipped bill, shaggy head, black legs and long, angular wings identify it. It is noticeably whiter-looking than the Common and Arctic terns. Migrant birds arrive with all-black crowns, but acquire white foreheads by the time the chicks hatch. Some birds show darker areas of wear on part or all of the wing. Flight is more powerful than the smaller species, with deliberate wing-beats. The wing proportions also create a distinctive flight action. The bird plunges for fish (especially sand eels). It has a distinct, loud "skee-rick" call. Highly gregarious, nesting in colonies on sand or shingle around coasts. 41 cm. Summer visitor: Apr–Oct. Occasionally, passage birds occur inland (especially Aug–Sept).

Manx shearwater
Puffinus puffinus

Large flocks of Manx shearwaters appear as flashing black and white crosses, flying close to the surface of the sea or, in fresh winds, rising and falling above the waves. Their stiff-winged flight and this alternate showing of their dark upperparts and pale underparts distinguish them from all other sea birds around British coasts. They travel long distances to feed on shoals of small fish far out at sea. They also feed in flight, hovering briefly, then making a shallow dive. They swim and dive well and come ashore only during the breeding season to nest in burrows, mainly on offshore islands round the W and Irish coasts. Birds arrive and leave the burrow in the dark to avoid predation by gulls. During breeding, loud, cacophonous screams indicate their presence. 30–38 cm. Summer visitor.

Fulmar
Fulmarus glacialis

One of the most familiar seabirds of rocky coasts and cliffs, often seen flying close to the cliff face to make use of all available updraughts. Fulmars also follow trawlers for offal. The same size as the Common gull (*p 211*) but the Fulmar's grey and white plumage pattern (without black wing tips or white in the tail), as well as its body and bill shape, and the typical banking, rising and falling petrel flight, distinguish it from all gulls. Note the dumpy body with long, narrow, central wings. Breeds from early March on all suitable cliffs around the coast and also nests on buildings. It is an extremely long-lived bird (up to 30 years), so the species can increase even though only a single egg is laid and maturity is not reached until six years old. Top Sixty. 45–50 cm. Resident.

Herring gull
Larus argentatus

The typical seaside gull, seen on promenades, following ships, and wheeling around cliffs with a relatively slow, powerful flight and the typical echoing gull cry. Also frequent inland (especially in winter) on fields, rubbish dumps, playing fields, and even city centres. It is the only grey-backed gull to nest on rooftops. Larger than the Common gull (*p 211*) or Kittiwake (*p 133*), the other two common gulls with grey backs and black wing tips. The adult Herring gull may be confused with the Common species, but it has a heavier build, pink legs and larger bill. Juveniles resemble Lesser black-backs (*p 211*), but the latter have darker wings and a different tail pattern. Immature birds (second year onwards) progressively show adult markings (the grey back in particular). Top Sixty. 56–66 cm. Resident.

SUMMER
Butterflies

Clouded yellow
Colias crocea

A powerful, fast-flying butterfly, The female has wider black margins enclosing yellow spots of uneven size. Her hindwing is dusky with prominent orange spots. Unable to survive the northern winters, the British population depends each year on fresh migrations from the Mediterranean. The first butterflies usually arrive late May and produce a "native" generation Aug–Sept. Migrants seen on the coast; otherwise on open spaces (such as heaths and moorland). The foodplants are Clover, Lucerne and Birdsfoot trefoil. Wingspan: 46–54 mm. Flight: Apr–Sept.

Grayling
Hipparchia semele

A complex species with many subspecies (several in Britain alone). The yellow postdiscal band on the forewing is poorly defined, suffused with brown in the male but more distinct and less dusky in the female. She is larger, with bigger eye-spots. The Grayling is difficult to spot with its wings closed. Its habitats are open: downs, hills, heaths and moors, but it tends to prefer sandy coastal areas. There is one brood of caterpillars a year and they feed on grasses. Wingspan: 42–50 mm. Flight: May–Aug.

Wild Flowers

Sea campion
Silene maritima
A common, cushion-forming plant of shingle and cliffs and occasionally mountains, with white flowers, 25 mm, on fat sepal-tubes and blue grey, stiff leaves. 15 cm. June–Aug.

Yellow-horned poppy
Glaucium flavum
Growing on shingle with large, noticeable yellow flowers, 60–90 mm, producing extremely long seedpods (up to 30 cm). The leaves are greyish-blue, the base ones being hairy. 90 cm. June–Sept.

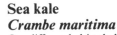

Wild carrot
Daucus carota
Growing on shingle and grassy spots, especially on the coast, with a bristly, solid stem, three times pinnate leaves and an umbel with many rays of white flowers which become concave when fruiting. The fruit is ridged and spiny. 80 cm. June–Aug.

Sea kale
Crambe maritima
On cliffs and shingle beaches, a tall erect perennial with large leaves, the base ones up to 30 cm long with wavy edges. It has whitish-yellow flowers in flat heads. The petals have green claws. 60 cm. June–Aug.

Golden samphire
Inula crithmoides
On cliffs and salt marshes, a hairless, succulent perennial with fleshy leaves, three-toothed at the tip, thickly clothing the stems, and yellow flowerheads, 20–25 mm across. 70 cm. July–Aug.

Rock samphire
Crithmum maritimum
A fleshy perennial growing on cliffs, with greyish leaves and an umbel of pale yellowish-green flowers producing egg-shaped fruits, 6 mm, which ripen purple. 30 cm. June–Aug.

Biting stonecrop
Sedum acre
On dunes, shingle, dry grassland and walls, a creeping evergreen, with bright yellow flowers, 10–12 mm, and fleshy leaves close against its stems. 10 cm. June–July.

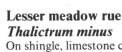

Lady's bedstraw
Galium verum
Forming mats on dry, grassy places, including dunes, with clusters of yellow flowers, 2–4 mm, above whorls of eight to twelve very narrow leaves. Stems go black when dry. Erect shoots to 1 m. July–Aug.

Ragwort
Senecio jacobaea
On sand dunes as well as meadows and roadsides, a very common perennial with clusters of yellow flowerheads, up to 25 mm, on a ridged stem. Pinnately lobed leaves. 1·5 m. June–Oct.

Lesser meadow rue
Thalictrum minus
On shingle, limestone cliffs and bare places, a tufted perennial, with flowers in loose clusters (compare Common meadow rue, *p 161*). Its pinnate leaves are divided three to four times. 85 cm. June–Aug.

Sea bindweed
Calystegia soldanella
Like that gardener's pest, the Field bindweed (*p 201*), but with much larger pink flowers (40–50 mm, similar-sized to that other garden pest, the white Hedge bindweed, *p 199*). Kidney-shaped leaves. On shingle and sand. Creeping to 60 cm. June–Aug.

Sea rocket
Cakile maritima
On sand and shingle near the high tide mark, a succulent with clusters of pinkish-lilac or white flowers, 20 mm. The leaves are lobed or toothed. Often prostrate to 45 cm. June–Aug.

Sea milkwort
Glaux maritima
Common on saltmarshes, a creeping succulent with pink flowers, 5 mm, interspersed with small leaves which are in opposite pairs. 20 cm. June–Aug.

Oyster plant
Mertensia maritima
A straggling, hairless succulent with clusters of flowers, 6 mm, opening pink and turning bluish-purple. The leaves are fleshy and oval. Grows on shingle. 60 cm. June–Aug.

Hound's tongue
Cynoglossum officinale
A softly hairy, greyish biennial with clusters of dark red flowers, 10 mm across, and long, narrow leaves. Grows on sand dunes and also dry grassy places. The fruit is covered with barbed spines all equal in length. 90 cm. June–Aug.

Bloody cranesbill
Geranium sanguineum
Brilliant rosy-purple flowers, 36 mm, crown this bushy herb which grows from creeping rhizomes on sand, as well as in woods and meadows. Leaves are deeply cut or almost whole. They have flat white hairs. 25 cm. July–Aug.

Common storksbill
Erodium cicutarium
Near the sea in the N, but elsewhere in dry places, such as roadsides. A stickily hairy plant with feathery compound leaves, the individual leaflets being cut. The purplish-pink flowers are 10–15 mm, clustered in nines. Fruits have long, twisted beaks. 30 cm. June–Sept.

Scarlet pimpernel
Anagallis arvensis
On shingle as well as on arable and wasteland, a well known, prostrate annual, with scarlet, five-petalled flowers on long stems. The leaves are opposite and spotted below. 20 cm. June–Aug.

Sea purslane
Halimione portulacoides
A perennial shrub growing in salt marshes, with untoothed, mealy leaves and dense clusters of tiny flowers. There are separate male and female flowers. 1 m. July–Sept.

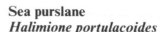

Lesser sea spurrey
Spergularia marina
A succulent prostrate annual of cliffs and salt marches, with pointed leaves in opposite pairs and clusters of pink flowers, 6–8 mm. Creeping to 20 cm. June–Aug.

Blue fleabane
Erigeron acer
A plant of sand dunes, meadows and dry chalky grassland. The bluish-purple flowers have yellow centres (12–18 mm). The leaves are hairy and the stems are reddish. 30 cm. July–Aug.

Eel grass
Zostera marina
Can grow actually *in* the sea from rhizomes, sometimes forming great beds on muddy shores. It has incredibly long, narrow leaves (up to 50 cm × 1 cm) and short spikes of tiny green flowers. To 60 cm. June–Sept.

Sea holly
Eryngium maritimum
A spiny, blue-tinged plant growing on sand dunes and shingle, with bluish flowers, in rounded heads. The base leaves have three lobes, the upper ones five, all with pronounced spines. 45 cm. July–Aug.

Sea plantain
Plantago maritima
On salt marshes and also by mountain streams, with succulent, much narrower leaves than the plantains found in garden lawns. The green flowerheads are tall and pointed, with yellow anthers. 13 cm. June–Aug.

Sea beet
Beta maritima
A succulent, sprawling plant of shingle and seashore, related to the cultivated beetroot with leathery leaves which may be large, and small clusters of flowers each at the base of a tiny leaf. 1 m. July–Sept.

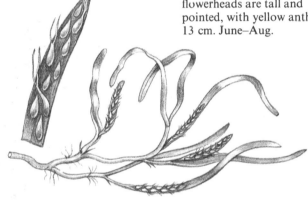

Fungi

Omphalina pyxidata
A small, delicate species usually found in small troops amongst short grass in sandy areas, including dunes, and near roads. The cap, 1–2 cm, can be funnel-shaped, and is orange-brown with dark striations. The gills are pale yellow. The stem, 2–3 cm, is paler than the cap and smooth. Aug–Nov.

Agaricus bernardii
Occasionally found in meadowland washed by sea spray from June onwards. Unlike most *Agaricus* species, it is inedible and has a very unpleasant foetid or fishy smell. The cap, 10–20 cm, is very irregular, white or greyish, cracking into large scales. The gills are pale grey to blackish-brown. The stem, 5–8 cm, is short, scaly and whitish; the ring is thin. The flesh is thick, white, and reddens on exposure. June–Oct.

Tephrocybe palustris
(Collybia leucomyosotis)
Found in bogs, always with *Sphagnum* moss, and smells of meal. The cap, 1–2 cm, is dark brown to greyish-brown. The gills are pale grey. The stem, 4–11 cm, is slender and smooth. May–Oct.

Birds

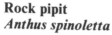

Rock pipit
Anthus spinoletta

The Rock pipit is much larger and greyer (with a dusky outer tail) than the ubiquitous Meadow pipit (*p 59*), but its extremely dark plumage makes it difficult to see against its rocky coastal habitat. (Young birds are more streaked than adults.) The bird has a pale eye ring, dark breast and dark brown legs. It is similar to the Tree pipit (*p 53*) in its deliberate gait, undulating flight and tail-wagging, and its distinct "tsup" call is more akin to the Tree pipit's call than to the shrill sound of the Meadow species. Seen mainly in rocky coastal areas in the breeding season and in coastal or wet areas inland in winter. 16–17 cm. Resident.

Puffin
Fratercula artica

Its small size, uniquely comical face and bill shape, and dumpy black and white body distinguish the Puffin from other auks. The bill changes in shape and colour, being less prominent in winter. Young birds have smaller bills and can be differentiated from young Razorbills (*opposite*) by their grey faces. Puffins are at home in the highest seas, often bouncing over waves to take off. They dive well. Flight is fast for a heavy bird and usually low over the waves. Huge colonies breed in clifftop burrows scattered round the coast, particularly in Scotland. Birds feeding young arrive with beaks full of small fish, all carefully laid across the bill, managing to catch more while still holding the first ones! Winters at sea. Top Sixty. 30 cm. Resident.

Dunlin
in summer plumage, see p. 141.

Grey Plover
in summer plumage, see p. 141.

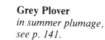

Sanderling
in summer plumage (only seen as
passage migrants, see p. 144).

Turnstone
in summer plumage,
see p. 145.

Black guillemot
Cepphus grylle

Smaller than the Guillemot
(*below*), the white on their
wings makes adult Black
guillemots unmistakable in
summer, and the shape,
combined with whitish
upperparts, identifies winter
birds. The legs are red. In the
summer the Black guillemot has
a white underwing and upper
wing patch. The winter bird is
much whiter. The Black
guillemot is normally seen on
the water, but rests on rocks.
Not a gregarious breeder like
the Guillemot, it nests in holes
under rocks, breeding in small
groups around coasts of
Ireland, W Wales and Scotland
and on offshore islands. 34 cm.
Resident.

Razorbill
Alca torda

Its remarkable short, deep bill,
heavy head and neck, and jet
black and white plumage,
identify the Razorbill. There is
more white on the face in
winter, *see p 145*. On water, its
long wing tips and pointed tail
create a pointed silhouette at
the rear. Nests with Guillemots
on cliffs and stacks (absent
from Humber to Isle of Wight).
Like the Guillemot, it lays a
single pear-shaped egg, but in
nooks and crevices in the rocks.
Top Sixty. 41 cm. Resident.

Guillemot
Uria aalge

Distinguished from the
Razorbill (*right*) by its larger
size and slender, dagger-shaped
bill. A Northern race, which
may winter with local birds,
looks as black as the Razorbill
and is best identified by shape.
Flight is fast and low with rapid
whirring wing-beats. In
summer, N and W sea-cliffs can
be alive with such auks. The
Guillemot lays a single,
pear-shaped egg on the open
rock. Top Sixty. 42 cm.
Resident.

Chough
Pyrrhocorax pyrrhocorax

By August, this small member of the Crow family of western sea-cliffs has finished breeding and is most often seen wheeling overhead in large, foraging flocks, calling noisily and performing aerobatics. Jackdaw-sized with large, broad, ragged-looking wings, its curved red bill and red legs distinguish it from other crows, though in mixed flocks Jackdaws and Choughs appear similar from the ground. In flight, its gliding profile shows upcurved wings (compare the Jackdaw, *p 109*), and it has a ragged look generally in the air. It inhabits cliffs, quarries and ruins and, unlike other crows, is not a carrion-feeder. It uses its pointed bill to dig out insects from the soil or cattle dung drying on coastal farms. Rarely inland. 39–40 cm. Resident.

Shelduck
Tadorna tadorna

Looks like a small goose (which it is not) and is distinguishable from ducks by its larger size and colourful, pied appearance. The female has almost no black on the belly and the male a red knob on the bill. Adult pairs may have a flotilla of chicks from several broods. Juveniles are duller with no chestnut in the body and some white on the face. Shelducks are sociable birds usually seen feeding on mud and sand flats, pools or beaches, by dabbling or up-ending. They have more rapid wing-beats than geese, but their flight is slower, with wings held well forward on take-off. The male call is a series of high whistles. Nests in burrows, sometimes on heaths a few miles inland. 58–67 cm. Resident.

Long-tailed duck
male in summer plumage, see p 148.

Black-headed gull
*in breeding plumage
see p 45.*

Arctic tern
Sterna paradisaea

Common tern
Sterna hirundo

Famous as the bird that migrates the farthest – some actually breed in the Arctic and winter in the Antarctic! Arctic terns are easily confused with the Common tern (*right*), but spring birds tend to be much greyer below than the Common species, and the blood-red bill transparent outer wing and very short legs further identify the Arctic. Flight and behaviour of both species is identical. The Arctic tern nests around the coasts of Britain and inland in Ireland. Also occurs inland on passage: Apr–June and Aug–Oct. 35 cm. Summer visitor.

The most widespread breeding tern in the British Isles, its black-tipped, orange-red bill and longer red legs distinguish it from the Arctic tern (*left*). The size of the transparent area on the wing (only small in the Common tern) is also diagnostic. Compare its dark primary feathers with the Arctic's clear grey ones. The Common tern dives for fish. It has a grating "kee-errrr" call. Breeds in colonies on the coast or inland waters. By August most birds have finished breeding and are back on the coast, preparing to migrate south to W Africa. 35 cm. Summer visitor: Apr–Nov.

Little Gull
*in breeding plumage,
see p 147.*

Great black-backed gull
*in summer, with unflecked head,
see p 149.*

Lesser black-backed gull
*in summer plumage with unflecked
head, see p 211.*

Kittiwake
Rissa tridactyla

The most marine of the gulls, but increasingly common throughout Britain. At close range, the combination of black on the adult and its yellow bill distinguishes it from all other gulls. Slimmer wing shape and distinctive wing markings (triangular, all-black wing tips and a thin white edge) on birds of all ages also distinguish Kittiwakes from the larger Common gull (*p 211*). The legs are black. Birds pick food from the surface in flight, or settle on the water and then dive. They may also plunge from a height like a tern. Flight is fairly fast, with shallow wing-beats. There is a diagnostic "kitiwaka" call. Nests in dense colonies on cliffs and also in groups on buildings. Only storm-driven birds are ever seen inland. Few are seen in winter which is spent far out at sea. Top Sixty. 41 cm. Resident.

Arctic skua
Stercorarius parasiticus

A marine pirate like the Great skua (*p 63*), forcing other birds such as terns or small gulls to disgorge their prey, the Arctic skua is the most widespread of the skuas along the coast. It is a medium-sized bird with a robust, sharply etched profile, identified by its shape, size and build, together with projecting tail feathers when adult. Its colour varies from pale to almost all-dark (more commonly seen in Britain). The pale form may have a brown breast band or none. Wing patches vary in size. The fast, flapping flight is interspersed with glides, giving the bird a falcon-like appearance. Breeds from SW coast of Scotland up to Shetland. 46 cm. Summer visitor, and also passage migrant in spring and autumn.

Shag
Phalacrocorax aristotelis

A large, black-looking bird with a distinctive profile, seen around rocky coasts. It normally frequents open water, rather than the more sheltered waters and estuaries of the Cormorant (*below*), and breeds on rocks and in caves. Occasionally seen inland after gales. It is markedly smaller, slimmer-necked and more slender-billed than the Cormorant, with an oily, sleek appearance. Adult breeding birds have bottle-green plumage with an often raised crest and a yellow gape. In winter, birds are browner and lack the crest. Immature birds have brownish, patchy underparts and differ from young Cormorants which usually have a pure white belly. Shags dive expertly with a noticeable jump and may surface some distance away. Both birds extend their wings to dry, but the Shag stretches its out further. Both fly low over water and land awkwardly, but the Shag has more rapid wing-beats and is more often seen alone. 65–80 cm. Resident.

Cormorant
Phalacrocorax carbo

Large, ungainly birds, usually seen perched erect and unmoving on a post or flying low and fast over the water. Adults are distinguishable from the very similar Shag (*above*) by their larger size and white on face and chin. Breeding birds are bronze above and steel blue below, with white patches on the thighs. Young birds show more variable plumage and are more difficult to identify, but their whitish underparts and yellow-bill distinguish them from young Shags (*see also p 145*). Behaviour and flight are very similar and both nest in colonies. On coasts, but also commonly winters on inland rivers and large areas of water including urban reservoirs. Breeds on coastal rocks and occasionally in trees inland. 80–100 cm. Resident.

Peregrine
Falco peregrinus

August is a good time to see Peregrines hanging on the wind high above sea-cliffs. The largest resident falcon, a magnificently powerful and fast flier and very heavily built (the female being much larger). Juveniles have dark brown upperparts, a streaked body and buff underparts. Adults look bluish below, with a pinkish or buff chest and a black moustache. Males may be pinker and plainer below than females. Flight is a series of fast, "winnowing" wing-beats followed by a glide. The Peregrine soars but does not hover. It takes birds in the air, either diving in a near-vertical "stoop" and bowling its prey out of the sky, or following in a direct chase. It nests in inaccessible places, favouring sea-cliffs, although also inland. 36–48 cm. Resident.

Gannet
Sula bassana

The largest British sea bird, the adult being unmistakable with dazzling black and white plumage, pale, dagger-shaped bill and creamy yellow head. Young birds are dark brown, acquiring adult plumage gradually over four years and looking very patchy meanwhile. Almost always in the air, resting on water only briefly after feeding. The wings flex noticeably at the tip, several deep flaps being followed by a glide on angled wings. Diving from up to 30 m with half-folded wings, Gannets plunge deep under water. Found inland only after storms, usually on the ground. Nearly three-quarters of the world's Gannets breed on cliffs (mainly on offshore islands) round the British Isles. 87–100 cm. Resident.

135

AUTUMN
Butterflies

Meadow brown
Maniola jurtina
Probably one of the most common and widespread of the brown butterflies, this species may be found throughout the British Isles, especially in coastal areas. The extent of orange on the wings is variable and several subspecies have been described. The male's uppers are predominantly grey-brown, with very little orange. The dark sex brand is visible under the cell area of the forewing. The female's upper forewing has extensive orange-yellow markings. The light and dark areas on her underside hindwing are more clearly defined. The Meadow brown can be found in all kinds of

grassy places on chalk and limestone – meadows, parkland, downs, hills, heaths, road verges – from sea-level up to 1,800 m and is even known to occur in the centre of cities. It will fly in cloudy weather, but usually remains in a fairly restricted area. The food plants are grasses, especially Meadow grass. Wingspan: 40–58 mm. Flight: June–Sept.

Wild Flowers

Haresfoot clover
Trifolium arvense
A neat little clover thriving in dry summers near the sea as well as on dry sandy meadows. It gets its name from the soft flowerheads, whitish-cream and like furry bottle brushes. The trefoil leaves are slightly elongated. 10 cm. June–Sept.

Purging flax
Linum catharticum
Grows on dunes, as well as grassland and heath, with delicate, slender stems, clusters of white flowers (8–10 mm) and opposite, oval leaves. The seeds are purgative. 15 cm. June–Sept.

Knotgrass
Polygonum aviculare
Very common on seashores and waste ground, with clusters of one to six white or pale pink flowers up the stem. Where the leaves join the stem, there is a silvery sheath. Leaves on the main stem are longer than on the branches. To 1 m. July–Oct.

Autumn lady's tresses
Spiranthes spiralis
On grassy coastal dunes, downs and chalky meadows, an orchid with a rosette of leaves that withers before the flowers appear. The flowers are tiny and twist in a spiral up the spike. 15 cm. Aug–Sept.

English stonecrop
Sedum anglicum
A creeping, succulent perennial which forms patches on shingle and cliff. The reddish, fleshy leaves are globular and alternate up the stem. The white flowers, 10–12 mm, are carried on short stalks. 4 cm. June–Sept.

Large-flowered evening primrose
Oenothera erythrosepala
On sand dunes, roadsides and wasteland, with spectacularly large yellow flowers, 80–100 mm, above red striped sepals, and big, spear-shaped, wrinkled leaves. A robust and hairy plant. 1 m. June–Sept.

Yellow wort
Blackstonia perfoliata
A grey-green annual with clusters of yellow flowers, 10–15 mm, on a short stalk. There is a rosette of leaves at the base. The stem leaves are triangular and grow in opposite pairs. On dunes and chalky grassland. 30 cm. June–Oct.

Black mustard
Brassica nigra
A member of the Cabbage family, greyish, with stalked leaves and pods flat against the stem. On cliffs and disturbed ground. 1 m. June–Sept.

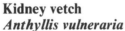

Kidney vetch
Anthyllis vulneraria
Pea-like flowers, 12–15 mm, vary in colour – yellow, orange, red, purple and even mixed. The plant has long silky hairs and can be prostrate or upright. Leaves are narrow and pinnate. Often near the sea and on chalky grassland. 50 cm. June–Sept.

Sea wormwood
Artemisia maritima
Growing on salt marshes, a very aromatic perennial with white woolly hairs all over its pinnate leaves and stem. The yellow flowerheads, 1–2 mm, droop. 50 cm. Aug–Sept.

Fennel
Foeniculum vulgare
A greyish, strong-smelling herb, with leaves cut into very fine, threadlike segments and crowned with yellow flowers. On disturbed ground, usually near the sea. 1 m. July–Oct.

Portland spurge
Euphorbia portlandica
A small version of Sea spurge (*right*), but with unbranched stems. The fleshy leaves are less leathery, with a prominent midrib underneath. The greenish flowers have long-horned glands. Often reddens with age. On sand dunes. 25 cm. May–Sept.

Sea spurge
Euphorbia paralias
A stiff, hairless, greyish perennial with thick, leathery leaves, close up the stem, each having a less prominent midrib than the Portland spurge (*left*). The greenish flowers are in clusters, and have short-horned glands. To 40 cm. Aug–Nov.

Autumn gentian
Gentianella amarella
On sand dunes in N and W, and on chalky grassland (where it is common), with dull purple, tubular flowers, 14–22 mm, growing in clusters. Its many, narrow leaves grow in pairs and are often also tinted with purple. 20 cm. July–Oct.

Common centaury
Centaurium erythraea
Another of the Gentian family, with clusters of pink flowers above a base rosette of rounded oval leaves (up to 50 mm long and 20 mm diameter). Only on sand dunes in Scotland, but common on grassland elsewhere. 30 cm. June–Oct.

Sea lavender
Limonium vulgare
Many flowers on short stalks grow within the much-branched head of this salt marsh perennial. The leaves, 12 cm, are succulent with prominent pinnate veins. To 30 cm. July–Oct.

Viper's bugloss
Echium vulgare
Grows on dunes and sandy grassland, including roadsides, a roughly hairy perennial having bright blue, tubular flowers with four protruding stamens. The leaves are long and narrow and can be wavy-edged. 65 cm. June–Sept.

Field gentian
Gentianella campestris
On dunes and pastures on chalk, an erect plant commoner in the N but less so in the S. It has seven to ten, bluish-lilac, four-lobed flowers visited by bees and butterflies. 20 cm. July–Oct.

Sea aster
Aster tripolium
A succulent perennial common on salt marshes and rocky cliffs, with flowerheads that are yellow in the centre and usually purple outside (though these ray florets may be missing). The leaves are narrow, the lower ones stalked. 1 m. July–Oct.

Curled dock
Rumex crispus
Very common on shingle and disturbed ground, with long, narrow leaves curled and crisp at the edges and dense clusters of tiny flowers on leafless spikes. Compare the other Docks (*see Index*). The fruit has three warts. 1 m. July–Sept.

Prickly saltwort
Salsola kali
A prostrate annual of sand dunes and shingle (also disturbed ground). Its leaves have spiny tips and the inconspicuous flowers are at the base where leaves join the stem. To 60 cm. July–Sept.

Glasswort
Salicornia europaea
A very succulent annual. The leaves are small scales and the tiny flowers are almost hidden at the stem-joints. The plant's colour changes finally to yellow or red-brown. Edible. Salt marshes and beaches. 20 cm. Aug–Sept.

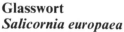

Annual seablite
Sueda maritima
A succulent plant of salt marshes, and sometimes sandy shores, with inconspicuous flowers. Plant colour varies from greyish-green to deep red. To 50 cm. Aug–Oct.

Fungi

Psathyrella ammophila
The stem is always buried deeply in sand, attached to roots of marram grass. The cap, 1–3 cm, is convex with an incurved margin at first, date brown then paler. The gills are pale grey brown to sepia and spaced. The stem, 4–5 cm, is whitish above and deeply rooting. Aug–Oct.

Conocybe dunensis
Grows amongst marram grass on sand dunes. The cap, 1–3 cm, is conical or convex, date brown drying to pale buff. The misty-brown gills are crowded. The stem, 4–10 cm, is pale ochre, partially buried in sand. Oct–Nov.

Inocybe dulcamara
Quite common in troops in sandy places. In more northerly areas this poisonous species is also found in coniferous woods. The cap, 2–5 cm, is ochre brown, felty-scaly, with a shaggy margin when young. The gills are olive-yellow finally cinnamon brown, narrow and crowded. The stem, 4–6 cm, is yellow-brown. Aug–Nov.

Rhodocybe popinalis
This species has a strong mealy smell, but the bitter taste renders it inedible. Occurs on dunes or in fields. The cap, 2–5 cm, is mouse grey, with an incurved margin. The gills are greyish or yellowish-pink and narrow. The stem, 1–8 cm, is grey. Aug–Oct.

Birds

Wryneck
Jynx torquilla

Britain's only brown woodpecker, the Wryneck's complex patterned plumage is unique. It has a curious habit of twisting its head slowly, so the black back stripe "snakes". It has orange wing spots and a barred grey tail. The sky-pointing display is used in courtship or when it is threatened. It feeds on insects licked up with its long tongue and nests in tree holes. The undulating flight is woodpecker-like. The "quie-quie" call is heard in spring. In early autumn migrants blown off course from Scandinavia can be found on British coasts, often among large numbers of Pied flycatchers and Redstarts. 16–17 cm. Summer visitor: Apr–Sept, especially SE England and parts of Scotland.

Grey phalarope
Phalaropus fulicarius

A wader that is usually seen swimming like a miniature gull. Autumn gales can blow it off course to land, sometimes in large flocks in SW Ireland or the Scilly Isles, but it basically spends the winter on the open sea. It is therefore rarely seen in its red breeding plumage. It has a chunky build, bold wing-bar and white area on the tail. There is often yellow at the base of the bill with pale, greyish or black legs. 20–21 cm. Passage migrant and winter visitor.

There is also a Red-necked phalarope (*P. lobatus*), not shown: a summer visitor (breeding in Scottish islands) and also a passage migrant.

Velvet scoter
Melanitta nigra

A thicker neck, heavier head, white round eye, yellow (not orange) bill and red (not black) legs of the adult male, and particularly the white wing patches on both sexes distinguish the Velvet scoter from the smaller Common species (*p 123*). The male has two prominent pale patches on his face. White is only visible on swimming birds when the wings are flapped. An expert diver, like the Common scoter, the Velvet scoter favours rougher water. It is much less numerous and usually seen in small parties of 15–20. It usually flies low over the sea but at a great height when migrating. 51–88 cm. Mainly winter visitor: Sept–May.

Storm petrel
(Mother Carey's chicken)
Hydrobates pelagicus

A tiny seabird whose white rump and white marks under the wing (though not always visible) are diagnostic. It has long wings and a square tail. Well known for following ships with its weak, fluttering flight at sea level (stronger on passage). It patters across the surface. Strictly a sea-going bird, mainly seen in onshore gales. Breeds W coast and around the coast of Ireland. When in nesting burrows it can be detected by a churring call and pungent smell. 14–18 cm.

Dunlin
Calidrus alpina

The commonest wader – a small dumpy bird seen in autumn and winter on all except the very rockiest shores, as well as on estuaries and mud-flats, and by inland pools. It has a white wing-bar, white patches on either side of the tail and a dark strip on tail and back. It may be confused with a number of wader species, but the fairly long, slightly down-curved bill and high-pitched rasping "sheeeeep" call are diagnostic. (*For summer plumage, see p 130*.) In the autumn, the adult moults into grey plumage above with a faintly streaked breast and white underparts, and can be confused with the much whiter Sanderling (*p 144*). Birds in summer and winter plumages occur together from Aug onwards. Birds normally walk. Flight is swift and twisting. Swirling flocks show as flickering dark and white masses. Breeds on open moorland. 17–19 cm. Resident. Also winter visitor and migrant.

Grey plover
Pluvialis squatarola

A large, usually wary plover with a bullet head and noticeably stout bill, longish black legs and spangled grey plumage. Its black armpits differentiate it from the Golden plover (*p 19*). The upperparts are greyish when breeding, not golden brown. Adults in full summer plumage are entirely black and white below (*see p 130*). Fairly fast flight with slower wing-beats than the Golden species. The yellow-tinged juvenile (*small picture below*) shows the typical hunched posture. The mournful "clee-er-whee" call is diagnostic. 28 cm. Winter visitor and passage migrant to coastal flats and estuaries. A few birds are seen in summer.

Brent goose
Branta bernicia

A small, stockily built goose with a short tail, neck and bill and comparatively long wings. It is the only goose with an all-black head. White upper tail coverts cover so much of the tail that only a thin black line shows at the tip. This separates the Brent species from all other geese. Pale or white wing-bars and no white nape patch distinguish juveniles. Most

Brent geese seen are the dark-bellied race, but a few pale-bellied geese can be seen in Ireland. They graze on salt flats but may up-end in shallows. Normally seen in flight or sitting out at sea but can be very tame, resting in harbours, where unmolested. They are very rare inland. Flight is fast with wing-beats more rapid than their larger relatives. Often gather in irregular flocks wheeling low over coastal flats. 56–61 cm. Winter visitor: Sept–May.

Pink-footed goose
Anser brachyrhynchus

Delicate birds, particularly in the shape of the head, and very active in flight and on the ground. They are the smallest of the common grey geese, distinguished by their pink bills and legs and dark heads and necks. They are very vocal with extremely high-pitched calls

and may occur in very large flocks. Roosting is on water or sandbanks. They feed largely on stubble, but may include cereals, potatoes and grass in their diet. 60–75 cm. Common winter visitor (late Sept–Apr/May) to parts of Scotland, N and E England and Severn estuary.

Barnacle goose
Branta leucopsis

Its white face, black neck and breast, grey and black body with mainly grey wings distinguish the Barnacle goose from all other geese, and it is further separated from the Canada species (*p 170*) by its grey-barred back and more white on its face. Flying birds show a contrast of black and white. The juvenile is slightly browner and duller. Barnacle geese graze on fields and marshes near the coast. Rising

flocks make a great clamour of guttural calls like yapping dogs and fly in close but untidy formations. The birds are vocal when swimming. Numerous in Hebrides and W and N coast of Ireland. Common in parts of Scotland. 58–69 cm. Winter visitor: Oct–Apr.

White-fronted goose
Anser albifrons

A medium-sized, angular-winged, square-headed bird. The white on its face and heavily barred underparts make it the easiest grey goose to identify. There are two races of White-fronted geese: the Greenland race has an orange-yellow bill, the European race a pink one. Both have orange legs. The Greenland race occurs in W Scotland and Ireland; the European mainly in the Severn area (at the Wildfowl Trust, Slimbridge). The white blaze and black barring on the belly is on adults only and juveniles have to be distinguished from the Pink-footed species (*p 142*) by their orange legs. It has a shrill call. 65–78 cm. Winter visitor: Oct–Apr/May.

Bean goose
Anser fabalis

Much scarcer than other geese, and slightly smaller than the Greglag (*below*), with a distinctive erect posture, long wings, neck and bill. The head and neck are noticeably dark. Its orange legs also separate it from the Greylag. Young of the Bean goose have pale yellow legs. Flight is less laboured than the Greylag's, and the neck is obtrusive. Feeds with other geese, but is a shy species. Its call is louder and deeper than the Greylag's. 66–84 cm. Winter visitor in small numbers in E England. A few birds occur elsewhere with other geese.

Greylag goose
Anser anser

The largest and heaviest goose, with a large head and thick neck very noticeable in flight. The Greylag has the palest forewing of all geese and pink legs which separate it from all except the Pink-footed species (*p 142*). Its wing-beats are slower and take-off less agile than in other species. It usually grazes for food, but may be seen up-ending in the shallows. It has a deep "arhung-ung-ung" call rather like the farmyard goose which is descended from it. 75–90 cm. Resident, also winter visitor (Oct–Apr) to coastal marshes and farmland.

WINTER
Birds

Lapland bunting
Calcarius lapponicus

Its bill, plumage, curious face pattern with black "triangle", and long wings and tail are the keys to distinguishing the Lapland bunting. The female and juvenile are very like the Reed bunting, except for the curious face pattern and the juvenile's yellow bill, more strongly patterned plumage and double wing-bars. A "creeping" feeder, often occurring on or near the coast with Shore larks (*below*) or Snow buntings (*p 66*). It has a typical swift, often high, "bunting" flight, a very clear "ticky-tik-tiu" call and also a rattling ticking sound. 15 cm. Winter visitor, from Nov onwards, mainly to E coast saltings.

♀

Shore (Horned) lark
Eremophila alpestris

Easily identified by the adult's black and yellow face pattern, duller in winter, and the black, horn-like feathering on the male's crown. The female has less black on her face. The tail is pale at the centre, but its outer panels look very dark. Compare its narrow white border with the Skylark (*p 44*). The back may be marked or fairly plain and the upperparts show a distinct pink flush at times. Feeds on shingle and marshy areas of coastal wasteland, blending well with the ground and usually seen only when flushed. The flight is undulating and low over the ground. There is a soft, rippling flight call. Has nested in Scotland, but is mainly seen on E coast, usually in small parties or flocks, often with Snow or Lapland buntings (*p 66 and above*). 16·5 cm. Winter visitor: Oct–Apr.

♂

Sanderling
Calidris alba

Characteristic of sandy winter seashores and seldom seem inland, the Sanderling is slightly larger than the Dunlin (*p 141*) and, in winter, ghostly pale. It is identified by its white wing-bar (more striking than on any small wader), short, straight black bill and short black legs. The dark shoulder spot helps distinguish it from the Dunlin. Habitually runs at great speed on twinkling black legs, as it searches for food left by the retreating waves. It has a typical fast wader flight and glides before landing. The "twik-twik" call is diagnostic. 20 cm. Winter visitor and passage migrant (*see p 131 for summer plumage*).

Purple sandpiper
Calidris maritima

The only sooty-plumaged small wader, slightly larger than the Dunlin (*p 141*), best identified by its yellow legs. It is a tame bird, restricted to rocky coasts and often found with the Turnstone (*below*). In winter, birds may also occur elsewhere on jetties or slipways. Flight is usually swift, Dunlin-like, and low over short distances, showing the sooty upperparts with white wing-bars and lozenges. The white underwing shows when the bird holds its wings up on landing. On the ground birds may be almost invisible against dark rocks or seaweed. Usually silent. 21 cm. Mainly winter visitor: Sept–Apr. Passage birds occur inland.

Cormorant
(in its second winter)   having less white on the head at this time than any other Cormorant (see p 134).

Ringed plover
in winter, see p 122.

Razorbill
in winter, see p 131.

Turnstone
Arenaria interpres

A tame, robust bird, typically seen flicking over stones and seaweed on the shore, an action from which it gets its name. The plumage varies from season to season and between individuals, but the bright pied pattern with white on back, wings and tail is unlike any other wader. It has a loud, mechanical "tuck-a-tuck" call and a rapid series of notes if flushed. It often occurs with the Purple sandpiper (*above*) on rocky coasts, but also on shingle and weed-covered flats. 23 cm. Winter visitor (though some stay all summer – *see p 131 for summer plumage*) and passage migrant: Apr–June, Aug–Oct.

145

Knot
Calidris canutus

A common, medium-sized shore-feeding wader, much larger than the Dunlin (*p 141*) with which it is often seen feeding. It is fat-bodied with long, thin wings, a fairly short, black bill, pale rump and white wing-bar which stands out against the dark wings, and crisp grey plumage. It lacks the white 'lozenge' patches seen on many other flying waders. All birds have greenish legs. Knots often occur feeding in very large flocks, forming a solid carpet of grey when the rising tide forces them to congregate thickly. They often walk (never run) along the shore, pausing to probe for prey. Flight is fast with rapid wing-beats. The call is a distinct low "knot-like" note and a double "kwik-ik" sound may also be heard. Breeds in Arctic tundra. However, some birds are seen in Britain in summer plumage (deep chestnut on head and body). 25 cm. Winter visitor to mud and sand flats, with occasional birds inland. Passage migrant.

Rock dove
Columba livia

The ancestor of all domestic pigeons and doves (from racers to ornamental), as well as of the Feral town pigeon (*p 205*). Pure flocks are likely to be all blue with a few natural chequers, and any other plumage variation indicates inter-breeding with others such as stray racing pigeons. The male Rock dove has a glossier green neck than the female. The bird is very broad-shouldered in profile and is distinguished from the Stock dove (*p 42*) by its pure white rump, greyish wing-tips and broad, black wing-bars. Seems to occur mainly on N and W coasts of Scotland and Atlantic coasts of Ireland, in flocks in winter. 33 cm. Resident.

146

Oystercatcher
Haematopus ostralegus

Probably the noisiest of the waders, these large, active birds with piping calls can be seen feeding in winter on muddy or sandy shores, often in huge numbers. Their pied plumage, orange bill and pinkish legs are unmistakable. They stand waiting for the tide to turn, all facing the same direction. Despite their name, they rarely eat oysters, but mostly molluscs like cockles and limpets. They either hammer them open or stab the muscle which holds the shell shut – which accounts for their bill formation. The bird flies strongly with rather shallow wing-beats, displaying its bold wing-bar and black tail with a white V up the back. It makes a ringing "kleep-kleep" alarm call and a persistent "pic-a-pic". Breeds inland on farmland and gravel pits. 43 cm. Resident.

Little gull
Larus minutus

The smallest of the gulls, easy to distinguish from them by size alone. However, its leisurely, dipping, tern-like flight can make it difficult to pick out in a flock of terns as it flutters over the water, pouncing on insects or picking food from the surface. A black head (compare with the Black-headed gull, (*p 45*) and red legs identify breeding birds (*p 133*). The juvenile has a white underwing like the Kittiwake, but its brown back identifies it. The adult is unmarked – pale grey above and smoky grey below. Seen round all coasts, but also occurs inland, spring, autumn and winter. 28 cm. Winter visitor and passage migrant.

Scaup
Aythya marila

Larger than the closely related Tufted duck (*p 177*) with a longer, wider body. The male's head shape, lack of crest, pearl-grey back and glossy green plumage further identify it. The female has a heavier build than the Tufted duck, but similar plumage below. Her large white face patch identifies her. The Scaup's tail trails low in the water. A marine species, also found on pools close to the coast, but uncommon far inland. Occurs in numbers near mussel-beds and sewage outfalls. Breeds very rarely (in Scotland). Males are less common in the S, where females and juveniles are usually seen. 42–51 cm. Winter visitor: mid-Sept–Apr/May.

Pintail
Anas acuta

More shy and wary than other ducks, and quick to take flight. The long-tailed, boldly patterned male is unmistakable with an elegant, attenuated profile in flight. His tail is not fully grown until mid Nov. His plumage is grey above and white below, relieved by patches of black, white and cream. The female differs from the female

Wigeon (*p 149*) in her bill colour, more pointed tail and plumage pattern. She is paler and greyer, with less warm colours than the female Mallard (*p 178*) or Gadwall (*p 181*). The long neck is unique. Flight is usually high and very fast with rapid wing-beats making a hissing sound. Breeds only rarely in scattered localities. Occurs mainly in winter (Oct–Apr), especially in flood waters and sheltered estuaries. 51–66 cm. Resident.

Long-tailed duck
Clangula hyemalis

The beautiful Long-tailed male is unmistakable in any plumage (*for summer, see p 132*). The female is a fairly small bird, distinguished by the combination of head and very short bill with a smudgy dark and pale pattern. Her head patches change very subtly from autumn to winter. Long-tailed ducks are essentially

marine birds, though also occurring singly on coastal pools or inland reservoirs. They are expert divers, quite at home in rough seas, and very energetic birds in flight with deep wing-beats, unlike any other duck. Flight parties may be seen carrying out a peculiar rolling action. A very localised bird with a variety of yodelling, hound-like calls. 40–47 cm. Common winter visitor in N Scotland and regular visitor to SE England, especially Oct–Mar.

Red-breasted merganser
Mergus serrator

Its long red bill, long body and crest distinguish the Merganser from other ducks, the bushy crest in particular distinguishing both sexes from the Goosander (*p 157*). It is distinctly smaller and more delicately proportioned than the Goosander. There is a clear distinction in flight: the male Merganser shows much less

white above than the Goosander and the female is dark brown above (compare the female Goosander's clear grey). Like the Goosander though, Merganser females and immatures are popularly called "Redheads". The birds are usually silent. They are much more marine in habit than the Goosander, but a ground nester by rivers and lakes in the W. 52–58 cm. Resident. Also winter visitor.

Wigeon
Anas penelope

Delicately featured ducks with sharp silhouettes and fairly short necks. Both sexes have high, peaked foreheads and black and grey bills, but the female is reddish brown on head and breast with ginger flanks, white wing-bar and brown back. Peaked forehead and greenish speculum separate from the female Mallard (*p 178*). The male's pale forehead differentiates him from the Pochard drake (*p 178*). A surface-feeding duck that dives only if injured and does not normally up-end. It spends more time feeding on land than any other duck and may be seen grazing on grass in large numbers. It leaps straight from the water into fast, direct flight. The male has a far-carrying "whee-oooo" call. The species is extremely gregarious. Breeds in scattered localities. Often seen on coast with Brent geese. 45–57 cm. Resident.

Great black-backed gull
Larus marinus

The largest of all gulls, dwarfing others on the ground: its broad wings, jutting head and huge bill create a very aggressive appearance. Most birds have very dark backs, but some may be paler than the darkest Lesser Black-backed (*p 211*). The head is flecked in winter only – *for summer, see p 133*. It is a fierce predator, taking seabirds and young during the breeding season and an imposing scavenger at other times. Size and appearance should identify it, but birds at a distance may be difficult to tell from the Lesser black-backed species. Although adults have dark backs and wings, juveniles are whiter on the head and paler above, with less brown on the tail than Lesser black-backed and Herring gulls (*p 125*). Flight looks slow and ponderous, but these gulls are fast enough to hunt down crippled birds. The deepest call of the gulls. Winter storms swell the number in sheltered bays with birds from further out at sea. Breeds Scotland, Ireland and W and S cliffs of England and occurs commonly inland on rubbish tips and farmland. 64–79 cm. Resident.

Marsh and Stream

This habitat, like the coastal one, has water as a common denominator, but now the water is fresh, not salt, so a different range of wildlife makes its home there. Freshwater habitats are those with open water in them – rushing mountain streams, placid rivers, tiny ponds and large lakes, flooded gravel pits and reservoirs, dykes and ditches. Another "watery" habitat is that of the wetlands – river banks and margins, bogs, marshes, fens, reed swamps and the like – which have less open water and much more soil, but still an overall impression of dampness.

Wildlife, especially flowers and birds, abounds in such prime conditions, with a ready supply of water, food and cover. Marginal plants such as the Great reed mace and Marsh marigold flourish in and around both fresh water and wetland, and there are also completely aquatic ones such as Pondweed and the exquisite Water lilies. Many birds revel in such surroundings. Ducks, coots, moorhens and herons are among the more noticeable ones, yet there are the shyer Reed and Marsh warblers, and above all the wonderful and unforgettable iridescent streak of the Kingfisher – the more highly prized because it is so rarely seen.

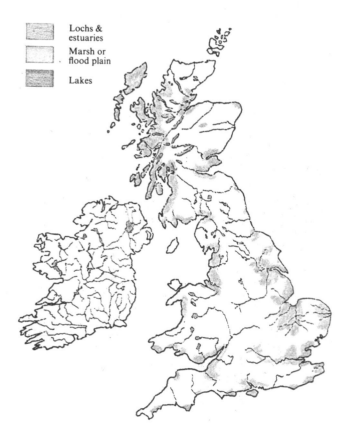

Lochs & estuaries

Marsh or flood plain

Lakes

SPRING
Butterflies

Swallowtail
Papilio machaon
The Swallowtail, easily recognized by its striking appearance, is a fast and agile flier. It is the only resident British swallowtail, and its range is restricted to the lowlying fens of East Anglia.

(The more widely distributed continental subspecies occasionally occurs as a migrant in southern England.) Sex differences are small: the female tends to be larger with less angular wings. The bright colours of the caterpillar warn off predators. Foodplants are Milk parsley, Wild carrot and Fennel. Wingspan is 64–100 mm. Flight: Apr–Aug. Protected by law.

Wild Flowers

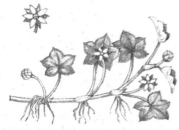

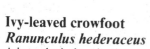

Water crowfoot
Ranunculus aquatilis
An aquatic, many-branched plant, with toothed, floating leaves, threadlike underwater leaves and white, Buttercup-like flowers, 10–20 mm, with long stamens. In still or slow water. May–Aug.

Ivy-leaved crowfoot
Ranunculus hederaceus
A branched plant both in shallow water and on river banks. It has creeping stems, opposite, stalked, ivy-shaped leaves, and small white flowers, 6 mm, with six to ten stamens. There are no submerged leaves. Creeping to 40 cm. Apr–Sept.

Large bittercress
Cardamine amara
Broader leaflets on the stem leaves than the Cuckoo flower (*p 15*) and having white flowers with violet anthers. A creeping plant with erect shoots. The lower leaves are stalked and pinnate. Marshes and river banks. 60 cm. Apr–June.

Butterbur
Petasites hybridus
Common by streams, and in damp meadows and shady woodlands, with dense spikes of pink flowerheads appearing before the huge (90 cm), heart-shaped leaves. 40 cm. Mar–May.

Wavy bittercress
Cardamine flexuosa
Larger than Hairy bittercress (*p 207*) with zigzag stems, pinnate leaves with up to 15 leaflets and flowers with six stamens. The pods hardly extend above the flowers. On banks and disturbed or shady places. 50 cm. Apr–Sept.

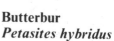

Marsh marigold
Caltha palustris
Common in marshes and damp woodlands, having bright yellow flowers, 10–50 mm, rising from round or kidney-shaped leaves with fine teeth. 20 cm. Mar–July.

Common wintercress
Barbarea vulgaris
On river banks, damp, disturbed ground and roadsides, with bright yellow flowers, 7–9 mm, pinnate leaves stalked in a base rosette and almost whole stem leaves. The pods are four-angled and upright. 90 cm. May–Aug.

Sweet gale (Bog myrtle)
Myrica gale
A strongly aromatic shrub. The catkins (male and female on separate plants) appear before the narrow, greyish leaves which are downy below and 20–50 mm long. Common in marshes and bogs. 60–150 cm. Apr–May.

Water avens
Geum rivale
Common in the N on river banks and damp woodlands, with nodding (15 mm) flowers which have purple sepals. Lower leaves are pinnate, the upper ones trefoil with the top leaflet large. 45 cm. May–Sept.

Ragged robin
Lychnis flos-cuculi
The deep pink flowers have lobed petals to give the typical "ragged" appearance. The plant is tall and branched, growing in marshes and other damp spots. The leaves are narrow. 60 cm. May–June.

Common comfrey
Symphytum officinale
Usually found near fresh water, with many branches of deep pink or cream flowers, 15–18 mm, in down-curled, nodding clusters. The leaves are large. 1·2 m. May–June.

Early marsh orchid
Dactylorhiza incarnata
Found in fens and damp meadows, with spikes of flowers ranging from salmon pink to dark red or creamy yellow. The edges of the lower lip always bend back. The leaves are narrow and long (to 30 cm). 50 cm. May–July.

Bogbean
Menyanthes trifoliata
An aquatic plant, also found in marshes, with pink flowers, 15–20 mm, on short stalks above the water, and large, trefoil leaves. The petal tube has fringed edges. 20 cm. May–July.

Birdseye primrose
Primula farinosa
Crinkly-edged leaves with mealy white undersides grow in a rosette below white stems and clusters of lilac pink flowers (8–10 mm). In marshes and damp places on limestone in N England. 10 cm. May–June.

Marsh valerian
Valeriana dioica
Growing in marshes and fens, with the base leaves oval and the upper ones pinnate. The pink male and female flowers are on different plants (males 4–5 mm, females 2–3 mm). 20 cm. May–June.

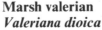

Marsh violet
Viola palustris

Common in bogs, marshes, fens, and wet woods. The small pale lilac flowers, 10 mm, have dark veins, a short spur and blunt sepals. The plant has no upright stems, but the leaf blade is 4 cm. Apr–July.

Water violet
Hottonia palustris

A floating, delicate perennial with pale lilac flowers (20–25 mm) in whorls on elongated stalks, as well as feathery leaves. 30 cm. May–June.

Water starwort
Callitriche stagnalis

Common in slow or still water and on mud, having narrow, submerged leaves and floating leaves in a rosette. The flowers are tiny and at the base of the rosette leaves. Floating to 60 cm. May–Sept.

Broad-leaved pondweed
Potamogeton natans

Common in still and slow water, with floating oval leaves, sometimes on longish stems. The flowers are in short, dense spikes. Underwater leaves are very narrow. Floating to 5 m. May–Sept.

Birds

Grasshopper warbler
Locustella naevia

A shy bird, adept at moving in thick vegetation and hiding in the scantest cover. It is best located by its high-pitched song (like a fishing line being reeled in) and is usually seen only when singing. It occurs in any rank grass, especially scrub and reeds at the edge of wetland areas, as well as on heaths or in forestry plantations. Its long central toe can grasp two flimsy stems. If it does emerge from cover, points to look for are its rounded tail, plain-coloured but streaked upperparts and pale eyestripe. Its shape can be dumpy or slim. A singing bird turns its head to reveal a yellow gape and the tail vibrates. The population fluctuates, but is widespread. 13 cm. Summer visitor; Apr–Sept.

Sedge warbler
Arcrocephalus schoenobaenus

An active, rather ebullient bird but with some of the skulking habits of other reedbed warblers, identified by its head markings, streaked pattern on the back and ginger rump. Distinguished from the Reed and Marsh species (*p 155*) by its white eye stripe and its varied song with harsher notes. It often emerges to sing noisily from low vegetation in damp or wet areas, especially edges of gravel pits, marshes and reedbeds. May look slim or quite stocky. It flies low, usually for a short distance. There is a hard "tuck" alarm call. Nests are well hidden in reeds. 13 cm. Top Sixty. Summer visitor: Apr–Sept.

Reed warbler
Acrocephalus scirpaceus

Marsh warbler
Acrocephalus palustris

Reed and Marsh warblers are slim, sharp-faced, active birds with sober colours. They are extremely difficult to tell apart, especially the juveniles, but the Màrsh warbler's plumage is colder-coloured and its plainer marking gives it a notably neater appearance. Reed warblers have slightly more rufous plumage, duller throats and darker legs. The Marsh warbler's general deportment is more horizontal. The Reed warbler is usually confined to reedbeds and their borders, whereas the Marsh warbler is found in low vegetation including osiers. The nests are quite different: the Marsh warbler's is bound to surrounding stems and the Reed's deep cup is built among reed stems. The Marsh warbler's song is far more melodious than the Reed's harsh, chattering jumble of "churrur-churrur" and "jag-jag-jag" notes. However, their bounding, jerky flights are identical and both are adept at moving in thick undergrowth, though Reed warblers often adopt a vertical head-down posture. The Reed warbler breeds S of Ripon, the Marsh warbler only in about 20 localities in the southern half of England and Wales, mainly the Severn valley. 12–13 cm. Summer visitor.

Sand martin
Riparia riparia

The smallest of the "swallows", with an unmistakable plumage pattern unique in a bird of its size. It is quite different from the Swallow and House martin (*p 189*): being sandy brown above and white below, with a brown collar. It has a short tail. Juveniles have the same plumage but duller. It is often the first arrival (before the Swallow), to be seen feeding over lakes and reservoirs. The brown and white underparts show up well as the birds fly low over the water. Sand martins have a more direct and flicking flight than House martins and a harsh, hard, rippling call. They breed in any vertical, exposed bank or excavation, such as a gravel pit or sand quarry, making a typical line of nesting burrows. They roost in reedbeds in spring and autumn. 12 cm. Top Sixty. Summer visitor: Mar–Oct.

Little ringed plover
Charadrius dubius

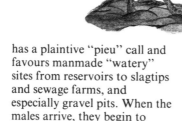

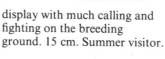

Scarcer, slightly smaller and more delicately built than the Ringed plover (*p 122*), but basically similar in appearance and behaviour. Its wings are more obviously flicked in its more erratic flight. Other differences are the lack of a wing-bar, a mainly black bill and a yellow ring round the eye. Notice the white on the forehead and over the eye. A lighter smudge on the forehead and a yellow eye ring distinguish a juvenile. The bird has a plaintive "pieu" call and favours manmade "watery" sites from reservoirs to slagtips and sewage farms, and especially gravel pits. When the males arrive, they begin to display with much calling and fighting on the breeding ground. 15 cm. Summer visitor.

Dipper
Cinclus cinclus

By February the Wren-like song of the Dipper can be heard loud above its background of tumbling water. The bird is never seen away from swift streams, lake edges or pools with gravelly or rocky beds (usually in its moorland or upland habitat, though a few winter in lowland areas). Bobbing up and down on a stone and cocking the tail, as well as its white breast against black plumage, identifies an adult. So does the bird's plump shape and its behaviour, which includes swimming, diving to feed on the stream bed, and collecting food as it "walks" on the bottom. The juvenile is grey above with more white below. Flight is generally fast and whirring. The call is a loud "zit-zit-zit". The large domed nest is often built under a bridge, in a hole in a bank, or even behind a waterfall. 18 cm. Resident.

Teal
Anas crecca

The smallest of the dabbling ducks (smaller than a pigeon). The drake has a distinctive red and green head, striking white wing-bar, white V above the tail and a cream breast. Tiny size and black bill and legs identify the female. The pale belly of both sexes shows in flight, which is very swift, wheeling, wader-like rather than duck-like, with rapid wing-beats. The Teal is a surface feeder. The male has a short, ringing "kwit-kwit" call, the female a more typical duck-like quack. Seen on ponds, floodwater and also at the coast. 34–38 cm. Resident and winter visitor.

Goldeneye
Bucephala clangula

In March the black and white Goldeneye males indulge in striking courtship displays while still on their wintering grounds. Small, dumpy, short-necked diving ducks, Goldeneyes are expert under water, jumping to dive and staying under for long periods. They patter along the surface to take off, drakes flickering black and white. Flight is very swift and the male's wings whistle. Females and juveniles look similar below, the humped back and odd domed head separating the female from other ducks (as does the drake's white face spot). A few breed in NW England and N Scotland. Fresh and salt water, shallow estuaries, bays and lakes. 42–50 cm. Mainly winter visitor.

Goosander
Mergus merganser

Unlike its close relative (the Red-breasted merganser, *p 148*), the Goosander is a freshwater species all year round. It is the largest sawbilled diving duck, with rather broad wings and a heavy, rectangular body. The pinkish tinge of the drake stands out from a distance. His bulbous head and white chest and the female's short crest distinguish them from the smaller Red-breasted merganser. The female Goosander is red-headed. The sawbill is serrated for catching fish. The bird dives well and for some distance. It is usually silent. Nests in holes by upland streams, rivers and lakes in England N of Lancashire and (rarely) in Wales and Ireland. 58–66 cm. Resident. Also winter visitor (Oct–Mar) to reservoirs, gravel pits and canals in the S.

Shoveler
Anas clypeata

The huge, spatulate bill easily distinguishes the Shoveler from other ducks and it often swims with this beak trawling the surface. Its blue forewing is also distinctive. Red on belly and white on breast picks out the males. The female has plumage similar to a female Mallard (*p 178*), but the bill shape distinguishes the two. When flying, the Shoveler's wings appear set far back because of its long neck and bill. It rises easily and flies with rapid wing-beats. On water it sits low in the front, dabbling with its bill. It inhabits freshwater lakes, marshes, ponds and sewage farms and breeds in scattered localities. March is when peak numbers can be seen as those birds which spent the winter in Britain are on their migration return to E Europe. 44–52 cm. Resident. Also winter visitor: Sept–Apr.

Ruff
Philomachus pugnax

The displaying male Ruff is unique and one of the most colourful of British breeding waders. All breeding males have a huge ruff and engage in mock battles, but vary greatly in plumage colour. Most birds seen outside the few marshland breeding areas are juveniles or winter adults. Then, non-breeding adults are Redshank-like birds, identified by a pale wing-bar and prominent white patches. The bird has a flicking action in an easy, Redshank-like flight. Standing birds show their deep bodies, long necks and small delicate heads. They can make a low "too-wit" call, but are usually silent. Breeds in a few places in East Anglia. 23–29 cm. Resident. Also passage migrant and winter visitor.

Red-necked grebe
Podiceps grisegena

Smaller than the Great crested species (*below*) and easily identifiable in summer with its yellow bill, black crown, pale grey cheeks and orange-red breast and neck (*see p 169*). It has less white in its wings than the Great crested species and lacks a well-defined eye stripe. In winter the head and body shape, yellow on the bill and lack of white above the eye distinguish the Red-necked species. It is an expert diver, like all grebes, and is usually seen singly. 42 cm. Normally a winter visitor (Aug–Apr), found inland or at sea, but has summered. Greatest numbers Oct–Mar.

Bittern
Botaurus stellaris

The only large, buff-coloured, heavily streaked "heron". Mainly seen at dawn and dusk, it looks vaguely owl-like in flight. More often heard than seen: in April when breeding its "foghorn" call booms around its reedbed habitat. Breeds infrequently in England, but is more widespread in winter. 70–80 cm. Resident.

Great crested grebe
Podiceps cristatus

The largest grebe, with distinct changes in seasonal plumage. In winter its very thin white neck with narrow black stripes at the rear stands out. The crest and frill show in summer (*see p 169*). There is a growling call. The chicks shelter in the adult's feathers. 46–51 cm. Resident.

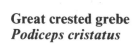

SUMMER
Butterflies

Marsh fritillary
Eurodryas aurinia

A local and variable species with many subspecies, a few examples of which are shown, including a very dark one (*above*), locally common in Ireland. Differences may occur even between individuals of neighbouring colonies, but generally the species is easy to recognise. The spots vary in size and the female is larger than the male. As well as liking wet, boggy areas, the Marsh fritillary also flies over dry mountain slopes up to 1,500 m.

Commoner in the W, with a few isolated populations as far north as W Scotland. The single brood of caterpillars lives gregariously under a silken web and hibernates in this form. Food plants are Plantain and Devilsbit scabious. Wingspan: 30–46 mm. Flight: May–June.

Wild Flowers

White water lily
Nymphaea alba

Beautiful, large white flowers up to 200 mm float on the water beside the even larger round leaves (300 mm) which are deeply cleft where they join the stalk. Rooted in the mud at the bottom of still or slow-moving fresh water. July–Aug.

Marsh pennywort
Hydrocotyle vulgaris

Growing both in water and in boggy places, a creeping perennial with circular leaves (50 mm) rising in long erect stalks. The flowers are minute, 1–2 mm, and often lurk under the leaves. 25 cm. July–Oct.

Frogbit
Hydrocharis morsus-ranae

A floating herb, with its roots in bunches with the rounded or heart-shaped leaves. The

flowers are white with a yellow spot in the centre. In still, shallow water. Can creep to 3 m. July–Aug.

Watercress
Nasturtium officinale

The hollow shoots of this plant creep or float in pure, shallow water and mud. The leaves are pinnate and dark green. The white flowers are 4–6 mm and the pods have two rows of seeds. 40 cm. May–Oct.

Canadian pondweed
Elodea canadensis
An aquatic plant in slow-flowing water, with submerged stems, tiny leaves in whorls of three and (occasionally) floating white flowers, 5 mm, on long stalks. Can extend to 3 m. May–Oct.

Water chickweed
Myosoton aquaticum
In boggy ground and by streams, a weak, spreading perennial with tiny white flowers (15 mm) and oval or heart-shaped leaves growing in opposite pairs. The stalks are hairy. 1 m. July–Aug.

Sneezewort
Achillea ptarmica
In marshes and damp grassland, a short perennial with narrow, serrated leaves and loose clusters of white flowers, 12–18 mm. The stems are ridged. 60 cm. July–Aug.

Common water plantain
Alisma plantago-aquatica
Growing on muddy freshwater banks, with large oval leaf blades (20 cm) and branches of flowers, 8–10 mm, only opening in the afternoon. 80 cm. June–Aug.

Amphibious bistort
Polygonum amphibium
An aquatic plant, varying in form; in water it has floating leaves and dense, rounded spikes of flowers. Also on muddy banks, growing to 75 cm high. July–Sept.

Water soldier
Stratiotes aloides
Hidden under water for most of the year, but in summer dense clusters of stiff, spiny-toothed leaves rise to the surface with solitary white female flowers, 40 mm (no male plants in Britain!) Rare naturally in E and C England, but often planted. 40 cm. June–Aug.

Great sundew
Drosera anglica
An insectivorous plant of marshes and bogs, with larger narrow leaves than Common sundew (*p 57*). The stalks are hairless and the flower shoots rise from the rosette centre. 20 cm. July–Aug.

Meadowsweet
Filipendula ulmaria
Very common in marshes and damp river banks, with dense, branching heads of tiny, creamy flowers (4–6 mm). The leaves are toothed and pinnate with several large leaflets alternating with smaller ones. 1 m. June–Sept.

Arrowhead
Sagittaria sagittifolia
An aquatic perennial in still and slow water with large arrow-shaped projecting leaves and oval floating ones. The white, three-petalled flowers, 20 mm, have purple centres, the male ones with many stamens. 70 cm. July–Aug.

Hemlock water dropwort
Oenanthe crocata
A very poisonous, tall perennial of damp, marshy places, growing from root tubers. The leaves are three or four times pinnate and the flower umbels are white. The fruits have conspicuous styles. 1·2 m. June–Sept.

Fool's watercress
Apium nodiflorum
Common in slow or still water, an often prostrate perennial with pinnate, toothed leaves and tiny flowers in umbels. Can extend to 1 m. July–Aug.

Yellow iris
Iris pseudacorus
Growing in marshy places and river banks, a striking yellow-flowered plant with sword-shaped leaves growing from a tuberous rhizome. Flowers are 100 mm across, two or three to a stem. 1 m. May–July.

Fringed water lily
Nymphoides peltata
An aquatic perennial with medium-sized yellow flowers (30–35 mm) whose petal lobes are fringed. The leaves are rounded and floating, very notched at the base, and often with purple spots. 7 cm. July–Aug.

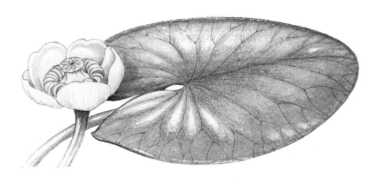

Yellow water lily
Nuphar lutea
An aquatic plant rooting in mud with almost globular flowers, 60 mm across, which rise out of the water on long stalks. The floating leaves, 40 cm, are cleft at the base. July–Aug.

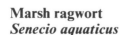

Lesser spearwort
Ranunculus flammula
Common in marshy places, a yellow-flowered perennial (sometimes creeping, sometimes upright. The base leaves are spear-shaped and the flowers are 7–20 mm across. 50 cm. June–Aug.

Common meadow rue
Thalictrum flavum
In marshes and damp meadows, with flowerheads making a sweet-smelling cloud of yellow. The leaves are two or three times pinnate and the whole plant is tall and unbranched. 75 cm. July–Aug.

Clustered dock
Rumex conglomeratus
In marshy places and damp meadows, with a slightly zigzag stem, narrow leaves and whorls on flowers on spikes. The fruits have three warty swellings. 55 cm. July–Aug.

Marsh ragwort
Senecio aquaticus
Similar to Oxford Ragwort (*p 193*) but with larger flowerheads (25–30 mm) and green rather than black-tipped bracts. Growing in marshy ground and river banks. 60 cm. July–Aug.

161

Greater bladderwort
Utricularia vulgaris
A carnivorous aquatic plant which has finely-segmented leaves, bladders to suck in small creatures for food, and flowers (18 mm) on spikes. Free-floating. 20 cm. July–Aug.

Great yellowcress
Rorippa amphibia
Growing in and beside slow-moving and still water with small yellow flowers, 6 mm, and toothed narrow or lobed leaves. Spreads by runners. 1.2 m. June–Aug.

Branched bur-reed
Sparganium erectum
Common in still and slow fresh water and by its banks, with long leaves and conspicuous, round yellowish-green flowerheads in spikes. The male flowers are at the branch tips. 1 m. June–Aug.

Marsh St John's wort
Hypericum elodes
On bogs but decreasing, a very hairy creeping perennial, with yellow, often only half-open flowers (15 mm) and reddish sepals. The leaves are rounded and greyish. 20 cm. June–Sept.

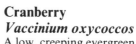

Bog pimpernel
Anagallis tenella
A creeping, mat-forming perennial of bogs and damp grassland, with tiny round leaves in opposite pairs and pink, upright bell-shaped flowers (10–15 mm) on long stalks. 10 cm. June–Aug.

Cranberry
Vaccinium oxycoccos
A low, creeping evergreen shrub growing in bogs, with the petals of its pinkish flowers turned back. Produces red edible berries. The leaves are small and oval. Creeps to 80 cm. June–Aug.

Meadow thistle
Cirsium dissectum
Growing in fens and damp grassland, like the Melancholy thistle (*p 27*), but not in the same habitat and shorter, with less hairy leaves and smaller (20–25 m) flowerheads. 80 cm. June–Aug.

Water mint
Mentha aquatica
Common in marshy places and often in water. Smells of mint. The flowers, 8–10 mm, are pinkish-lilac and in dense clusters, the toothed leaves are oval and the reddish stems are hairy. 70 cm. July–Oct.

Spiked water milfoil
Myriophyllum spicatum
An aquatic plant of still water having branched submerged stems covered with whorls of four pinnate leaves bearing grasslike leaflets. The whorls of tiny flowers are at the end of the leaf spikes. Trailing to 2·5 m. June–July.

Pale butterwort
Pinguicula lusitanica
On bogs, with delicate, pale pinkish-lilac, spurred flowers, 7 mm, which have two lips, the lower having three lobes. The leaves grow in a rosette. Insectivorous. 10 cm. June–Oct.

Great willowherb
Epilobium hirsutum
In marshy places, ditches and river banks, a very common tall perennial with very hairy stems and large, magenta flowers, 25 mm. The leaves are large and hairy, and the seed pods are very long, up to 80 mm. 1·2 m. July–Aug.

Flowering rush
Butomus umbellatus
Widespread in and by fresh water, a very tall perennial with long, narrow, twisted leaves and clusters of pink (25–30 mm) flowers. 1 m. July–Sept.

Purple loosestrife
Lythrum salicaria
In marshy places and by river banks, a tall perennial with long spikes of bright magenta flowers in whorls mixed with leaves. The main leaves are narrow, in opposite pairs or threes. 1 m. June–Aug.

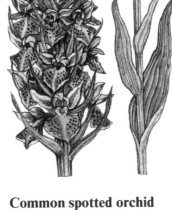

Southern marsh orchid
Dactylorhiza majalis
subsp. *praetermissa*
In marshes and fens with dark green, unspotted leaves and a dense spike of pinkish-purple flowers, each with a broad, fat lower lip and a definite, short, fat spur. Widespread in S and as far as N England. 45 cm. June–Aug.

Common spotted orchid
Dactylorhiza fuchsii
In marshy places, the commonest British orchid with narrow, darkly spotted leaves, and a dense spike of pink or occasionally white flowers spotted purple. The three-lobed flower lip is 10 mm across. 17 cm. June–Aug.

Common sorrel
Rumex acetosa
In marshy ground, including meadows and roadsides, with arrow-shaped leaves and loose spikes of reddish-orange flowers (compare the Docks). The fruits have no swelling. 1 m. May–June.

Marsh cinquefoil
Potentilla palustris
Common in marshy places and growing from a creeping rhizome. It has five to seven serrated leaflets. The flowers, 20–30 mm, have small purplish petals surrounded by conspicuous brownish-purple sepals. 35 cm. May–July.

Ivy-leaved bellflower
Wahlenbergia hederacea
In damp and marshy places and stream banks, an uncommon delicate creeping perennial with sprawling stems to 30 cm. The leaves are ivy-shaped and the pale blue flowers, 6–10 mm, nod on very long thread-like stalks. 4 cm. July–Aug.

163

Water speedwell
Veronica anagallis-aquatica
Growing in mud at the edge of water, with upright spikes (in opposite pairs) of pale blue flowers, 5–6 mm, and long leaves. 30 cm. June–Aug.

Northern marsh orchid
Dactylorhiza majalis subsp. *purpurella*
Similar to the Southern marsh orchid (*p 163*), but with deep purple flowers which have a narrow lip and a tapering spur. Distributed in Scotland, N England and N Wales. 20 cm. June–July.

Water lobelia
Lobelia dortmanna
Grown in water, mostly in Scotland and occasionally the Lake District and Wales, with a tuft of short, narrow leaves (4 cm). Stems up to 60 cm of nodding, two-lipped lilac-blue flowers, 15–20 mm, emerge from the water. July–Aug.

Marsh helleborine
Epipactis palustris
In marshy fens and on dunes, mainly in the S, an orchid forming patches from rhizomes. It has flowers with brownish-purple sepals hairy on the outside, and the lower petal has a frilly lip. The leaves are often tinged with purple. 30 cm. June–Aug.

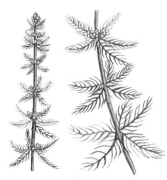

(Great) Reedmace
Typha latifolia
Very common on edges and actually growing in water, with broad leaves up to 2 cm wide and unmistakable flower spikes (sometimes popularly known as "Bulrushes"). The fat brown sausage is made of the female flowers, the upper thin spike being the male ones. 2 m. June–July.

Lesser reedmace
Typha angustifolia
Growing in similar situations to the Great reedmace (*left*), but less common and with narrower leaves (to 5 mm wide) and a smaller flowerspike with the male and female parts separated by a gap of 10–90 mm. 2·5 m. June–July.

Whorled water milfoil
Myriophyllum verticillatum
Similar to the Spiked species (*p 162*), but with leaves in whorls of five, not four. The flowerspike grows 25 cm above the water. The submerged shoots reach 3 m long. July–Aug.

Common duckweed
Lemna minor
A minute plant very common on still water. The leaves are round, flat floating discs, 4 mm in diameter, with a single unbranched root. June–July.

Marestail
Hippuris vulgaris
In slow or still water, but not common, with whorls of six to twelve leaves, some submerged, some emerging from the water. In chalk and limestone areas. Grows from a rhizome. 60 cm. June–July.

Fungi

Mycena tortuosa

Easily overlooked, this minute species is always found in wet places on the underside of rotting fallen logs, often alder but also other trees in moist situations. Both the cap and stem are covered in very fine hairs. The cap, 1–8 mm, is small, pure white, finely hairy. The narrow white gills are fairly crowded. The stem, 1–3 cm, is short, slender, white and finely hairy as the cap. July–Nov.

Cortinarius delibutus

A fairly common species occuring in groups or tufted. Found in wet places in a wide range of habitats, including under conifers, birch and beech. The cap, 3–9 cm, is yellow and very sticky. The gills are at first deep blue, then yellowish to cinnamon brown. The stem, 5–10 cm, is club-shaped, white, with a yellow sticky veil. Aug–Nov.

Naucoria escharoides

Often in large numbers in boggy alder carrs. The cap, 1–3 cm, is yellowish to reddish-brown and scurfy. The gills are brown, narrow and crowded. The stem, 3–5 cm, is yellowish-brown. Aug–Oct.

Gyrodon lividus

Known only from the Cambridgeshire fens in Britain, but more frequent elsewhere in northern Europe. Grows in groups near alder and has a soft, spongy texture. The cap, 3–10 cm, is irregular, sticky when wet, shiny when dry, olive beige to reddish-brown, with a thin, wavy margin. The tubes are short and lemon yellow. The shallow pores are ochre yellow to olive, bluing to the touch. The stem, 4–10 cm, is curved and the same colour as the cap. The flesh is thin. Aug–Oct.

Pholiota myosotis

Frequently found in *Sphagnum* bogs and easily confused with *Hypholoma udum* (*p 173*). The cap, 2–4 cm, is convex then flat, olive green to light yellowish, darker at the centre, smooth and sticky. The gills are olive green then rusty brown and fairly spaced. The stem, 7–15 cm, is slender and cylindric, with a white, powdery apex. July–Sept.

Galerina sphagnorum

One of several brown-spored *Galerina* species with long, slender stems, found amongst *Sphagnum* moss. *G. paludosa* is similar but has a ring on the stem. *G. sphagnorum* smells of meal. The cap, 1–4 cm, has an umbo, is yellowish-brown, lined and smooth. The gills are ochre and fairly crowded. The stem, 4–12 cm, is ochre brown and silky. July–Oct.

Psilocybe inquilina

Grows on dead grass and herb stems. Like many of the *Psilocybe* species it has a sticky pellicle which can be peeled off, but the gills remain brown and do not acquire a purplish tint. The cap, 0·5–1 cm, has an umbo and is dingy brown drying to pale tan, lined when moist. The gills are clay to red-brown and rather spaced. The stem, 1–3 cm, is slender, and the same colour as the cap. It is often wavy. July–Oct.

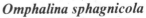

Omphalina sphagnicola

Always with *Sphagnum* moss. The cap, 1–2 cm, is funnel-shaped, olive brown to sooty brown and lined. The gills are pale grey-brown and narrow. The stem, 2–4 cm, is paler. June–Sept.

Russula nitida

Often in *Sphagnum* moss. A small to medium species, not eaten because the flesh is too thin. The cap, 3–7 cm, is shiny, wine red or purplish, sometimes with ochre or olive tints, darker at the centre; the margin is grooved. The gills are pale cream to ochre yellow and fairly spaced. The stem, 4–8 cm, is white flushed with pale pink. July–Oct.

Birds

Yellow wagtail
Motacilla flava

The male is the brightest yellow British bird, though the brilliance and extent of its yellow varies widely. The yellow-headed form is the most common, but a blue-headed variety also occurs in the SE (only the males differ). Females and juveniles are duller. These wagtails are active birds, tail-wagging and darting after insects on the ground. By August, the breeding season is over and flocks exploit the summer insect population. The birds have a dipping, skipping flight and a distinctive "tsweep" call. Found in marshes and watery meadows and a few drier habitats S of Clyde. 16–17 cm. Summer visitor: Apr–Sept.

Pied wagtail
male in summer, see p 179.

Redshank
Tringa totanus

The noisiest bird in any marsh, taking wing with an explosive melodious "teu-he-he" call, especially in summer to protect its young. It is the only wader with a bold white triangle on its wing. An alert posture, red legs and dark-tipped, fairly long, orange bill identifies the summer bird. Red projecting legs, white underparts, white on wings, the typical white on the back, as well as the noisy call, identify it in flight. (In winter the legs are orange.) Flight is erratic with jerky deliberate wing-beats. An alighting bird shows a white V and tail, but a flying bird has a white diamond on its back. Very widely distributed. Breeds on all wet areas inland and coastally. Winters on coast. 28 cm. Resident. Also passage bird and winter visitor.

Spotted redshank
Tringa erythropus

A lanky wader, larger than the Redshank with longer bill and legs and lacking white on the wings. The white oval on the back and its red legs distinguish it from all other birds. (*For winter plumage, see p 180*). Breeding birds have sooty black plumage, unlike other waders. Those just in or out of this breeding plumage look very patchy – the small picture shows a partial summer plumage. There is a white eye ring and stripe over the eye and an orange bill. The loud, deep "cheewit" call is diagnostic. 30 cm. Passage birds may be seen on coast (May and especially Aug–Oct). Increasing winter visitor.

Green sandpiper
Tringa ochropus

The first of the autumn's returning Green sandpipers will appear in July and any small muddy pool, marsh, ditch or farmyard pond will provide a home for this freshwater wader that avoids the coast. It is a noisy, easily alarmed bird which looks almost black and white, with its white rump conspicuous in flight, when its greenish legs only just project beyond the tail. The flight is twisting and erratic, with a rapid climb after take-off. On the wing, the bird resembles a huge House martin. It makes an explosive "klerweet-weet" call in flight. When standing, its dark breast, well-defined but tiny spots, and stocky build are noticeable. Spring birds have streaked breasts and pale heads. (*For winter plumage, see p 181.*) It has a typical sandpiper habit of tail and head bobbing. 23 cm. Winter visitor: Oct–Apr. Also passage migrant (Apr–June, July–Oct) to wet areas inland.

Black-tailed godwit
in summer, see p 181.

Greenshank
Tringa nebularia

A lanky, pale wader larger than the Redshank (*p 166*), with plain-coloured, darkish-tipped wings. It is rather more angular in form than other waders and the only one with a slightly uptilted bill, green legs and a white V on its back. The back is well marked and blackish in the breeding plumage. Flight is swift and direct, sometimes high. The bird's presence is usually indicated by a characteristic ringing "tew-tew-tew" call in an emphatic and deliberate manner. Breeds in Scotland and Hebrides on wet moorland. A number winter on S and W coasts. 30–31 cm. Summer visitor to inland waters.

Black-necked grebe
Podiceps nigricollis

Often seen in company with other grebes, including the Slavonian which it closely resembles, except that the Black-necked has an uptilted bill and less white on its face. Summer birds have a golden head fan. (*For winter plumage, see p 180.*) The Black-necked grebe dives well, but feeds more from the surface than other species. Fairly common on inland water and sheltered marine areas, especially Aug–Mar. Scattered breeding. 28–34 cm. Resident.

Little grebe
in summer, see p 180.

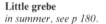

Red-necked grebe
in summer, see p 158.

Great crested grebe
in summer when its crest and frill show, see p 158.

Great northern diver
Gavia immer

Black-throated diver
Gavia arctica

Red-throated diver
Gavia stellata

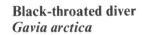

The Red-throated is the smallest and most common of the divers seen in Britain. All are superficially like Cormorants (*p 134*), but have thicker, tube-like necks and pointed bills. The legs are set well back and the birds are virtually tailless. Summer birds are easy to tell apart. The Red-throated diver has a grey head and a brick-red throat. The Black-throated species has a grey head and a black throat. The Great northern has a black head and neck with a striped collar. It is much the largest of the three. (*For winter plumage, see p 182.*) In flight, the three divers have a characteristic flight profile with their long, narrow wings set midway along the body. Keeling over in the water to reveal the underside and just touching the water with the tip of the bill are typical of divers. They may also put their heads underwater briefly before diving, often for long distances. The Red-throated species (55–65 cm) breeds N Ireland and W coast of Scotland. The Black-throated (60–70 cm and the least common) breeds W coast of Scotland and the Hebrides, and usually winters on the coast. The Great Northern diver (70–90 cm) is a winter visitor to coastal waters, sometimes inland. (Sept–May). Breeds very rarely in Scotland.

Marsh harrier
Circus aeruginosus

One of Britain's rarest breeding birds of prey, virtually confined to East Anglian marshland. It is the largest and most heavily built of the harriers, its size and shape alone distinguishing it from other species. Plumage is variable, but the pattern remains constant. Adult males have pale grey wings and tail gradually acquired over three to four years. They may be whitish or patterned below. Females and juveniles have dark eye stripes and yellowish heads which show up as a pale "beacon" at a distance: this distinguishes them from other harriers. The birds feed on small amphibians, mammals and birds and have a typical, low, slow, flapping harrier flight, with frequent V-shaped glides and occasional leg trailing. Their shrill call is not unlike the Buzzard's (*p 67*). Though some are resident, many are summer visitors who may breed irregularly, always nesting in extensive wet reedbeds. Food-gathering adults may range over neighbouring farmland. Passage birds occur in many places in spring and autumn, some wintering in marshy and coastal areas. 48–56 cm.

Canada goose
Branta canadensis

In July the Canada geese are flightless, so are most frequently seen. They are the commonest of the urban park geese and the largest of the three black-necked geese, much the most likely to be seen inland. A species introduced to ornamental lakes in Europe from N America, they are well established and breed on inland waters throughout Britain. Seen occasionally in coastal areas, especially in winter, but they usually graze inland on marshes or fields near fresh water. The white patch contrasting with the black neck and head is diagnostic, but the contrasting black and white seen from below is also noticeable. The bird flies fast with strong, measured beats of its very large wings. It is often seen in V-shaped flocks, especially in autumn. The upperparts are fairly plain brown before the autumn moult, but some birds have distinct barring on the back. Deep "an-huck" flight call. 90–102 cm. Resident.

AUTUMN
Wild Flowers

Grass of Parnassus
Parnassia palustris
Commoner in the N, in marshy spots, a hairless herb with a rosette of heart-shaped leaves on longish stalks. The flowers are large, 15–30 mm, and white. 30 cm. July–Oct.

Lesser water parsnip
Berula erecta
In marshy ground and on banks, with finely divided, underwater leaves (having seven to ten pairs of leaflets) and an umbel of white flowers. 1 m. July–Sept.

Common fleabane
Pulicaria dystenterica
In wet places and on river banks, with a large bright yellow flowerhead, up to 30 mm across, and wavy-edged heart-shaped leaves, very hairy below. 40 cm. Aug–Sept.

Nodding bur marigold
Bidens cernua
Grows on damp banks and edges, with drooping heads, 25 mm. It also differs from the Trifid bur marigold (*below*) in having unlobed leaves, 15 cm long, without stalks. 60 cm. July–Sept.

Marsh hawksbeard
Crepis paludosa
In marshy places in the N, having narrow, toothed leaves and heads each carrying a few yellow flowers, 25 mm across, with black, hairy bracts. 90 cm. July–Sept.

Trifid bur marigold
Bidens tripartita
Differs from the Nodding bur marigold (*above*) in having three-lobed, serrated leaves, with erect heads of yellow flowers, 15–25 mm. Grows on muddy edges by ponds and streams. 45 cm. July–Sept.

Greater spearwort
Ranunculus lingua
The largest British buttercup, growing in marshy land from long runners. It has long spear-shaped leaves, 25 cm long. The flowers, 20–40 mm, grow on branching stalks. 1·2 m. June–Sept.

Perennial sow thistle
Sonchus arvensis
A robust perennial of marshy ground and damp, grassy roadsides, having a sticky, hairy stem, branching clusters of flowerheads, 40–50 mm, and softly spiny-edged, greyish leaves. 1·5 m. July–Oct.

Orange balsam
Impatiens capensis
Similar to the Touch-me-not variety, but with leaves only 8 cm long having fewer, smaller teeth. The flowers are orange, often spotted with red, 20–30 mm. They may not open. Common by rivers and canals in the S and E. 80 cm. June–Sept.

Monkey flower
Mimulus guttatus
Widespread on banks and marshy ground, except in the E. It has rounded, toothed leaves and large, yellow flowers, with small red spots inside, 25–45 mm. Rather weak-stemmed. 50 cm. July–Sept.

Touch-me-not balsam
Impatiens noli-tangere
The name of this upright annual comes from its habit of shooting out its seeds if the fruit is touched. The leaves are 12 cm with largish teeth. The flowers, 40 mm, have curved spurs. On river and canal banks and in damp woodland. 40 cm. July–Sept.

Celery-leaved buttercup
Ranunculus sceleratus
A robust annual of muddy banks, with inconspicuous, small-petalled flowers, 5–10 mm, producing fruits with 100 or more seeds to a head. The upper leaves have three narrow segments. 45 cm. July–Sept.

Himalayan balsam
Impatiens glandulifera
An introduction from the Himalayas and common by rivers and canals. An erect robust annual, with a stout, translucent and reddish stem, leaves either opposite or in groups of three round the stem, and large, purple-pink flowers (40 mm) having short, bent spurs. 1 to 2 m. July–Oct.

Water pepper
Polygonum hydropiper
The flowers in the slim, nodding head of this short, untidy annual have yellow glands. They are white, tinged with green or pink. The plant has a burning taste. Common on damp ground by and sometimes in fresh water. 75 cm. July–Sept.

Water dock
Rumex hydrolapathum
Growing by and in water, a tall, robust perennial with leaves up to 1 m long. The flowers are in dense branching spikes and the fruits are triangular, 6–8 mm, with three warts. 2 m. July–Sept.

Hemp agrimony
Eupatorium cannabinum
Another tall, upright perennial growing in marshes and by streams, with opposite pairs of three-lobed leaves which give the appearance of a whorl of six. The flowerheads are a dull pinkish mauve. 1·2 m. July–Sept.

Common hemp nettle
Galeopsis tetrahit
Grows frequently on marshy and also disturbed ground, a straggling, coarsely hairy annual, with white, pink or purple flowers (15–20 mm). The petals are often spotted. The leaves are toothed. 1 m. July–Sept.

Marsh thistle
Cirsium palustre
Very common in marshes and damp woods (and also meadows), with dense flowerheads, 20 mm, either purplish-red or white. The stems are spiny-winged and the leaves are spiny. 1·5 m. July–Sept.

Skull cap
Scutellaria galericulata
A hairy perennial growing by and in water, with pairs of bluish-violet, two-lipped flowers scattered up the stem. The flower tubes are up to 20 mm long. 50 cm. June–Sept.

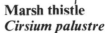

Fungi

Naucoria scolecina
The cap, 1–2 cm, is convex, rusty brown then paler, with a lined margin. The gills are pinky-brown. The stem, 3–7 cm, is thin and curved. Sept–Oct.

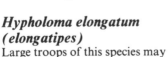

Hypholoma elongatum (elongatipes)
Large troops of this species may be found pushing up through the *Sphagnum* moss. The cap, 1–3 cm, is honey yellow with olive tints, and a thin, lined margin. The gills are lilac-grey, darkening to chestnut brown. The stem, 5–10 cm, is slender, white at the apex and yellowish-brown below, hollow and smooth. Sept–Nov.

Yellow swamp russula
Russula claroflava
Usually found amongst moss. The slimy, bright yellow cap fades with age. Mild-tasting, with a strong, fruity smell and edible after cooking. The cap, 5–10 cm, is convex to depressed and shiny. The gills are whitish and crowded. The stem, 5–9 cm, is white to greyish. Aug–Sept.

Pholiota alnicola
Usually in tufts on old roots and fallen trunks of Alder and Willow in boggy ground, it has a mild, fruity smell reminiscent of pear drops. The cap, 2–8 cm, is fleshy, yellow with olive or brownish tints; the margin is inrolled. The gills are straw yellow to cinnamon brown and quite crowded. The stem, 4–8 cm, is lemon yellow above, rust brown below. Sept–Nov.

Laccaria proxima

Closely related to the Deceiver
(p 102) but confined to
marshland and it is usually
larger with a longer stem. The
cap, 2–7 cm, is pinkish-brown
and scurfy-scaly. The gills are
flesh pink, powdery and spaced.
The stem, 3–10 cm, is the same
colour as the cap, slender and
fibrous. Sept–Nov.

Cortinarius paleaceus

A graceful, slender species of
boggy heathland, and
sometimes damp woods. It has
a distinctive smell of geraniums
(*Pelargonium*). The cap,
1–3 cm, is conical with a
pointed umbo, and deep brown
with whitish scales. The gills are
lilac then cinnamon brown, and
crowded. The stem, 4–7 cm, is
wavy and brown with several
zones of white scales. The flesh
is brownish-lilac. Sept–Nov.

Dermocybe uliginosa

Found in woodland in boggy
places, especially under Willow
and Alder. It grows in groups,
often amongst *Sphagnum* moss,
on ground that may be
submerged for part of the year.
Although not recorded as toxic,
it could be confused with the
deadly *Cortinarius
speciosissimus*. The cap,
2–5 cm, is bright tawny orange.

The gills are lemon yellow, then
ochre to rusty. The stem,
3–8 cm, is cap colour or paler,
yellow at the apex, with a
yellow cortina. The flesh is
lemon yellow and smells of
radish. Sept–Oct.

Birds

Bearded tit
Panurus biarmicus

Activity in November is quite
high at reedbed sites where this
tiny bird occurs. Its minute size,
tawny colour overall, long tail
and fast wobbling flight ending
with an abrupt dive into cover
identify the Bearded tit
(actually not a tit at all). It feeds
on insects in summer and seeds
in winter. The grey head and
black moustache of the male
and the plumage and profile of
both sexes are unique. The
juvenile is much blacker than
the female. The "ping" call (like
two coins being flicked
together) often betrays its
presence. It is rarely, if ever,
seen away from reeds and at
present breeds sporadically, but
increasingly in England.
16·5 cm. Resident.

Cetti's warbler
Cetti cetti

More robustly built than other marshland warblers, this recent arrival is confined to the extreme SE of England, but is spreading. Dark, rich brown plumage above a grey breast and a long, ragged-looking, rounded tail make identification easy. It has a white eye stripe. Its flight is low and fairly rapid. It usually skulks low in scrub, but occasionally emerges into full view with intermittent upward flicks of the tail. It makes a typical warbler's churring alarm call or a more emphatic single "chic". The song is loud and explosive, usually erupting from low vegetation. In wet areas and nearby ditches and hedges. 14 cm. Summer visitor.

Reed bunting
Emberiza schoeniclus

Perhaps the most familar of the buntings, typically seen in the vegetation bordering overgrown lakes and reedbeds. It is an active, conspicuous bird which usually perches prominently, yet it is easily overlooked on the ground. The breeding male has a bold black and white face in spring. When freshly moulted he is similar to the female. She has chestnut wings and a well-streaked back. The white outer tail (often flicked) distinguishes her from the Sparrow (*p 179*). Flight is undulating and erratic, and only over short distances. There are a "seep" contact call, a metallic "chink" and an irritating, tinkling song. The habitat now includes drier marshy areas, and the Reed bunting even visits garden bird tables in winter. 15 cm. Top Sixty. Resident.

Grey wagtail
Motacilla cinerea

By November the Grey wagtail has left its breeding areas besides fast-flowing NW streams for the quieter waters of the lowlands. It is also often seen on roofs in city centres! Its grey upperparts against yellow underparts are distinctive. Yellow encircles the tail at all times of the year. It is the largest-tailed and slimmest-winged wagtail with a dipping, exaggerated flight and constantly wagging tail. The breeding male is distinctive with its black bib; its back is always greyer than the Yellow wagtail (*p 166*). The winter female has a buff breast – *see p 179*. Only males have a white wing-bar. Sharp "tizpeep" call. 18 cm. Resident, though mainly summer visitor to N and W.

Kingfisher
Alcedo atthis

A wonderfully exotic-looking bird usually seen in flight as an iridescent blue streak following the line of a river or stream. The blues and greens in its plumage alter with the light. Apart from the stunning coloration, its small size and shrill whistle identify it. Juveniles have shorter bills than adults. The female has an orange patch on the bill. The bird often perches on a branch just above the water. It will dive straight in from this perch or hover to spot its prey before plunging in. It gives a high-flying display in spring. Often found by very small streams in winter. Throughout British Isles, though absent from much of Scotland. 16–17 cm. Resident.

Common sandpiper
Actitis hypoleucos

The most likely small wader to be seen inland, breeding by hill streams, lakes and other inland waters. In autumn, freshwater areas near the coast will also attract large numbers preparing to migrate. The Common sandpiper is an extremely active bird with a bobbing head and tail in constant motion, easily identified by its sober colour and distinctive white wing-bar. It has a white eye ring and dark breast with a white "slot" against its drab olive upperparts. When disturbed, it flies out in a low arc over water, on stiff, flicking wing-beats and uttering a "teetering" call. Its flight profile, with bill down, wing slightly forward and tail partly spread, is unique. It then also shows its white wing-bar and white outer tail. A few winter birds occur. 20 cm. Summer visitor: Mar–Oct.

Coot
Fulica atra

A noisy, quarrelsome bird, common on inland waters (including park lakes), and recognisable by its white bill and frontal plate. It differs from the smaller Moorhen (*below*) in having no red and yellow bill, but more white on its face. Its chicks have reddish heads. Juveniles are grey and white.

Coots also seem to prefer wider waters than Moorhens and spend more time swimming and less on land. The body is round and blue-grey, but black-looking from a distance. Birds often graze in groups near water. Flight is weak, but the birds can actually travel long distances and even fly quite high. They make loud explosive "keuk", "k-towk" and "t'uck" calls. Top Sixty. 36–38 cm. Resident.

Moorhen
Gallinula chloropus

Very common on town park lakes, rivers, streams and ponds, usually preferring more confined water spaces like ditches and narrow canals than the Coot (*above*). Moorhens spend much time walking over soft ground on their long toes. The red frontal plate and yellow-tipped bill, dark-looking plumage with a white flank line and undertail are unmistakable and differentiate them from the Coot. Juveniles are a two-toned buff-brown with a green frontal plate. The bird runs, walks, swims and dives with ease. Swimming birds nod their heads and flick their tails. They trail their legs in their fluttering, weak flight. They make explosive "kurruk" and "kityik" calls and softer "kok-kok" call at night. Top Sixty. 32—35 cm. Resident.

Tufted duck
Aythya fidigula

A rapid increase in their breeding population has changed Tufted ducks from being only winter visitors to one of the more numerous resident breeding ducks, in places actually outnumbering Mallards. Tufted ducks are small, round, and very active, continually jump-diving and bobbing up to the surface. The crest, glossy purple head, yellow eye and grey bill unmistakably identify the male, but care is needed to tell the female and young apart from the larger, longer-bodied Scaup (*p 147*). However, the square, domed head of the Tufted duck separates its females from the flatter, round-headed female Scaups. Flight is rapid with a pattering take-off. 40–47 cm. Resident and winter visitor: Oct–Apr.

Pochard
Aythya ferina

In summer fewer of these squat ducks, expert at diving and rarely out of water, are seen, but the autumn migration brings many thousands more. The male has a striking contrast of silver grey against his dark areas. Bill colour and shape separate him from the Tufted duck (*p 177*) and Scaup (*p 147*). His red head contrasts with the female's brown one. Her round shape and grey innermost wing feathers separate her from other ducks. She has pale marks around bill and eye. In flight, compare the dark and pale underneath areas with the Tufted duck and Scaup. On fresh water, also occasionally at sea. 42–49 cm. Resident.

Mallard
Anas platyrhynchos

The most common duck in town parks and village ponds, and the many resident ducks are greatly increased at the autumn migration. A fairly heavy bird in weight and proportion, but a good flier and walker. It feeds by up-ending and dabbling, but may be seen away from water in spring, as well as grazing in fields after harvest and in winter. Young birds dive well, but adults only when injured. Females and juveniles have streaked bodies and white wing linings, unlike any other duck except the female Shoveler (*p 157*), but the Mallard's bill shape separates it. Females can be told from other brown ducks by the blue and white speculum (bar) on the wing. Only the drake has the all-yellow bill and curled tail feathers. He has a soft call and the female the familiar deep "quack-quack" repeated more and more softly. Both a freshwater and marine species. Top Sixty. 50–65 cm. Resident. Also winter visitor: Sept–Apr.

Grey wagtail
female in winter, see p 175.

WINTER
Birds

Pied wagtail
Motacilla alba

With deliberate gait and bobbing and wagging tail, a familiar sight on open land in town and country. In winter, many roost communally in lowland water meadows, reedbeds and dense waterside vegetation. Plumage varies and can look similar to that passage visitor, the White wagtail. But all black and white wagtails seen in winter and almost all in summer will be Pieds. The summer male is black and white with smoky grey flank feathers (*see p 166*). His back looks almost black, but is greyer in winter. The female has a dark grey back, sometimes with an olive-grey tinge. Wingbars are prominent in both sexes. The call is a distinct shrill "chizzick". Nests in holes, walls and sheds. Top Sixty. 18 cm. Resident.

Jack snipe
Lymnocryptes minimus

Smaller than the Snipe (*right*), with a much shorter bill and tail, and broader wings, it is also much more secretive, only taking wing at the last moment. Jack snipes rarely show themselves on the ground. The flight is slower and less zigzagging than the Snipe. The back stripes are very vivid on a flying bird. Usually silent but may give a faint Snipe-like call. On marshes and inland waters. 19 cm. Winter visitor (Sept–Apr) and passage migrant.

Snipe
Gallinago gallinago

A medium-sized game bird, rare on the ground, though, if so, seen on inland wet areas such as marshland or fields (in winter) or at the water's edge. Its stocky build, boldly striped head and back identify it then. It has a dashing, zigzag flight, with a "squelch-like" call: its brownish, long-billed look identifies it (the bill is held at a shallow angle to the body and the creamy back stripes contrast with the dark brown plumage). Flight is swift and erratic. Birds twist and turn low down after take-off and then climb rapidly. There is also a diving, tail-vibrating display flight. 27 cm. Resident. Also winter visitor: Oct–Mar.

Little grebe (Dabchick)
Tachybaptus ruficollis

The commonest and smallest of the grebes, with a fluffy rear in water and a large head for its small body. In winter it is buff-brown. In summer it has a reddish patch on the face and throat (*see p 169*). The belly and underwing are white, but lack of white on the upperwing separates it from the other grebes. It is an energetic diver and often patters along the surface. Flight is fast with rapid wingbeats. It is a secretive bird, keeping to vegetation at the water's edge. At the first sign of danger it dives. Unlike other grebes, it stays on fresh water during the winter. Large numbers leave the quieter waters where they nested and gather on more open water. Only if this freezes do they go to the coast and then they frequent sheltered harbours and estuaries rather than exposed beaches. 25–29 cm. Resident.

Spotted redshank
in winter, see p 166.

Black-necked Grebe
in winter, see p 169.

Water rail
Rallus aquaticus

Loud, pig-like squealing and staccato "kik-ik-ik" calls are often the only indication of the Water rail, but if all is quiet it may be seen clambering in bushes. Recognisable by its long red bill, buff streaked upperparts and grey below, with a Moorhen-like tail and pinkish-brown legs. It has a weak, leg-trailing flight, very like the Moorhen. Breeds in limited numbers in reedbeds, marshes and swampy rivers, but occurs more widely in winter when migrants swell the population. 23–28 cm. Resident.

Smew
Mergus albellus

The smallest and shortest-billed of the sawbills. The dazzling black and white of the male (though he looks almost white at rest) and the red, white and grey plumage combination of the female and juvenile distinguish Smews from other ducks. They have white on the wing like the Wigeon (*p 149*), but compare their heads and tails. The Smew sits high in the water and dives expertly, sometimes in pairs and small groups. It flies in oblique, waving lines or in loose groups. Usually on fresh water in the SE. 38–44 cm. Scarce winter visitor: Nov–Apr.

Green Sandpiper
in winter, see p 167.

Gadwall
Anas strepera

One of the rarer dabbling ducks, easily identified by its white wing patch. The male is a uniform mealy grey, the female has tiny crescent greyish breast marks. Shyer than the Mallard (*p 178*), the Gadwall up-ends to feed. Wing-beats are faster than the Mallard's. The male's call is a series of whistles and grunts, the female's a progressively softer quacking call somewhat like the female Mallard's. 46–56 cm. Resident and winter visitor: Oct–Mar.

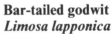

Black-tailed godwit
Limosa limosa

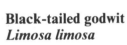

Smaller than Curlews, a long, lanky bird with a very long, almost straight bill, the Black-tailed godwit can be told by its Oystercatcher-like, black and white appearance and in summer by its reddish plumage (*see p 168*). The winter bird is grey-brown and white. (Only Oystercatchers have a similar white wing-bar.) Compare the white beneath the tail and on the belly with the Bar-tailed species (*right*). Flight is swift, powerful and direct. Has a loud "wiker-wiker-wiker" flight call. Breeds on meadowland and marshes. 41 cm. Resident. Also passage migrant and winter visitor.

Bar-tailed godwit
Limosa lapponica

More stockily built with a less erect carriage than the Black-tailed species (*left*), the summer bird has all-red underparts (seldom seen in Britain since it breeds in the high Arctic). The female's bill is longer than the male's. Often seen in loose flocks, its flight is fairly rapid when the white V, shorter legs and lack of wing-bar can be compared with the Black-tailed species and also with Curlew and Whimbrel (*p 61*). May perform aerobatics on descent. Low chattering call. Rare inland. 35 cm. Winter visitor (when it is commoner than the Black-tailed) and passage migrant to coastal flats.

Black-throated diver
in winter, see p 169.

Great northern diver
in winter, see p 169.

Red-throated diver
in winter, see p 169.

Short-eared owl
Asio flammeus

The Short-eared owl is
patchy-looking and
buff-coloured, more likely to be
seen in daytime than other
owls, especially when hunting in
winter low over marshes or
moorland. It tends to look like
a giant-sized moth with its dark
wing patches. It is also very
active at dawn and dusk. Flight
is silent and wavering, with
glides on its noticeably long,
crooked wings. The eartufts are
so short they are difficult to see,
but the bird can be
differentiated from the Tawny
owl (*p 110*) by its yellow eyes.
Numbers vary from year to
year depending on its food
supply of voles. Usually it
roosts in a tussock of coarse
grass. 38 cm. Resident, but
more widely distributed as
winter visitor.

Grey heron
Ardua cinerea

The largest common land bird in Britain, the Grey heron flies with slow, very deep beats of its bowed wings, trailing its legs and with its black and white head drawn back into its neck. On land it often adopts a one-legged stance as it stands patiently above the shallows waiting for its prey. It favours fresh water for feeding, hunting stealthily by day or night for fish, amphibians and the occasional small mammal or water bird. It also hunts fish in urban ponds and can be a great trial to trout farmers. May be seen alone or in groups in fields. It nests in colonies. In early February birds re-establish their pair bond and rebuild the previous season's nest. A breeding bird has longer head plumes and white back plumes. Immature birds lack the black eye stripe and the black on neck and breast of the adult. The call is a very harsh "hraak", often heard from flying birds. Frequents any watery area, especially marshland but also upland and urban areas. 90–98 cm. Resident.

Swans:
Mute swan (*Cygnus olor*)
Bewick's (*C. columbianus bewickii*)
Whooper (*C. cygnus*)

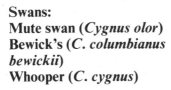

The Mute is the common swan of park and river, also sometimes seen at sea and identified when swimming by its arched neck and wings held raised. It has an orange bill and a black round eye. The adult male has a larger knob at the base of the bill than other birds. In flight wings make a throbbing sound. Snorting call. 152 cm. Resident. The Whooper is the same size, but not so heavily built and distinguished by its ringing "whoop-a-hoop" flight call, its straighter neck and silent wings. Its black and yellow bill looks elongated. No knob. Wilder than the Mute. 152 cm. Common winter visitor (Oct–Apr), especially to Scotland. The smallest is Bewick's, best identified from afar by its size and shorter, thicker neck. Loud, baying call like a pack of hounds. Its yellow bill patch is smaller and rounder, not going beyond the nostrils. The central black stripe may go up to the forehead. 122 cm. Winter visitor.

Whooper Bewick's Mute

Town and Garden

Urban habitats are a severe challenge to wildlife, yet many creatures and plants come to terms with the bricks and concrete, the bustle of feet and traffic, and the air pollution. Indeed, it is not always realised that towns and villages, with their gardens, parks, roadsides, waste and disturbed ground, walls and industries, are actually one of the more important wildlife habitats – richer in numbers of animals and wild plants than many "natural" habitats such as moorland and sand dunes.

Wild flowers find a niche in many an odd corner and quiet nook and some such as Rosebay willowherb positively thrive on wasteland and even high up on walls. Oxford ragwort arrived in Britain accidentally and finds buildings and rubble conveniently similar to its native volcanic sites!

Many creatures appreciate the easy "pickings" in towns, and not just the ubiquitous House sparrow and Town pigeon. Even Kestrels have been known to nest in the inner city and are often seen hovering above a motorway to clean up the small mammals and birds killed by cars. Fungi often find conditions in gardens and compost heaps to their liking and, though butterflies have a bit of a struggle, they *can* be seen, especially in those gardens that make an effort to attract them with scented plants and patches of rough ground and nettles for caterpillars.

184

SPRING
Butterflies

1st generation

2nd generation

Small white
Artogeia (Pieris) rapae

The favourite haunt of the Small white, one of the commonest British butterflies, is likely to be the cabbage rows of market gardens, although it may be found in a variety of habitats – from urban parks to open countryside. Its small green caterpillars are even more frequent than those of the Large white (*p 199*). The Small white is noticeably smaller, but more numerous than the Large white and feeds on a greater

variety of plants especially Wild mignonette and Cabbage. The resident population is augmented each year by large numbers from abroad. There

are two generations which differ slightly in appearance (*see pictures*). Wingspan: 46–55 mm. Flight: Mar–Sept.

Wild Flowers

Daisy
Bellis perennis

One of the flowers that everybody recognises, very common in lawns, with a stout rootstock, a rosette of leaves and single white and yellow flowers, 15–25 mm, usually pinkish-red on the backs of the ray florets. 8 cm. Mar–Oct.

Common mouse-ear
Cerastium fontanum

A creeping hairy perennial, found as a weed in gardens, and also on other disturbed ground and meadows. It has narrow, greyish-green leaves in pairs and white flowers, 10–15 mm. 40 cm. Apr–Sept.

White dead nettle
Lamium album

A common weed on disturbed ground and roadsides, with hairy stems. Its heart-shaped leaves are like the Stinging nettle's but without the sting. Two-lipped flowers, 20–25 mm, are in whorls at the base of the leaves. 60 cm. May–Dec.

Dandelion
Taraxacum officinale

A very well-known garden weed, also in meadows, disturbed ground and roadsides, with edible leaves, stems with milky juice and large flowerheads, 35–50 mm, whose fruit is the familiar "clock". 40 cm. Mar–Oct.

Creeping buttercup
Ranunculus repens
A short creeping perennial growing from runners, very common in damp places, and sometimes a troublesome garden weed. The flowers, 20–30 mm, differ from the Meadow buttercup (*p 23*), in having hairy stalks. To 60 cm. May–Aug.

Coltsfoot
Tussilago farfara
The round, toothed leaves (20 cm) appear after the flowers on this very common plant of bare ground including sand dunes. The flowerheads, 15–35 mm, are carried on white stems with purple scales. 10 cm. Mar–Apr.

Wallflower
Cheiranthus cheiri
An alien plant from Europe naturalised on old walls, castles and rock cuttings, with woody ridged stems, leaves 5–10 cm long (covered with forked hairs) and flowers 25 mm across. To 60 cm. Apr–June.

Red dead nettle
Lamium purpureum
A very common weed of disturbed ground, with smaller, purplish-pink flowers (10–15 mm) than those on the White dead nettle (*p 186*). It is a bushy annual and purple-tinged. 45 cm. Mar–Oct.

Yellow corydalis
Corydalis lutea
Introduced on walls in many places, a much-branched perennial with pinnate leaves (the leaflets being trefoil) and flowers, 12–18 mm, with a short spur. 30 cm. May–Aug.

Black medick
Medicago lupulina
Common in grass (lawns, meadows and roadsides), with trefoil leaves and dense heads of flowers (3–8 mm) which turn into curled pods. 35 cm. Apr–Aug.

Thyme-leaved speedwell
Veronica serpyllifolia
Very common in moist grass and disturbed ground, a prostrate perennial with upright flowering shoots. The leaves are opposite, and the flowers grow on long, loose spikes. Creeping to 30 cm. Mar–Oct.

Ivy-leaved speedwell
Veronica hederifolia
A very common weed of cultivated ground, with ivy-shaped leaves and blue flowers, on short stalks.

(Compare other Speedwells, *pp 16, 50, 75* and *164*). Prostrate to 60 cm. Mar–Aug.

Petty spurge
Euphorbia peplus
A common weed on cultivated ground, hairless, with oval leaves (3 cm) and an umbel of greenish flowers with horned glands (see also the other Spurges, *pp 36, 75, 88, 137* and *187*). 30 cm. Apr–Nov.

Fungi

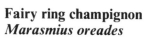

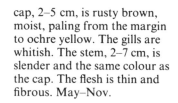

Lawyer's wig, Shaggy ink cap
Coprinus comatus

Occasionally these may cover entire fields, but are more typically found in small tufts on lawns, compost heaps and roadside verges. Edible when young, but they soon spoil. The cap, 6–15 cm, is high, white then pink or brown, with thick scales, becoming blackened to produce a thick black ink. The gills are white then purplish-black, and very crowded. The stem, 10–25 cm, is white and tapers above; the ring is thin. Apr–Nov.

Common ink cap
Coprinus atramentarius

Young specimens with white gills are delicious after cooking, but with alcohol produce palpitations and vomiting. In clusters on ground. The cap, 3–6 cm, is high, fleshy and grey, and scaly at the centre. The gills are white then black, broad and densely crowded, soon dissolving into a black ink. The stem, 6–20 cm, is white, tapering below, and smooth with a small ring near base. Apr–Nov.

Fairy ring champignon
Marasmius oreades

Much disliked by gardeners because it occurs in large numbers forming fairy rings on lawns and edges of paths. A well-known edible species, excellent when fried, but the tough stems are usually discarded. Do not mistake it for the poisonous *Clitocybe* species e.g. *C.dealbata (p 40)* which grows in the same locality. The cap, 2–5 cm, is rusty brown, moist, paling from the margin to ochre yellow. The gills are whitish. The stem, 2–7 cm, is slender and the same colour as the cap. The flesh is thin and fibrous. May–Nov.

Little Jap umbrella
Coprinus plicatilis

Common on lawns and grass verges; often solitary. The thin, pleated cap, resembling a Japanese parasol, is 2–3 cm, light grey or brownish with a brown central disc, and radially grooved. The gills are grey to black. The stem, 4–8 cm, is white, smooth and fragile. May–Nov.

Spring agaric
Agrocybe praecox

Found in spring, often by roadsides. Edible after cooking, but mediocre, it is recognized by its large thin ring and pale to reddish-brown gills. The cap, 2–6 cm, is ochre yellow to pale brown, with a shaggy margin. The stem, 6–9 cm, is slender and whitish discolouring brown. Apr–July.

Coprinus domesticus

Similar to the Glistening ink cap (*p 114*), but solitary or in groups of two or three. On dead wood, in gardens, on old walls or damp houses. The cap, 2–4 cm, is date brown and deeply grooved, often with a few granular scales. The gills darken, dissolving into black ink. The stem, 3–7 cm, is white and silky. Apr–Dec.

Weeping widow
Lacrymaria velutina
(*Psathyrella lacrymabunda*)

Near buildings and roads, also fields. The cap, 5–10 cm, is dull clay brown, with an incurved margin. The gills are mottled, brown to black with black droplets on the white edge. The stem, 5–12 cm, is clay colour, with a white ring which turns black. Apr–Nov.

Birds

House martin
Delichon urbica

A familiar species that has abandoned its historical cliff breeding sites to build its tiny nest of mud under the eaves of houses. It is smaller than the Swallow (*below*), with steel-blue (black-looking) underparts, white rump and white underparts from chin to tail. The adult has a pure white throat in contrast to its black head. The bill is small. The bird is an avid feeder, usually swooping low over water when it first arrives in spring from Africa, but generally flying higher than the Swallow. There is a flicking wing action in its wheeling flight and the triangular tail is very noticeable. There is a "tchirrup" call. In autumn birds gather on telephone wires, prior to migration. Some late broods are abandoned. Top Sixty. 12–13 cm. Summer visitor: Apr–mid Nov.

Swift
Apus apus

The most aerial of all species, built for speed and unmistakable with its torpedo body, scimitar-shaped wings and dark brown (black-looking) plumage. The throat is pale and the pale underwings flash in the sun. The long wings, short tail, all-dark plumage and custom of screaming in parties on summer evenings distinguish Swifts from Swallows and Martins. A Swift makes rapid, windmilling wing-beats in its careering flight. It has a distinctive, high, thin scream. Swifts breed exclusively under roof eaves in town and country. Otherwise, they spend all their lives in the air – feeding, mating, collecting nest material, drinking and even sleeping on the wing. Top Sixty. 16–17 cm. Summer visitor, seen everywhere late Apr–end Aug (stragglers until Oct).

Swallow
Hirundo rustica

The Swallow nests in buildings like barns and outhouses, reaching its nest unerringly and at high speed. Pairs tend to return to the same spot. The low-level, insect-catching flight is a common sight in early summer in parks and fields. Distinguished from Swifts and Martins by its flight, plumage (blue-black upperparts, redface, pinky-buff underparts – pure white in Sand martin, *p 155,* and long, forked tail. The female's tail streamers are shorter than the male's. The juvenile is pale, with a markedly shorter tail. Swallows spend much time in the air, but are often seen perched on wires or fences. They also land to gather mud for nest-building. The call is an emphatic "tswit-tswit" and the song a repeated twittering "feeta-feet". Top Sixty. 19 cm. Summer visitor (Apr–Oct), with very early arrivals Mar, stragglers Nov.

Magpie
Pica pica

Its shape, black and white plumage, weak-looking flight and harsh, chattering call make the Magpie unmistakable. The long green tail and the iridescent blue in the wings look black from a distance. The wings are rounded. Juvenile tails are shorter. Magpies have a deliberate tail-up walk and they also hop. Long glides are typical in flight. They are wary birds, occupying treetops and hedgerows in farmland, larger gardens, parks and even squares in many cities. Usually in pairs but also in greater numbers in winter. An early-nesting species, building being well under way by mid-March. The nest differs from other members of the Crow family: it is domed – usually in inaccessible places. Top Sixty. 46 cm. Resident.

Rook
Corvus frugilegus

Superficially resembling the Carrion crow (*opposite*), the shape is different and the Rook's major distinguishing feature is the adult's conspicuous bare "face" (a bare patch at the base of the bill). Rooks also have drooping flanks, giving them a "baggy trousers" look. Flight is faster and more flexible than Crows, showing more pointed wings and a wedge tail. Rook gait is more waddling. They are highly gregarious birds, nesting in colonies. There is an old birdwatchers' saying: "One Rook seen is a Crow, several Crows are Rooks"! Rook colonies are alive with activity and noisy squabbling during February as the old nests, standing out starkly at the top of the leafless trees, are patched up. The prolonged "kaak" call is higher-pitched than the Crow's. Mainly on farmland, but also gardens and towns. Top Sixty. 46 cm. Resident.

Hooded crow
Corvus corone cornix

Behaviour and habits are exactly the same as the Carrion crow's and only its grey body finely streaked with black sets the Hooded crow apart. However, they occupy different breeding ranges, although there is some overlapping and even interbreeding, resulting in half Carrion, half "Hoodie" hybrids. Hooded crows have a typical crow gait (more deliberate and less waddling than the Rook's). In flight their grey underwings are most apparent. Hooded crows always nest solitarily and are territorial. There is a very subtle distinction between the voices of the two species. In fields, scrub and near people. The Hooded crow replaces the Carrion species in Ireland and NW Scotland. Occasional winter visitor to England and Wales, especially on coast. 47 cm. Resident.

Carrion crow
Corvus corone corone

A common and widespread bird, with deep, croaking, cawing "kraah" and "kerwark" calls and all-black face which distinguish it from the Rook (*opposite*), although it may resemble a juvenile Rook. It has neat leg feathers without the Rook's "baggy trousers" and a shorter head than either Rook or Raven (*p 69*). Compare also the grey back of the Hooded crow (*above*). The Carrion crow's wings are square and the tail is rounded when soaring. It is a very wary bird, usually seen singly or in pairs, but may form small flocks (see the old saying about Crows and Rooks (*opposite*). It occupies very large urban centres, where the Rook is absent. The flight is slow and measured, the most deliberate

flight of all non-predators. Common except in Ireland and NW Scotland. Top Sixty. 47 cm. Resident.

SUMMER
Butterflies

Painted lady
Cynthia cardui

The Painted lady butterfly will feed on many sources of nectar and so will frequent a variety of habitats from gardens and farmland to hills and even mountains. A rapid flier and strong migrant, it may appear and breed anywhere in Europe. The first migrants may not arrive until June. The sexes are similar. The caterpillars' foodplant is Thistle. Wingspan: 54–58 mm. Flight: Apr–Oct.

Comma
Polygonia c-album

A lighter-coloured, less heavily marked first generation (*top*) is produced from eggs laid by overwintering Comma butterflies in the spring. A rapid flier, looking like a ragged Small tortoiseshell (*below left*), its name comes from the white mark like a comma on the underside hindwing. Apart from gardens, other habitats include meadows, hills and farmland where its foodplants (Nettle and Hop) are available for its two broods of caterpillars. Wingspan: 44–48 mm. Flight: Mar–July.

Small tortoiseshell
Aglais urticae

One of the commonest butterflies and generally easy to recognise. Apart from being smaller than Large tortoiseshell (*p 98*), it is usually brighter in colour, but this may vary between individuals. The hindwing has a large black basal area, whereas the Large tortoiseshell has a single black costal patch. Small tortoiseshells are common in gardens and often hibernate in houses. Other habitats are meadows, farmland generally and hills. The two broods of caterpillars feed on Stinging nettle. Wingspan; 44–50 mm. Flight: Mar–Apr, June–Oct.

Holly blue
Celastrina argiolus

The Holly blue prefers wooded areas to grassland and will visit gardens and clearings with trees and shrubs up to 1,500 m. The two generations of caterpillars have different foodplants – in spring, the female lays her eggs on Holly or Dogwood, while in summer the eggs are laid on Ivy. Adults of the two generations differ, (top and middle are first generation, bottom is second generation). The species has increased in recent years in S and C England, but is rare in Ireland. Wingspan: 26–34 mm. Flight: Mar–Apr, July–Aug.

Wild Flowers

Stinging nettle
Urtica dioica
A familiar weed of disturbed ground and woods, indicating past human occupation. It has creeping stems with erect shoots at intervals. The stems and leaves have stinging hairs. Flowers grow as long catkins. 1·5 m. June–Aug.

Annual nettle
Urtica urens
An annual like the Stinging nettle (left), but not so tall. It has both male and female flowers on leafy branches, whereas the Stinging nettle has them on separate plants. The leaves are long-stalked (Stinging nettle's are short). 45 cm. June–Sept.

White melilot
Melilotus alba
One of the Pea family, growing on disturbed ground and roadsides, with long spikes of white flowers and trefoil leaves. (Compare with Tall melilot, p 24). The fruit is hairless and brown. 1 m. July–Aug.

White stonecrop
Sedum album
Similar to English stonecrop (p 137), but with longer green leaves and branching, flat-topped heads of smaller flowers (9 mm). It is an evergreen, forming a carpet on walls and road edges. 15 cm. June–Aug.

Fool's parsley
Aethusa cynapium
A common weed in the S on disturbed ground, with two or three times pinnate leaves, and an umbel of 10–20 rays of white flowers. It is a perennial and hairless. The fruit is 4 mm and ridged. 1 m. July–Aug.

Ground elder
Aegopodium podagraria
A weed much dreaded by gardeners, forming extensive patches from runners. The leaves and leaflets are trefoil. The flowers are minute, in an umbel 60 mm diameter. Creeps to 1 m. May–July.

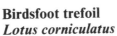

Birdsfoot trefoil
Lotus corniculatus
Very common on meadows and disturbed ground, with heads of two to six yellow or orange flowers and pods which twist spirally when they split. There are five leaflets, but two bend back to give a trefoil appearance. 20 cm. June–Sept.

Catsear
Hypochoeris radicata
Common on roadsides and meadows, with a rosette of hairy leaves. The top of the branching flower shoot is swollen and has scale bracts. The flowerheads are 25–40 mm across. 50 cm. June–Sept.

Oxford ragwort
Senecio squalidus
Spread by being carried along railway lines from its home in the Physick Gardens in Oxford and common on walls, disturbed ground and woods. Much shorter than the 1·5 m Ragwort (p 127) and Marsh ragwort (p 161). 25 cm. May–Dec.

Hedge mustard
Sisymbrium officinale
Very common on disturbed ground and road edges, a stiffly erect annual with downward-pointing stem hairs and base leaves in a rosette. The flowers, 3 mm, are pale yellow. The pods are cylindrical. 90 cm. June–Aug.

Wall lettuce
Mycelis muralis
Growing on walls and in shady places, with thin, often reddish leaves which have a large top lobe itself three-lobed. The flowers are 7–10 mm. 1 m. July–Sept.

London rocket
Sisymbrium irio
Not unlike Hedge mustard (*left*), growing on roadsides, walls and disturbed ground, but much rarer, shorter and with no base leaf rosette. Appeared in quantities after the Great Fire of London in 1666. 40 cm. June–Aug.

Smooth sowthistle
Sonchus oleraceus
A common weed, with hollow branching stems giving out a milky juice. The leaves are spiny and the flowers 25 mm. (Compare other Sowthistles, *p 23, 171*). 1·5 m. June–Aug.

Broad-leaved willowherb
Epilobium montanum
Much shorter than the Rosebay and with tiny flowers, 6–9 mm, this is the commonest willowherb growing in wasteplaces and walls. The leaves are broad and rounded at the base. 40 cm. June–Aug.

Creeping cinquefoil
Potentilla reptans
On road edges and disturbed ground, a prostrate plant with long rooting stems and erect flowering shoots. The flowers are 17–25 mm. The leaves have five to seven lobes. 30 cm. June–Sept.

Snapdragon
Antirrhinum majus
Naturalised on old walls and rock cuttings, a woody perennial varying in flower colour. The flowers (40 mm) do not have spurs. 80 cm. July–Sept.

Rosebay willowherb
Epilobium angustifolium
A very common, tall perennial of disturbed ground and heaths. The large flowers, 20–30 mm, are rosy-purple and the resultant pods break open to give a cottony appearance. 1 m. July–Sept.

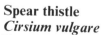

Spear thistle
Cirsium vulgare
Very common on disturbed ground and roadsides, with spiny wings up its ridged stem and very spiny leaves. The flowerheads are globular and pale purple, 20–40 mm across. 1·5 m. July–Oct.

Teasel
Dipsacus fullonum
On roadsides and by hedges, a very tall, prickly biennial whose flowerheads are extremely noticeable, being large, spiny and round (60 mm across and up to 80 mm long). The dead heads survive through the winter. 2 m. July–Aug.

Fungi

Agaricus nivescens

The fruitbody is pure white and although it bruises yellow it does not acquire the overall ochre yellow appearance of the Horse mushroom (*p 43*) growing in groups under trees. The cap, 5–15 cm, is white and silky, with pale pink then black gills. The stem, 8–10 cm, is not swollen at the base, white discolouring yellow; the ring is white. The thick flesh smells of almond. Edible. June–Sept.

Agaricus bitorquis (edulis)

An edible species, often found in towns, always away from trees, and may appear between paving stones. The cap, 5–9 cm, is smooth, not scaly, white to slightly ochre, yellowing to the touch. The gills are pale pink to chocolate brown and very crowded. The stem, 4–6 cm, has two persistent rings; the lower ring is thin, the upper one more complex. The flesh is thick, white and firm. May–Oct.

Lyophyllum connatum

Forms pure white clusters by the sides of paths, sometimes in long rows. Likes rich, cultivated peaty soil. It has a distinctive alkaline smell and although edible when young it should always be boiled first. Do not confuse with the poisonous white *Clitocybe* species (*see Index*). The cap, 5–10 cm, is white to pale cream, greyish when moist, with a wavy margin. The gills are white to cream. The stem, 3–8 cm, has a swollen base, and is white to greyish. The flesh is white and firm. Aug–Oct.

Stinking parasol
Lepiota cristata

The thin white flesh of this poisonous species of grassy places and garden refuse smells rubbery. The cap, 2–5 cm, is white, with small red-brown crowded scales. The gills are white. The stem, 2–6 cm, is slender and white, with a narrow white ring. Aug–Oct.

Giant clitocybe
Leucopaxillus giganteus

A large white mushroom, exceptionally up to 45 cm tall, which often forms fairy rings in grassy places in parks and gardens. The cap, 15–30 cm, is creamy white, sometimes with silky scales at the centre, with a thin margin at first incurved. The gills are white to pale brown, and very crowded. The stem, 3–10 cm, is stout, whitish and fibrous. The flesh is white and firm. Poisonous. July–Sept.

195

Rose-gilled grisette
Volvariella speciosa
Resembles an *Amanita* species, but has pink gills and lacks a ring. Found on rich soil, often on compost heaps and in woodland. Edible after cooking, but not recommended. The cap, 8–14 cm, is sticky, whitish-grey to brownish. The gills are cream then flesh pink. The stem, 10–18 cm, is satiny white, bruising brown. June–Oct.

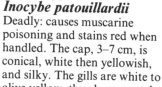

Shaggy parasol
Macrolepiota rhacodes
Delicious when grilled or fried, but often avoided because the flesh turns red when broken. It is smaller and sturdier than the Parasol mushroom (*p 30*), with large scales on the cap and a smooth stem. Grows in rings on disturbed soil and compost heaps. The cap, 5–15 cm, is dry, grey-brown with a central disc and shaggy margin. The gills are whitish-grey, reddening. The stem, 10–16 cm, is greyish-white, smooth and dry; the very thick moveable ring is white and scaly. The flesh is white, turning saffron red on exposure. There is a large, bulbous stem base. Aug–Oct.

Inocybe patouillardii
Deadly: causes muscarine poisoning and stains red when handled. The cap, 3–7 cm, is conical, white then yellowish, and silky. The gills are white to olive yellow, then brown, and crowded. The stem, 4–7 cm, is robust and white. May–Nov.

Brown cone cap
Conocybe tenera
Usually grows singly, but several of the tall, slender fruitbodies may occur together amongst grass. The cap, 1–3 cm, is conical, ochre brown paling to yellowish. The gills are cinnamon brown. The stem, 8–10 cm, the same colour as the cap, darkens towards the base, and is powdery. May–Nov.

Brown hay cap
Panaeolina foenisecii
Sometimes called "Mower's mushroom". Very numerous on lawns. Has caused mild poisoning in children. The cap, 1–2 cm, is dull brown, drying paler from the centre. The gills are mottled, pale brown then umber. The stem, 2–5 cm, is brown with a pale apex. June–Oct.

Melanoleuca brevipes
Found often by cinder paths. Similar to the more common *M. melaleuca* (*p 104*), but the stem is dark brown and shorter than the cap diameter. The cap, 5–8 cm, is convex then flat, umber brown becoming paler, smooth and moist. The gills are white and crowded. The stem, is short, 2–4 cm. Edible after cooking. June–Oct.

Lepista sordida
The grey or lilac flesh has a watery appearance and is thinner than other *Lepista* species. Can occur in very large numbers on compost heaps and is often found under hedgerows. Edible after cooking. The cap, 2–7 cm, is greyish-lilac to brownish-violet, drying paler. The gills are lilac to grey-brown, and fairly crowded. The stem, 4–6 cm, often curved, is the same colour as the cap. July–Nov.

Birds

Robin
Erithacus rubecula

The bold, tame bird on a million Christmas cards, familiar in gardens, parks and fields, yet also a shy, little seen woodland bird. In summer juveniles have speckled plumage which does not moult into the adult red breast until the end of October. A highly aggressive bird, especially in the breeding season when it may resort to physical fighting (rare among birds). Both sexes, which are alike, hold territories in winter. The habit of cocking the head and precise deliberate movements on the ground are distinctive. The rear view (*left picture*) shows the narrow head and the typical drooping wing position. The bird has an easy, undulating flight and quizzical alert feeding behaviour. The call is a persistent "tick-tick" and also a low "tsip". It sings all the year round. Top Sixty. 14 cm. Resident.

Bullfinch
Pyrrhula pyrrhula

A retiring bird whose bright colours identify it. The male has a black cap, pink breast and white rump. The female is duller, but always seen with the male. Juveniles have no cap but otherwise are like females. Flight is slow and gently undulating. Common in gardens and hedges, though usually feeds on woodland fringes. Bullfinches are disliked by orchard owners as they eat buds in spring. They also pick seeds on the ground, Located by the distinct, soft "pheeu" call. Young birds have a squealing call. Top Sixty. 14–16 cm. Resident.

House sparrow
Passer domesticus

A cheeky, aggressive, garrulous bird going wherever man goes and almost always breeding in buildings. In July, vast flocks gather in rural areas to feed on cereal crops and are a serious pest. Sparrows have catholic appetites. Town birds are dingier than country birds. Shape and colour pattern varies with posture. Can be slim and erect or low and rounded. The birds have a thick bill (compare Dunnock, *p 198*). Only the male has a black bib. The female is lighter overall and the juvenile is like her. Flight is direct and swift, but undulating over a distance. Sparrows build untidy nests in wall cavities, hedges or ivy. They make chirruping calls, but have no song. Top Sixty. 14–15 cm. Resident.

Dunnock (Hedge sparrow)
Prunella modularis

Quieter than the House sparrow (no relation), from which it is distinguished by its thin bill, grey head, breast and underparts, speckled buff flanks and orange eye. It occupies many habitats (parks, gardens, scrub, wood and farmland) as it picks delicately for food. It frequently flicks its wings and tail. Flight is unhurried and undulating. The call is a high, piping "tseep" and a trilling note. The song is a pleasant warble heard all year round. Top Sixty. 14–15 cm. Resident.

Grey wagtail
occasionally nests in urban habitats. see p 175.

Black redstart
Phoenicurus ochrurus

Larger than the Redstart, but not very common, the Black redstart has similar behaviour including the distinctive tail-shivering, but spends more time feeding on the ground. The summer male has a jet-black body and white wing panel. In winter his black upperparts are replaced with sooty grey (*see p 204*). The sooty brown female lacks the Redstart's eye ring and pale throat. Nests in S England in city buildings like power stations. The song is like jangling keys. 14 cm. Resident. Some winter and passage birds.

AUTUMN
Butterflies

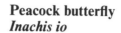

♀

♂

Large white
Pieris brassicae

Capable of completely stripping a cabbage of its leaves, the caterpillars of the Large (or Cabbage) white butterfly can be a serious garden pest. (Other habitats are fields and meadows, especially on chalk and limestone.) Surprisingly, the resident population is fairly small, numbers being increased each year by an influx of migrants from across the Channel. Specimens from the first summer generation are larger with more black on their wing tips than those seen in spring and autumn. Foodplant: Cabbage (especially). Wingspan: 57–66 mm. Flight: Apr–Oct.

Peacock butterfly
Inachis io

The Peacock must be one of the most conspicuous butterflies, impossible to confuse with any other, with its large "peacock eye" on each wing. It is well camouflaged by its very dark underside when at rest, but, if disturbed, the eye-spots on its upperside can startle predators. The female is slightly larger. Although not migratory, the Peacock is both common and widespread in many habitats. The adult overwinters often in buildings from late summer and autumn onwards, though it may emerge during mild winter spells. Apart from gardens and meadows, it is found on hills and farmland generally, especially in chalk and limestone areas. There is one brood of caterpillars a year, feeding on Nettle. Wingspan: 54–60 mm. Flight: July–Oct and spring.

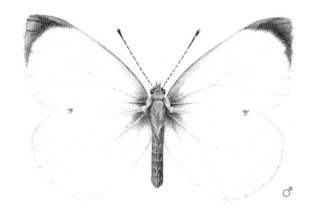

♂

♂

Wild Flowers

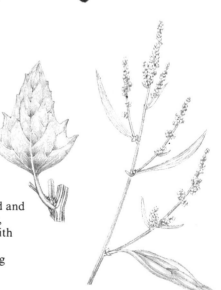

Hedge bindweed
Calystegia sepium

A very common and persistent garden weed (also growing in hedges), which climbs and clings anticlockwise. The large white flowers, 60 mm, are trumpet-shaped. The leaves are also large, and arrow-shaped. To 2 m. July–Sept.

Common orache
Atriplex patula

Very common in cultivated and disturbed ground, an erect, branching mealy annual with spikes of tiny flowers. The lower leaves have spreading lobes, the upper ones are narrow. 90 cm. Sept–Oct.

Gallant soldier
Galinsoga parviflora
A weed of disturbed ground
with opposite pairs of oval
leaves and small white flowers
with yellow discs. 60 cm.
May–Nov.

Mugwort
Artemisia vulgaris
Common in waste places
generally, on roadsides and
disturbed ground and by
hedges. It is a tufted aromatic
plant with dense spikes of small
flowerheads, 2 mm. The stem
has scattered hairs. 1·2 m.
July–Sept.

Nipplewort
Lapsana communis
A tall branching annual with
pale yellow flowerheads
(15–20 mm), a rosette of lower
leaves with a large end lobe and
oval upper leaves. Common on
roadsides and by hedges. 90 cm.
July–Sept.

Smooth hawksbeard
Crepis capillaris
Common on disturbed ground
and in meadows, with lobed
base leaves and arrow-shaped
stem ones. The flowerheads,
10 mm, are in loose clusters.
70 cm. June–Sept.

Common toadflax
Linaria vulgaris
The yellow flowers, 25 mm,
look like small Antirrhinums,
but with a spur. The leaves are
very narrow and grow up the
stem. Common on roadsides
and meadows. 60 cm. July–Oct.

Creeping thistle
Cirsium arvense
A persistent garden weed, and
very common on roadsides and
in meadows where it forms
patches. It has dull mauve
flowerheads, 15–25 mm, and
spiny leaves. The stems do not
have spiny wings. 1 m.
July–Sept.

Black horehound
Ballota nigra
Common on disturbed ground,
roadsides and by hedges, a
nasty-smelling perennial with
very branched stems, hairy oval
leaves and dense whorls of
purplish-pink flowers
(12–18 mm). 1 m. June–Oct.

Pellitory of the wall
Parietaria diffusa
A typical plant of walls and
rocks, also hedges, covered in
non-stinging hairs. The male
flowers are in clusters on the
side of the stems, female flowers
at the stem tips. Leaves are
oval. 1 m. June–Oct.

Field bindweed
Convolvulus arvensis
A widespread and persistent weed dreaded by gardeners, and also found at roadsides. It climbs anticlockwise. The pink flowers, 20 mm, often have paler stripes and the leaves are arrow-shaped. To 75 cm. June–Sept.

Redshank
Polygonum persicaria
Very common on disturbed ground, roadsides and meadows, a hairless, branched perennial with lance-shaped leaves, often having a dark blotch. The flowers are in dense spikes. 80 cm. June–Oct.

Self heal
Prunella vulgaris
Found on disturbed ground and also meadows, the stems and oval leaves, 50 mm, are often purplish. The violet flowers which grow in dense clusters are two-lipped. 20 cm. June–Sept.

Lesser burdock
Arctium minus
Common on roadsides, waste places and woods, a thick-stemmed bushy biennial with large heart-shaped leaves. The arching stems have many egg-shaped flowerheads, 15–30 mm, with spiny bracts which become burs on the fruit. 1·3 m. July–Sept.

Ribwort plantain
Plantago lanceolata
One of the commonest grassland plants, by roadsides and in meadows, with long, narrow leaves (15 cm) and flowerheads which are blackish-brown with creamy anthers. They are carried on a very long deeply furrowed stalk. 40 cm. Apr–Oct.

Greater plantain
Plantago major
Very common on lawns and paths, with large leaves (15 cm long and almost as broad, though they can be much narrower in long grass). The flowerheads can be 15 cm tall and have purple anthers that turn yellow. 20 cm. May–Sept.

Fat hen
Chenopodium album
An ancient food plant replaced by spinach and common everywhere on disturbed ground. It has erect, often red-tinged stems, dark green or mealy leaves, varying in shape. The flowers are tiny and in spikes. 1 m. July–Oct.

Broad-leaved dock
Rumex obtusifolius
Very common on disturbed ground, with broad leaves to 25 cm long and hairy underneath. The flowers are in whorls. The fruit has a prominent red warty swelling. 70 cm. June–Oct.

Ivy
Hedera helix
A common woody climber on walls and trees, clinging by its aerial roots. The leaves have three to five lobes and are glossy. The green flowers are in umbels and the berries are black. To 30 m. Sept–Nov.

Fungi

Yellow-staining mushroom
Agaricus xanthodermus
Poisonous: one of the few *Agaricus* species to cause discomfort when eaten. The white surface bruises bright chrome yellow and has an inky or carbolic smell. In clusters amongst leaf mould. The cap, 6–15 cm, is white or slightly greyish at centre, with very fine scales. The gills are pale then flesh pink, and finally black-brown. The stem, 8–15 cm, is white staining yellow at the base with a large, thick ring. The flesh is white, chrome yellow in the stem base. July–Oct.

Cultivated mushroom
Agaricus bisporus
The only commercially grown mushroom in Britain, representing a multi-million pound industry; also produced in nearly every other country. The history of its cultivation dates back to 1700. (Distinguished from the Field mushroom (*p 30*) mainly by its large, fleshy ring.) The cap of the cultivated form is smooth and pure white, but in the wild it may develop dark brown fibrous scales. Grows in groups on rich soil. The cap, 5–10 cm, is white to greyish-brown with small, brown scales. The gills are bright pink to blackish-brown. The stem, 3–5 cm, is thick, white, with a rather cottony surface; the ring is white, thick and membranous. The flesh is white, turning slightly red on exposure. July–Sept.

Honey fungus
Armillaria mellea
Kills many trees in gardens and woodland, growing in tufts from stumps in huge numbers, thereby dreaded by gardeners since it spreads by black, bootlace-like structures under bark. Edible after cooking but reject stems and old caps. The cap, 5–25 cm, is scaly and honey yellow to rust. The gills are white to yellow and rust-spotted. The scaly stem, 10–20 cm, is tough with a fleshy ring. June–Nov.

Psathyrella gracilis
Tall and graceful with a brittle cap, sometimes found in large numbers, often in long grass. The cap, 1–3 cm, is reddish-brown drying to pale tan. The gills are greyish-black with a pink edge. The stem, 3–10 cm, is long and slender, smooth and white. Aug–Nov.

Conocybe rickenii
Often found in enormous numbers in gardens where the soil has been enriched with horse manure. The cap, 1–4 cm, is pale ochre yellow to cream. The gills are yellowish-brown. The stem, 2–10 cm, is white to pale brown and powdery. Aug–Oct.

Liberty cap
Psilocybe semilanceata
Found in small to large groups on grass but not tufted. Poisonous, it may produce delirium within a couple of hours. The cap, 5–10 mm, is sharply conical, and a pale tan drying to creamy buff. It is sticky when wet, with an incurved margin. The gills are purplish-brown with a white edge. The stem, 4–8 cm, is tough, wavy and pale. Aug–Nov.

Agrocybe erebia

Typically found on shady embankments amongst loose soil but only in the autumn. It lacks the mealy smell of the Spring agaric (*p 188*). The cap, 2–6 cm, is dark brown when moist, drying to a clay colour. The gills are pale to cinnamon brown. The stem, 2–5 cm, is grey-brown, with a white, narrow, membranous ring which finally turns brown. Sept–Nov.

Lyophyllum decastes (*Tricholoma aggregatum*)

The dense clusters occur around stumps or on buried roots from summer onwards. The tough flesh is edible after cooking but may cause a burning sensation. The cap, 4–12 cm, is fleshy, and umber to reddish-brown. The gills are white to yellowish and crowded. The stem, 5–10 cm, is whitish to greyish-brown and fibrous. The flesh is white. July–Oct.

Tricholoma terreum

A very common, widespread species found at the edge of woods or paths. It is edible after cooking and suitable for soups, but if in doubt all grey *Tricholoma* species should be avoided. Has a fungal not mealy, smell. The dark grey scaly cap, 4–8 cm, is dry, radially fibrillose, exposing white flesh. The gills are white, often greyish towards the margin. The stem, 3–8 cm, is solid, dry and whitish. Sept–Nov.

Panaeolus subbalteatus

Larger and more robust than other *Panaeolus* species and quite commonly found forming tufts of two–four fruitbodies on newly manured soil in gardens. Poisonous. The cap, 2–4 cm, is dark brown when moist, drying paler from the centre. The gills are mottled, dark brown and crowded. The stem, 4–8 cm, is paler than the cap and hollow. July–Oct.

Birds

Greenfinch
Carduelis chloris

By autumn the Greenfinch is flocking and roosting communally, returning to gardens for bird tables and nut bags. It is a heavy, muscular finch with a strong bill, long wings and a short, forked, black and yellow tail. Males have grey in the wings. Females are browner above and not as bright and the juvenile is streaked. An aggressive and quarrelsome bird, the call is a rapid, harsh trill and a drawn out, nasal "sweee". The flight is very undulating. Top Sixty. 14–15 cm. Resident.

Chaffinch
Fringilla coelebs

One of the commonest birds, in gardens, parks, meadows, woods and scrub, as it hops with low, jerky movements. Often the slight head peak is visible. The white shoulder patch is a good field mark, and so are the male's wing pattern and bright colours. Unlike the Brambling (p 108) it has a pink (not orange) breast and black and white tail. Females and juveniles are duller. Feeds sometimes in flocks with other finches. Its extremely undulating flight shows its green rump and double white wing-bars as well as its white underwing. Its usual loud "chink-chink" call can be confused with the Great tit's, but not its "chip" flight call song. Top Sixty. 15 cm. Resident.

Starling
Sturnus vulgaris

Very common, aggressive, garrulous birds, carrolling and chattering away on rooftops or swooping down to waddle about and vie for food. Very common in all urban and agricultural habitats, with a vast influx from the Continent in winter. The heavily marked plumage is glossy and iridescent with buff-tipped back feathers, spotted underparts and heavily spotted, almost greyish head. The juvenile is grey-brown with a pale throat, later acquiring semi-juvenile, semi-adult plumage. It is the only bird that pecks at the ground with an open bill when feeding and also that sings with open mouth and wings flapping slowly. There is a very wide vocabulary of songs and calls (generally a harsh, churring call and pleasant, gurgling song). Flight is swift and direct with a series of wing-beats followed by a glide. The tail looks fan-shaped then and the contrast between the pale underwing and black underparts distinguishes Starlings from Blackbirds. Top Sixty. 21–22 cm. Resident.

Black redstart
*in winter,
see p 198.*

Blackbird
Turdus merula

The male Blackbird is the only member of the thrush family and the only common garden bird that is jet black. It has a yellow eye-ring and bill. The bill has a brown tip in winter. The female is a dark brown version of the male with indistinct spots on her breast and a black tail. The juvenile is like a ginger-bodied female, but its shape identifies it. Many whitish mutations occur. A flicking, gliding flight as well as its profile identify a Blackbird. It is a noisy, excitable bird, given to much tail-flicking, with a rattling alarm call, low "tchook-tchook" call and "chink" call at dusk. It sings its lovely song from a roof, tree or wall. In parks, gardens, woods, scrub and farmland. In November, there are large-scale communal roosts in dense thickets (up to 2000 birds have been recorded) in company with other thrush species. 25 cm. Top Sixty. Resident and winter visitor.

Feral (Town) pigeon
Columba livia

This domesticated descendant of the Rock dove occurs in a wide variety of forms. Flocks may sometimes be seen in fields feeding with racing pigeons and they are often seen with Jackdaws (*p 109*) on large, ornate buildings which provide breeding ledges. Feral pigeons occur in every sort of plumage from white through chequer patterns to black. They have stouter bills than the Rock dove. The lower picture (*far right*) shows a Feral pigeon in the plumage phase which most resembles the Rock dove. There is a typical sailing display flight, often preceded by slow, deliberate flaps of the wing. The birds have an extended breeding season, nesting through the winter, as a result of the abundant food supply in towns. Top Sixty. 33 cm. Resident.

Collared dove
Streptopelia decaota

A heavy dove, very pale with a long tail and broad wings, which are held back in its deliberate, flicking flight. It is larger than the Turtle dove (*p 18*), with duller grey plumage, a different tail pattern, much more white in the tail and a noticeable black neck bar. In display, it rises almost vertically and sails around on spread wings. Its fawn and grey, as well as dark wing tips, are unlike other doves. It raises its tail on landing. Its ground feeding and other habits are very like those of Pigeons. It has a "coo, coo, cuck" call which can be irritating (unlike the Wood pigeon's soothing "coo-coo-coo") and a buzzing nasal display note. First nesting in Britain in 1955 and now distributed widely, the Collared dove population has expanded to such proportions that the species can now be controlled legally as a pest. In gardens, parks and city centres, as well as farmland, grain stores and scrub. 32 cm. Resident.

Kestrel
Falco tinnunculus

The commonest bird of prey occurring everywhere from city centres to bleak moorland, but probably most frequently seen hovering above motorway verges to clean up the bodies of animal car victims. It is distinguished from the Hobby, Merlin and Sparrowhawk by its long tail and its habit of continuous hovering. It has a typical falcon flight – a series of flaps interspersed with glides and it frequently soars. It "slides" down steeply to take prey from the hover. The principal food is voles, but it will take small birds and large insects. A kestrel may be seen perching on trees, buildings and power lines. The male has a blue-grey head, rump and tail (though this colour is often hard to see), with a black band on the tail and darker wing tips (also possessed by the female). She and the juvenile are reddish-brown above with a strongly barred, black-banded tail. Kestrels nest in buildings, trees or suitable nest boxes. It has a high-pitched "qui-qui-qui" call. 32–35 cm. Resident, but also winter visitor.

WINTER
Wild Flowers

Common chickweed
Stellaria media
A very common, straggly weed on disturbed ground having tiny, white flowers with cleft petals (to 10 mm) and hairy stems. The leaves grow in pairs and are oval. To 40 cm. All year round.

Hairy bittercress
Cardamine hirsuta
Common on bare ground and walls, with a neat rosette of pinnate leaves and inconspicuous white flowers, 2–4 mm, often concealed by its long pods. 20 cm. Flowers nearly all year round.

Shepherd's purse
Capsella bursa-pastoris
One of the commonest weeds of disturbed ground, most conspicuous by its rows of pods. The triangular shape of the pod gives it its name. Leaves are usually mainly in a base rosette. 25 cm. All year.

Groundsel
Senecio vulgaris
Very common on disturbed ground, with clusters of yellow flowerheads and lobed leaves, often with woolly hairs. The flowers, 10 mm, seldom have ray florets. 45 cm. All year.

Fungi

Scurfy tubaria
Tubaria furfuracea
Commonly found in large numbers in the autumn, but may occur throughout the year, growing both on the soil and on woody debris. The scurfy cap, 1–4 cm, is much paler when dry. It is wavy, cinnamon brown drying to pale tan. The gills are cinnamon brown. The stem, 2–5 cm, the same colour as the cap, has a white, woolly base. Jan–Dec.

Blewit
Lepista saeva
One of the best edible species with thick, white flesh, but not easily found. Likes chalky soil and may form large rings. Can tolerate very cold weather. The cap, 5–12 cm, is fleshy, dull grey-brown and smooth. The gills are grey to whitish, thin and crowded. The stem, 5–10 cm, is stocky, violet to mauve and fibrous-scaly. Roadsides, parks and wasteland. Nov–Feb.

Birds

Wren
Troglodytes troglodytes

Brownish upperparts, greyish underparts and quick, jerky movements create a mouse-like appearance in one of Britain's smallest birds. It is often seen on a branch bobbing confidently with its remarkably short tail cocked. The bill is slightly curved. The flight is direct, whirring and fast. It has a loud, scolding "tit-tit-tit" call, often changing to a "churring" note. The song is amazingly loud for so small a bird and can be heard in a mild January. The commonest British bird, found everywhere. It is severely hit by hard winters when large groups of Wrens huddle together for warmth – even an amazing 61 in a nest box! Top Sixty. 9–10 cm. Resident.

Blue tit
Parus caeruleus

The commonest British tit, a woodland bird that has adapted well to man and is frequently seen in gardens, especially at peanut bags in winter. It readily takes to nest boxes. Bold patterns on its face and body and the white wing-bar catch the eye. The black eye stripe shows clearly, but the central belly streak is always very variable. There is a small compact blue crown, raised when the bird is excited or angry. The flight is fast and undulating with flicking wing-beats. Males spread their wings (*right hand picture*) for an unusual floating "butterfly" display flight. Top Sixty. 11–12 cm. Resident.

Great tit
Parus major

The largest of the tits and so less acrobatic. Great tits are active, inquisitive and quarrelsome, frequent visitors to bird tables and users of nest boxes. They are sparrow-sized, with a bold black and white head pattern, yellow breast and apple-green back. There is a pale nape patch and a well-marked tail with white outer feathers. The pale wing-bar and white cheeks show in flight. There is less black on the female. The juvenile has a brownish crown and yellowish cheeks. Great tits often feed agilely on nut bags, especially in winter. Note the thicker black belly stripe of the male lower down the string of nuts. There is a distinctive "tsink-tsink" call, a "teecher-teecher-teecher" call in spring and many other sounds. Common in woods and gardens, also fields and scrub. Top Sixty. 14 cm. Resident.

Nuthatch
Sitta europaea

An ebulliant, restless, noisy bird, whose loud, whistling call, constant movement up, down and around branches and trunks (habitually descending them head downwards) and demonic facial expression are unmistakable. So also are its blue-grey back, bold black eye stripe and pale underparts. It will suddenly take swift flight in a jerky, hesitant, woodpecker-like way which shows its grey upperparts and its variable orange-buff underparts.

However, often only a silhouette of a flying bird is visible. Nuthatches nest in tree holes whose size they may reduce with a mud lining. Found in deciduous woodland, farmland and wooded gardens. On a December day its loud whistling "hweet-hweet" call, similar to a human wolf whistle, can be heard from the topmost branches. 14 cm. Resident.

Redwing
Turdus iliacus

The smallest and darkest of the thrushes, seen feeding gregariously in open fields. It is generally retiring and only in severe weather moves from the berry hedges, woods and open farmland into gardens to exploit food put out for birds. The red flanks, prominent eye stripe and heavily streaked underparts show at close range.

The Redwing has a yellow bill. It looks small in flight, with a characteristic wing-flicking action. From above, it looks similar to the Song thrush, (*p 210*), but its red underwing may be compared with the Song thrush's orange one. The Redwing hops when feeding on the ground. It takes berries (e.g. Hawthorn). It has a penetrating "steep" call. Breeds in Scotland. Top Sixty. 21 cm. Winter visitor in huge numbers: Oct–Apr.

Fieldfare
Turdus pilaris

Larger than the Song thrush (*p 210*) with long wings and tail, the Fieldfare resembles the Mistle thrush in build and flight (*p 210*). It feeds on berries or on open ground in fields, woods and scrub and, in severe weather, gardens. Both sexes have a creamy, spotted breast, grey head, chestnut back, grey rump and black tail.

It is an extremely wary bird, with a harsh, chattering "cha-cha-chack" call. Flying in loose flocks is typical of the species, and the waving, erratic flight resembles that of the Mistle thrush. Now breeding sporadically from Shetland to Pennines. Top Sixty. 25–26 cm. Common winter visitor: Oct–Apr.

Song thrush
Turdus philomelos

One of the commonest and most widespread garden birds, also seen in woods, farmland and other open countryside with trees and bushes. It has arrow-shaped breast spots, a crescent behind the eye and a dark streak on either side of the throat which distinguishes it from the Mistle thrush (*below*). It has no obvious marks on its back. Its underparts are creamy yellow and heavily spotted. Its feeding behaviour is distinctive – hops interspersed with short runs are broken by upright, watchful pauses. Song thrushes use a large stone or rock as an anvil to break open snails for a meal, although sometimes Blackbirds steal the opened snail from them! Song thrushes also eat worms and berries. They have a "tick" or "tsip" flight call and a song of repeated phrases. They usually sing in a tree, whereas the Mistle thrush prefers a treetop perch for its song. Top Sixty. 23 cm. Resident.

Mistle thrush
Turdus viscivorus

The largest and boldest of the thrushes, known as the "Storm cock" because it sings loudly in a storm. Its pot belly and long wings and tail in flight, together with the very upright, barrel-chested stance, are distinctive. The bird is greyer than the Song thrush (*above*), with heavier build and shape. Its breast is more boldly patterned. From behind, the pale edges to its wings contrast with the uniform back of the Song thrush. The flight is deeply undulating with periodic closure of the wings and the white underwing shows. There is a loud, chattering "football-rattle" call and a ringing song with no repeated phrases. The song starts very early in the year, peaking in February when the bird is sitting on eggs. Top Sixty. 27 cm. Resident.

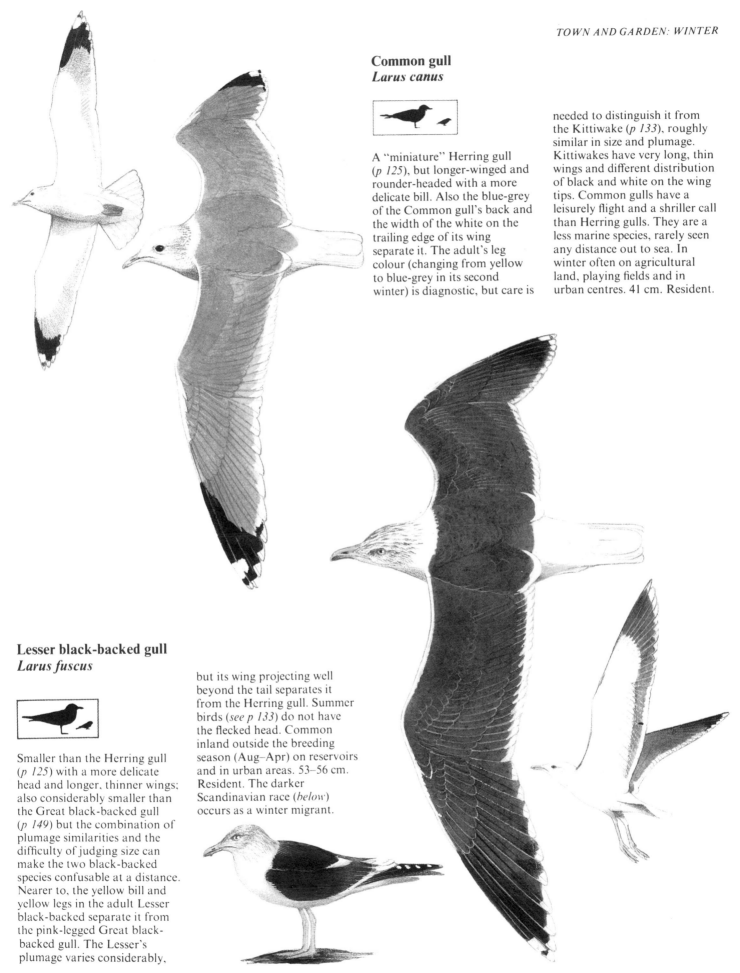

Common gull
Larus canus

A "miniature" Herring gull (*p 125*), but longer-winged and rounder-headed with a more delicate bill. Also the blue-grey of the Common gull's back and the width of the white on the trailing edge of its wing separate it. The adult's leg colour (changing from yellow to blue-grey in its second winter) is diagnostic, but care is needed to distinguish it from the Kittiwake (*p 133*), roughly similar in size and plumage. Kittiwakes have very long, thin wings and different distribution of black and white on the wing tips. Common gulls have a leisurely flight and a shriller call than Herring gulls. They are a less marine species, rarely seen any distance out to sea. In winter often on agricultural land, playing fields and in urban centres. 41 cm. Resident.

Lesser black-backed gull
Larus fuscus

Smaller than the Herring gull (*p 125*) with a more delicate head and longer, thinner wings; also considerably smaller than the Great black-backed gull (*p 149*) but the combination of plumage similarities and the difficulty of judging size can make the two black-backed species confusable at a distance. Nearer to, the yellow bill and yellow legs in the adult Lesser black-backed separate it from the pink-legged Great black-backed gull. The Lesser's plumage varies considerably, but its wing projecting well beyond the tail separates it from the Herring gull. Summer birds (*see p 133*) do not have the flecked head. Common inland outside the breeding season (Aug–Apr) on reservoirs and in urban areas. 53–56 cm. Resident. The darker Scandinavian race (*below*) occurs as a winter migrant.

Index

Each of the four categories in the book, Butterflies, Wild Flowers, Fungi and Birds, are indexed separately. English names appear in Roman, Latin names in *Italic* throughout. Where an individual bird, butterfly, fungus or wild flower has both an English and a Latin name, both names appear in the Index as separate entries.

Fungi

Fungi are listed under their full names, for example, "Death cap" is listed under "D" whereas "False death cap" is listed under "F".

Birds

To look up a bird in the Index, find the species or family name first. Individual members will then be listed alphabetically underneath the species or family name. For example, "Tern" is followed by "Arctic", "Common", "Little" and "Sandwich", all Tern varieties.

Acknowledgements

PHOTOGRAPHER
Martin Dohrn

ILLUSTRATORS
Butterflies
Richard Lewington
Fungi
Patrick Cox, Colin Emberson, Gill Tomblin
Wild Flowers
Jac Jones, Josephine Martin, Nina Roberts,
Kathleen Smith, Gill Tomblin
Birds
Peter Hayman

Where applicable text has been
adapted from the following titles
published by Mitchell Beazley
Publishers:
Butterflies   Paul Whalley
Mushrooms and Toadstools   David N. Pegler
Wild Flowers   Peter D. Moore
Birdwatching   Peter Hayman